OPUS DEI IN THE CHURCH

OPUS DEI IN THE CHURCH

AN ECCLESIOLOGICAL STUDY
OF THE LIFE AND APOSTOLATE
OF OPUS DEI

Pedro Rodríguez

———

Fernando Ocáriz

———

José Luis Illanes

With a foreword by

BISHOP ALVARO DEL PORTILLO

Scepter

Originally published in 1993 as
El Opus Dei en la Iglesia
Ediciones Rialp, S.A.

First English edition copyright © 1994, Four Courts Press, Dublin
New English edition copyright © 2003 Scepter Publishers, New York

ISBN 1-889334-93-6 PB

Scepter Publishers, Inc.
P.O. Box 211, New York, N.Y.
www.scepterpublishers.org

Text composed in Linotype Janson Text
PRINTED IN THE UNITED STATES OF AMERICA

CONTENTS

Chapter 1 / *Pedro Rodriguez*

THE PLACE OF OPUS DEI IN THE CHURCH

Page 17

Chapter 2 / *Fernando Ocáriz*

VOCATION TO OPUS DEI AS A VOCATION IN THE CHURCH

Page 99

Chapter 3 / *José Luis Illanes*

THE CHURCH IN THE WORLD: THE SECULARITY OF MEMBERS OF OPUS DEI

Page 147

FOREWORD

BISHOP ALVARO DEL PORTILLO

In preparing to write a short foreword for this book I thought immediately of the love Blessed Josemaría Escrivá had for the Church. For, if it is true that to understand Opus Dei one needs to study its founder, that applies even more when one intends to examine that aspect of Opus Dei which is the subject of this volume.

Anyone who knew Blessed Josemaria even slightly can attest to his enthusiasm whenever he spoke about the Spouse of Christ, and the intensity with which he embraced wholeheartedly anything which in one way or another had to do with the Church. In the forty years I lived by his side, I was a daily witness to the fact that our Holy Mother the Church was one of his great loves. The Church was the family to which he belonged and he heroically dedicated himself to its service.

In 1918, while still an adolescent, he first experienced intimations of love for God, a love which grew from that moment on. He decided to become a priest so as to be more available to carry out God's plans. Over the years, on more than one occasion, when referring to himself he said that his sole, ardent desire was to be "a priest of Jesus Christ." That priest, on October 2, 1928, felt himself called by God to found Opus Dei. From that moment on, with the grace of the Holy Spirit, he devoted himself entirely to that institution, motivated by the love for Christ and for the Church that filled his heart.

The holy zeal of Blessed Josemaría on behalf of Christ's Church showed itself constantly in his words and deeds, at times in an especially marked and dramatic manner. One example of this was an event that occurred in 1933. He was praying in a Madrid church, and during his fervent conversation with our Lord, he began to experience great anxiety. He began to imagine that all his efforts to found and develop Opus Dei might be misguided; that perhaps he had been misled, and might mislead others. He reacted by making a humble act of faith, and told God, "Lord, if Opus Dei is not here to serve the Church, destroy it!" The reasoning behind his reaction is evident: the Church was all he lived for. His thoughts and actions reflected his conviction that the Church was the Body of Christ—Christ himself present in the souls of the faithful, as he liked to see it.

Among the published homilies of Opus Dei's founder, there is one which he delivered on the campus of the University of Navarre—"Passionately Loving the World." I remember very well that it was Blessed Josemaría himself who chose the title when the Italian edition of the homily was published. He really did have a great capacity for love, and he cherished all that was noble, wholesome and beautiful in this world. This honourable passion of his had very deep roots. His love for and dedication to Jesus Christ and his Church led him to see in the world, in society and in any noble human endeavour, a reflection of God's love for mankind and our capacity to respond to our Creator's affection by sanctifying our work. Blessed Josemaria's passionate love for the world was simply an extension of his love for Christ and the Church. One can say that he took to heart what St Augustine once declared: *Ecclesia, hoc est mundus reconciliatus*. Love for the world and for the Church did not constitute two separate things in the mind and heart of the founder of Opus Dei.

This theological view of history led him to see Christians as men and women, as children of God, whose rightful place it is to be in the very heart of civil society in order to bring the world back to its Creator, thereby contributing to the work of Redemption in and through their ordinary human occupations. It was this acute awareness of the transcendent destiny of man which led the founder of Opus Dei, in his actions and through his preaching, to stress the great value of all earthly realities, even those which seem ordinary and unimportant. He always saw the Church not only as an institution or structure, but also as the People of God, the sum total of all Christians. He saw the Church in the heart of each one of Jesus' disciples, to the point where he asserted, with a deep conviction, that "the Church is present wherever there is a Christian who strives to live in the name of Christ."[1] This Church, which is both institution and charism, structure and life, hierarchy and fraternity, is the same Church which Monsignor Escrivá de Balaguer loved with all his heart, without any limits or reservations. That is why I feel I can say quite confidently, glossing the title of that homily, that he spent his life "passionately loving the Church."

---

[1] *Conversations*, no. 112.

It was in that Church to which Blessed Josemaria devoted his life that Opus Dei was born. This book is a study of the prelature and its place in the Church: "An Ecclesiological Study of the Life and Apostolate of Opus Dei," as the subtitle says. The authors have produced a profound and insightful study on the nature of Opus Dei as a personal prelature within the structure of the Church, on vocation to Opus Dei as a specific manifestation of baptismal vocation, and on secularity as the proper condition of ordinary Christians and therefore of the faithful of the prelature.

Throughout these pages, one can see that the authors have understood and expounded the ecclesiality of Opus Dei using two principal sources—the writings of its founder and the living reality of the prelature. Naturally, before it became the object of theological study, that ecclesiality was lived out in the priesthood of Blessed Josemaría Escrivá de Balaguer, and in the apostolates of Opus Dei. I frequently heard the founder speak about a criterion for interpreting the history of the Church which he found verified in the very institution which God had inspired him to found. "First," he would say, "comes life, the living pastoral phenomenon. Next comes the juridical norm, usually derived from custom. Finally, the theological theory which is developed from the living reality." [2] This approach has allowed the authors to emphasize how the founding of Opus Dei and its historical development can only be understood as an expression of the living reality of the Church, which is the source and touchstone of everything Christian. Precisely because of this, in writing the foreword to this book, I have tried to set it in the framework of Blessed Josemaria's contemplation of the mystery of the Church. That contemplation, and the love which it involves, underlies the reality of Opus Dei and explains its apostolic activity, that is, the specific pastoral task for which the Pope established this ecclesiastical circumscription, the prelature, some ten years ago.

+ Alvaro del Portillo
Prelate of Opus Dei
Rome, 9 January 1993

[2] Letter, 19 March 1954.

PREFACE

Ten years ago today, on November 28, 1982, Pope John Paul II signed the Apostolic Constitution *Ut sit*, establishing Opus Dei as a personal prelature. This was a decisive event in the process whereby Opus Dei assumed the canonical structure suited to its theological and spiritual reality. A few months later, On March 19, 1983, the oral promulgation of the Constitution took place in a ceremony during which Archbishop Romolo Carboni, papal nuncio to Italy, solemnly presented the papal bull to the prelate of Opus Dei.

At the beginning of this year, 1992, the year of the beatification of the founder of Opus Dei, we all happened to be in Rome at the same time on academic business. All three of us are involved in theological research and teaching and, more to the point in the present case, we are all members of Opus Dei. These two things have a connection since there is a profound relationship between theology and life. The spiritual experience which comes from belonging to Opus Dei encourages theological thought; and in turn, our analytical turn of mind naturally leads us to reflect on the spirit and apostolic approach of Opus Dei.

At our meeting in Rome, with the beatification of the founder looming ever closer, we reflected on how important an ecclesial event the establishment of Opus Dei as a personal prelature had been. That was when we began to think of jointly writing a theological study The first step was to determine the exact content and structure of the work. From our original discussions it was clear that the approach should be ecclesiological. Accordingly, the first chapter would explain and analyze from a theological perspective the structure of Opus Dei and its particular place within the Church.

Without abandoning that ecclesiological approach, it seemed advisable to allow for anthropological and spiritual perspectives in the subsequent chapters, for completeness' sake. So, we decided on a second chapter which would start by studying Christian vocation and go on to look at vocation to Opus Dei. Since vocation to Opus Dei is a call to holiness and apostolate in the world, that is, in secular occupations and situations, it seemed necessary to round off the book with a third chapter, on the lay status of the members of the prelature.

From the beginning we agreed that the book should have a certain cohesiveness, even though it would consist of separate contributions by the three authors. We accordingly kept in contact with each other after our early meeting in Rome; we exchanged ideas and read each other's drafts, providing observations and suggestions and arriving at shared conclusions. It is therefore true to say that the book is the result of a combined effort.

Having explained our objectives and methodology, it remains to set out our sources, of which there were essentially two—our personal experience of Opus Dei and, above all, the writings of its founder, St. Josemaría Escrivá de Balaguer. These writings include, on the one hand, his published works,[1] and, on the other hand, various unpublished works addressed to the members of Opus Dei. Among the latter, we call particular attention to those which the founder called "Letters" and "Instructions," two series of documents in which he commented on aspects of the spirit of Opus Dei and various events in its history; the content and authority of these documents justify their being called "foundational."[2]

Another source should be mentioned—the *Statuta* of the Prelature. This document, by which Opus Dei governs its life and activity, was approved ten years ago today. It was the result of the foundational light and apostolic experience of the founder, and was written by him. The text was later presented by his successor, Bishop Alvaro del Portillo, to the Holy See for approval. This approval was granted via the above-mentioned Bull *Ut sit*, by which the Holy See established Opus Dei as a personal prelature. Because of their importance and the frequency we use them in our work, we thought it appropriate to include these two documents as Appendices, that is, *Ut sit* and the *Statuta* (Code of Particular Law of Opus Dei). The translations of passages from these documents quoted in the book are unofficial.

To end this brief introduction, we would like to express our gratitude to the Prelate of Opus Dei, Bishop Alvaro del Portillo, who encouraged us throughout our endeavour. We hope that this study will contribute to a better and more profound understanding of the ecclesial reality of Opus Dei.

November 28, 1992

---

[1] See list on p. 15.

[2] The abbreviation RHF ("Registro histórico del Fundador" or Historical Register of the founder), followed by the corresponding number, refers to documents in the Archives of the Prelature.

PUBLISHED WORKS OF ST. JOSEMARÍA ESCRIVÁ

These works are cited in the text by title or abbreviated title
(without the author's name).

La Abadesa de las Huelgas. Estudio teologico-juridico. 1st edition,
Madrid, 1944.

Christ is passing by, 1st edition, Dublin, 1974 (a translation of *Es
Cristo que pasa*, 1st edition, Madrid, 1973).

Conversations with Monsignor Escrivá de Balaguer, 1st edition,
Dublin, 1968 (a translation of *Conversaciones con Mons. Escrivá
de Balaguer*, 1st edition, Madrid, 1968).

The Forge, 1st edition, London and New York, 1988 (a translation
of *Forja*, 1st edition, Madrid, 1987).

Friends of God, 1st edition, Dublin, London and New York, 1981
(a translation of *Amigos de Dios*, 1st edition, Madrid, 1977).

Furrow, 1st edition, London and New York, 1987 (a translation of
Surco, 1st edition, Madrid, 1986).

Holy Rosary, 1st edition, Chicago, 1953 (a translation of *Santo
Rosario*, 1st edition, Madrid, 1934).

In Love with the Church, 1st edition, London and New York, 1989
(a translation of *Amar a la Iglesia*, 1st edition, Madrid, 1986).

The Way, 1st edition, Cork, 1953 (a translation of *Camino*, 1st
edition, Madrid, 1934).

The Way of the Cross, 1st edition, Dublin, London and New York,
1983 (a translation of *Via Crucis*, 1st edition, Madrid, 1981).

CHAPTER I.

THE PLACE OF OPUS DEI IN THE CHURCH

PEDRO RODRÍGUEZ

Rome, October 2, 1958: a handful of people were informally gathered at mid-morning with Monsignor Escrivá. Looking back on the Work of God's first thirty years, Opus Dei's founder, nothing if not grateful, called them "a history of God's mercies." He was, of course, conscious of the fact that Opus Dei's institutional development had not been an easy one—and that even greater difficulties lay ahead (things would not be settled until after his death, when Opus Dei was established as a personal prelature).[1] Back in 1958, however, in reply to a query about the Work (as members usually call it) he simply said, "Opus Dei is a little bit of the Church."

With that non-technical expression the founder doubtless meant to ignore the legal framework into which the Work was slotted at the time, in order to highlight better its essence as a "little bit of the Church." It struck me at the time (and still does) that he was pointing the way to understanding the ecclesiology of Opus Dei—getting to the very core of the question. To think and speak of Opus Dei soon sends us back to what the Church essentially is, to its saving riches. All that Opus Dei is, it is within the mystery of the Church. Consequently, to study Opus Dei one

---

[1] Note that Pope John Paul II, in the Apostolic Constitution *Ut sit*, explicitly says that the Second Vatican Council, in *Presbyterorum Ordinis*, no. 10, introduced the figure of personal prelature into the framework of the Church to carry out specific pastoral tasks. Therefore I take it (cf. my *Iglesias particulares y Prelaturas personales*, Pamplona, 2nd ed., 1986, p. 133 [the first ed. of this work was translated into English (Dublin, 1986) as *Personal Prelatures and Particular Churches*]) that the technical name for these institutions is that employed by the two Constitutions—Paul VI's *Regimini Ecclesiae universae* and John Paul II's *Ut sit*: "Prelatura personalis ad peculiaria opera pastoralia perficienda." For brevity's sake, we will simply say "personal prelature." But let us not forget that the specific pastoral remit of each personal prelature will determine its role within the Church.

needs to have a good grasp of ecclesiology. The better we understand the Church, the better will we see how the "little bit" fits in. That is what this first chapter is about.

Opus Dei was given its definitive juridical configuration as a personal prelature in the Church by the Apostolic Constitution *Ut sit* (November 28, 1982). In its introduction John Paul II said this step was taken "bearing in mind its true nature and theological characteristics."[2] Both "true nature" and "theological characteristics" lie at the basis of its canonical configuration and therefore will always be a key to understanding the institution. So, we need to dwell theologically on Opus Dei's true nature in order to understand its place and role in the structure of the Church. That will also help us to understand how and to what extent the various elements of the Church are to be found in Opus Dei; finally, we shall examine those institutional elements that are unique to Opus Dei.

(1)

OPUS DEI IN THE CONTEXT OF THE MISSION OF THE CHURCH

St. Josemaría Escrivá often spoke of "the pastoral phenomenon of Opus Dei."[3] That expression covered the spiritual, institutional and apostolic reality that God caused him to see on October 2, 1928, a reality which gradually took shape in the Church under God's loving guidance.[4] The ecclesiological development of that

---

[2] "Natura theologica et primigenia Institutionis perspecta." The Constitution's text (see the first appendix) appears in *AAS* 75 (1983) 423–25 at 423. [The Spanish reads "después de examinar la naturaleza teológica y originaria de esta institución"—*originaria* being its rendering of *primigenia*. Professor Rodriguez often uses the word *originario* in this chapter. Where he quotes *Ut sit* or refers directly to it, we use an available English translation of that document, which gives "bearing in mind its true nature and theological characteristics." In the absence of a direct English equivalent of *originario*, that word is translated variously in the text as: original, identity-setting, basic, basic and aboriginal (a special sense of aboriginal, implying the "DNA" of an institution, etc., something that establishes its basic pattern), pristine, foundational.—Translators' note.]

[3] "It is clear that, through our vocation, by our specific way of sanctifying ourselves and of working apostolically, we are a new pastoral phenomenon in the Church's life, although we are still as old as the Gospel": letter, Feb. 14, 1944, no. 7.

[4] "And to make way for this divine project, truly a theological, pastoral, and social phenomenon in the Church, God led me by the hand": letter, Jan. 25, 1961, no. 4.

pastoral phenomenon has many facets; it affects many difficult aspects of Church life. For example, what we call Opus Dei is not merely a personal prelature, strictly speaking; properly and inseparably united to it is the Priestly Society of the Holy Cross, an association of secular clergy. Prelature and Society make up a single entity, even though they are distinct in themselves. Thus those members of the Priestly Society who are incardinated in dioceses are part of Opus Dei; yet they neither fall under the jurisdiction of Opus Dei's prelate nor in any way form part of the prelature's clergy, since they answer only to their respective diocesan bishops.[5] Moreover, Opus Dei's "spirit" or "spirituality" is so evidently at work in the lives of very many Christians that it clearly overflows the limits of Opus Dei as an institution.

On October 2, 1931, Josemaría Escrivá noted down: "It was *three years ago* today... that, in the house of the Vincentians, I managed to make sense of the various notes I'd been jotting down up to then. From that day on, this mangy donkey *came to see* the beautiful yet heavy burden that God, in his unfathomable goodness, had laid on his back. On that day the Lord founded his Work: from then on I began to have contact with souls of laymen, students and others, but all of them young people. I also began to bring groups together. I began to pray and to get others to pray. And I began to suffer...."[7] Three years later in an Instruction to Opus Dei members, he claimed: "Opus Dei is not a human invention.... Years ago God inspired it in a clumsy and deaf instrument, who saw it for the first time on the feast of the Guardian Angels, October 2, 1928."[8] Josemaría Escrivá thus testifies to a divine

---

[5] See section IV, 5, later in this chapter. Also associated with Opus Dei are Cooperators, who, while not faithful of the prelature or members of the Priestly Society of the Holy Cross, form another association linked to the prelature. See `Statuta`, no. 16.

[6] Also here, as in any true ecclesial experience, this tendency is verified. "C'è una communicazione fra persone, storicamente sperimentabile, che dà origine ad un rapporto interpersonale e a un fenomeno de aggregazione ecclesiale constatabile, e c'è una communicazione dello Spirito che amplia e muove il processo che sta accadendo in spazi non più definibili e in una profondità inaccessibile all'indagine": S. Dianich, *Chiesa in missione. Per una ecclesiologia dinamica* (Milan, 1987), p. 184.

[7] "Apuntes íntimos," no. 306. In the privacy of his diary, later gathered into these Notes, Opus Dei's founder called himself a "mangy donkey," for so did he humbly see himself in God's eyes.

[8] Instruction, March 19, 1934, nos. 6–7.The subject is explored and the texts analyzed in J. L. Illanes, "Dos de octubre de 1928: alcance y significado de una fecha" in *Mons. Josemaría Escrivá de Balaguer y el Opus Dei* (Pamplona, 1985), pp. 65ff. See also A. de Fuenmayor, V. Gómez Iglesias, and J. L. Illanes, *El itinerario jurídico del Opus Dei. Historia y defensa de un carisma*, 4th ed. (Pamplona, 1990),

initiative. In other words, the "little bit" of the Church, before becoming an established thing, was charism, grace, light, inspiration. Or, rather, the institution was born of a charism, of an intervention by God in the Church's life at a particular time through a man called to this task. This charism declared God's will, an imperative command of Christ pointing to a task, to an apostolic mission. This was followed, first, by subjective awareness of both mandate and mission; then, by immediate action—what Scripture calls the "obedience of faith." Vatican II teaches that the Holy Spirit enriches and directs his Church with various gifts, both hierarchical and charismatic.[9] We have here a further clear example of how he continues to endow the Church.

The charism Josemaría Escrivá received on October 2, 1928 is crucial to this study; it is the enduring root of the "pastoral phenomenon" born at that time and extending down to our days, with its already long history of apostolic experience and institutional development. What Opus Dei's founder "saw" on that day (because God showed it to him) also constitutes the theological (and "foundational") criterion for understanding the nature of this "little bit" of the Church.

There is nothing new in all this. What we have here is an instance of the "rule" that governs the whole plan of salvation. Christ—God's very Word who became man to redeem us by his cross and resurrection—is what he is by reason of his redemptive mission: *propter nos homines et propter nostram salutem*. The very make-up of Christ's being—his "exodus" from the Trinity to man in hypostatic union—is a mission from the Father to redeem us:

"Behold, I have come to do your will, O God."[10] And Christ's Church, imitating its Lord, shares in that divine way of salvation: "As the Father has sent me, so I send you."[11] The Church is not self-explanatory nor does it live for itself; it exists for Christ and for mankind. It originates in the trinitarian mission (of both Son and Spirit) and it exists for a strictly redemptive mission. Consequently, like Christ, the Church's being is determined by its mission.[12]

---

chap. 1. An English translation of this work was published with the title *The Canonical Path of Opus Dei: History and Defense of a Charism* (Princeton, 1994).

[9] *Lumen gentium*, no. 4: "diversis donis hierarchicis et charismaticis instruit ac dirigit."

[10] Heb 10: 7; see Ps 40: 9.

[11] Jn 20: 21.

[12] Consequently, in carrying out its mission, the Church experiences its being: "la missione è il luogo nel quale si pone il problema dell'autoidentificazione della Chiesa": S. Dianich, p. 143.

Its founder and head has given his Church a precise, fundamental structure, sacramental as well as charismatic, so that it may carry on the mission, continue the "sending" that originates in the Father. A similar connection between mission and structure is found in Opus Dei. We shall now examine the imperative command and the mission that gave rise to Opus Dei in the bosom of the Church.

1. *Message, mission and institution*

As earlier quotations show, Josemaría Escrivá was clearly conscious from the start, of the meaning, for himself and for the Church, of what happened on October 2, 1928: "That day the Lord founded his Work." He saw the Work as God's, not as his own invention; its mission defined it, created it. What did the twenty-six-year-old priest see that October morning, as he sorted out some papers? [13] What divine lights, what enlivening graces did the Holy Spirit infuse into his soul? At the heart of the event was something obviously mystical. Finding the right words to convey an ineffable divine communication is a challenge both for the person who receives the message and for any later researcher who wants to analyze what happened. Useful studies have been written that shed both biographical and theological light.[14] What interests us here are the ecclesiological implications of the event. (We know there is the risk of "desiccating" what was, above all, an ineffable intimacy of God with his creature.)

We can discern two aspects of that divine illumination. On the one hand, for Josemaría Escrivá, it takes the form of what we could call a "message," a word from God for his Church. Then, within the bosom of that Church illuminated by that message, he "sees" that God wishes to raise up an "ecclesial community" (Opus Dei) entirely devoted to serving that message. There was to be an institution, a *coetus fidelium*, whose *raison d'être* was wholly defined by that message and whose nature and ecclesial structure would be intrinsically conditioned by it. There was no "background" of any kind; or rather, the only background was the message itself and the Church in which it arose. Let us now examine these two aspects of what happened on October 2, 1928.

That event, as we have said, involved a "message" above all; this was what we might call its "prophetic" dimension. God engraved

---

[13] "I received an illumination concerning the whole Work, while reading over those papers": "Apuntes íntimos," no. 306.

[14] Cf. J. L. Illanes, "Dos de octubre . . . ," cited above.

with fire on Josemaría Escrivá's soul a fundamental fact of Christian faith and life—the call to holiness God addresses to every Christian by virtue of baptism. Indeed, no dimension of Church life is more radical and primary than that: it sums up the very reality of salvation in Christ. In this sense there is nothing new about what happened on October 2; or rather, to put it positively, it partakes of the ever-newness of the Good News. Really, nothing can be "founded" in the Church, since everything personal or institutional is "founded" on the Church itself. That is self-evident. Every authentic realization of Christian life, every true following of Christ—whatever the path and spirituality, whatever the ecclesiological position of the person or institution concerned—can be nothing other than faithfulness to, and unfolding of, the baptismal vocation. Holiness in the Church is, always and objectively, a response to God's goodness, who calls us to unite ourselves to the mystery of his Son. Nonetheless, this is compatible with the often verified fact that this radical demand that baptism makes is something many Christians have been unconscious of or have done little about.

Therefore, in trying to understand the "message" of October 2, 1928 we need to go deeper. Josemaría Escrivá did not receive a general insight into the universal call to holiness; he was being shown that the holiness originating in and founded on baptism to which God is calling Christians is *holiness in the midst of the world*. In other words, God calls this multitude of Christians in three ways: first, *baptismally*: they are called to be configured to Christ in the Church, called to holiness; secondly, *personally*: they are called, not *en masse*, but one by one, each by name (*"vocavi te nomine tuo"*: I have called you by your name);[15] thirdly, they are called *in the midst of ordinary life*: they must seek holiness in and through the ordinary realities of life, among which everyday work plays a key part.[16] In this way God causes them to experience that positive acceptance of human affairs as a road to salvation which the Incarnation implies.[17] A "new light" shed on baptism is thus inseparably linked to this other aspect of the "message." Those crowds of Christians (whom Josemaría Escrivá will repeatedly call "ordinary Christians", a term he will give a technical

[15] Is 43: 1. This biblical quotation was a *leit-motif* for Monsignor Escrivá.

[16] Cornelio Fabro says the spirit of Msgr. Josemaría is a "complete spirituality of complete work": "El temple de un Padre de la Iglesia" in *Santos en el mundo. Estudios sobre los escritos del Beato Josemaría Escrivá* (Madrid, 1992), p. 68.

[17] Isn't this what John Paul II often says: "Man is the way for the Church"? See *Redemptor hominis*, no. 14.

meaning)[18] are the true protagonists of what began on October 2, 1928.

Both aspects of the "message,"[19] while conceptually distinct, are in fact closely connected. Indeed, the "universal" call to holiness would be utopian (or illusory), if the wide range of human situations (all human life) could not be sanctified and absorbed into the redemption. This was an aspect of the message often referred to by Josemaría Escrivá in these words: "The divine paths of the earth have been opened up!"[20] Everything truly human has become a way to God, to salvation.

The "message" also shows that the universal call to divine intimacy includes, as a necessary consequence, the fact that everyone is called to the apostolate.[21] In keeping with what we have just said, this is a call to discover and act on the apostolic possibilities latent in all the various situations where secular Christians find themselves, especially in the wide world of work. The vista of human sanctification which Opus Dei's founder perceived through the special light God gave him also reveals the apostolic mission ordinary Christians are called to, by virtue of their baptism.

In the historical circumstances of our time, explaining and spreading this message (about holiness, ordinary life, and apostolic mission) necessarily took the form of asserting *the laity's* call for holiness. For centuries the prospect of deep friendship with God seemed linked, or even restricted, to the canonical and institutional forms of the religious life (or approximations thereto). Josemaría Escrivá never tired of saying, in many different ways, that "holiness is not something for a privileged few," that is, it is not limited to people called to follow some very special route. Rather, God was having him focus his attention on the ordinary lives of ordinary people. Here is his message: "God is calling us all, he expects all of us to love him—wherever we are, whatever our state in life, whatever our job or role. That common, ordinary, humdrum life can be a means to holiness. To seek God there is no need for us to leave our place in the world (so long as God doesn't call us to the religious state): every walk of life can lead to an encounter with Christ."[22]

[18] See chapter two and, above all, chapter three.
[19] Chapter II, section II, 1, will call them "subjective and objective universality" of the call to holiness.
[20] *Christ Is Passing By*, no. 21.
[21] So has the Church understood it, as reflected in the opening prayer of the Mass for St. Josemaría: "Deus, qui beatum Josephmariam presbyterum *universalis vocationis ad sanctitatem et apostolatum* praeconem in Ecclesia effecisti. . . ."
[22] Letter, March 24, 1930, no. 2.

Religious life (and what we today call "consecrated" life) always merited his heartfelt respect and veneration.[23] He numbered among his best friends many prominent members of religious orders or congregations. For this authentic *vir Ecclesiae* (man of the Church), moreover, the Church's life and apostolate would be inconceivable without the contribution of religious. Long before Vatican II formulated it, he had always taught, in similar terms, what we read in *Lumen gentium*: the religious state "belongs to the Church's life and holiness" (*ad Ecclesiae vitam et sanctitatem pertinent*).[24] Yet, we must emphasize that the core of his message was that, for "ordinary Christians," answering God's call to holiness and radical imitation of Jesus Christ need not involve becoming religious. What they have to do is to respond to God, with all the Gospel's vigour, wherever they may be, fully involved in their affairs and responsibilities, for "all the earth's paths can occasion an encounter with Christ."[25]

Josemaría Escriva's life and his life's work were, then, determined by this "message." Earlier we called this aspect of what he "saw" on October 2, 1928, its "prophetic" dimension. That is in fact what a prophet does—proclaim a message to God's people. From that day on, he realized that his whole life would be tied up with spreading this good news. And so it was until he died. "How loudly did God make this truth resound when he inspired his Work!", he wrote early on. But on that autumn morning in 1928 there was more than a "message," even though, as we have just seen, that was a key element in that supernatural event. For Josemaría Escrivá was not just someone who proclaimed a word, a divine design: the "light" that flooded his soul showed him that God wanted something more. He grasped the message and his duty to spread it tirelessly—but God showed him that to make the message truly part of the Church's social fabric he had to bring about an enduring "convocation of men and women"—that is, establish an institution wholly dedicated to spreading the news and incarnating the message.

Thus once again in Church history the essential structure of salvation is clearly to be seen—word *and* realization of the word;

---

[23] "You know well that we always rejoice to see many vocations to the seminaries and religious families. Moreover, we thank God for them, because not a few of those vocations arise as fruits of the spiritual and doctrinal training we impart to young people. When we raise the spiritual temperature around us, making it more supernatural and apostolic, it is only natural that more souls dedicate themselves to God in all the Church's institutions": letter, March 11, 1940, no. 39.

[24] No. 44.

[25] *Christ Is Passing By*, no. 110.

proclamation *and* God's power at work, effecting salvation. There-fore, Josemaría Escrivá was not only a *prophet*; he was also a *pastor* (in this case a *founder*). Essential to that October inspiration was what we can call its "institutional dimension." God made Josemaría see that he was to be used to call others to an "organic and vocational commitment"—not just a commitment to take to heart the content of that message (personal holiness, ordinary life, apostolate, a mes-sage for the multitude), but also a commitment to make it resound throughout the Church and the world. He was to bestir himself to show people that the message was not utopian; it was something down-to-earth, made of flesh and blood. This organic reality within the Church, which St. Josemaría began simply calling "the Work," is Opus Dei as an institution. Getting others to commit themselves is what he called "doing Opus Dei." He himself tells us: "As part of God's providence in caring for his holy Church and preserving the Gospel spirit, the Lord entrusted to Opus Dei, from October 2, 1928 onwards, the task of showing and reminding all souls, through your exemplary life and word, that there is a universal call to Chris-tian perfection that and it is quite possible to follow it.

"God wants each of you, amid the particular circumstances of his or her position in life, to strive to be holy: *haec est enim voluntas Dei, sanctificatio vestra* (1 Thess 4: 3), this is God's will, your sanctifi-cation. Often this will be a hidden (inconspicuous) holiness, daily, heroic, designed to co-redeem with Christ, to save creatures with him, to direct human affairs towards him.

"God wishes to avail himself of your personal holiness, sought according to the Work's spirit, to teach everyone, in a specific and simple way, what you yourselves know well—that all the faithful, incorporated in Christ by baptism as they are, are called to seek the fullness of Christian life." [26]

Our analysis has shown that, from the very beginning, the pas-toral phenomenon of Opus Dei involved two things—a prophetic message and its institutionalization (Christian community or orga-nization). In the founder's eyes both dimensions were related. Still, the message transcends the organization, and it is in fact an essen-tial feature of the Church itself—the universal calling to holiness. (Vatican II's *Lumen gentium* will later devote all its fifth chapter to this subject.) However, this prophetic element is not merely pro-claimed; it also becomes the prime purpose and mission of an institution, from which will stem that institution's ecclesial struc-ture and its place within the structure of the Church.

---

[26] Letter, March 11, 1940, no. 25.

The linkage of message and institution in Opus Dei is a primary datum or foundational fact and therefore a key to theologically understanding the position of the Work in the structure of the Church. This key will guide us in this chapter as in the following two. We plan to use it circumspectly, because it is easy to go wrong. For example, if one concentrated on the (true) fact that Opus Dei members are fully committed to following Christ, one could (wrongly) think that Opus Dei (whatever its canonical position, which is a secondary matter) is theologically a "form" of the "religious life." Such misunderstandings are easy to explain. They stem from ways of thinking which have been around for centuries and which in part derive, I think, from an evident fact—that historically the Church has scarcely any experience of institutions featuring a profound commitment to follow Christ that are not in fact forms of consecrated life. If this circumstantial historical experience were allowed to *identify* the search for holiness with consecrated life, the prospect of radically imitating Jesus in any existential and institutional setting other than that of the religious life would be inconceivable. But such thinking represents an unwarranted freezing of history: it would "forbid" the Holy Spirit to bring about new structural and communitarian developments in the Church.

The tenacity with which the founder fought the Work's inclusion in the moulds of the religious state or any of its many varieties or derivations, witnesses to his deep conviction that the Church's experience of the mystery of Christ is not restrictive but openended. More specifically, he was convinced that in our day God had sought to open new horizons. As far as the present study is concerned, this means that Opus Dei's institutional newness must be examined in the light of both its new message and the specific way it is called upon to promote it (its mission).

2. *The institution in the light of its mission*

The message of the universal call to holiness is as we have seen, central to the very message of the Church. It is to be found at the very root of the historical accomplishment of Christ's work of salvation. This means that it is not up to any particular ecclesial institution, but rather to the Church as such, to muster every human and supernatural resource to carry out this wide-ranging pastoral task. The warp and the woof of the Church as *sacramentum* must everywhere clearly show, by word and sacraments, that God calls everyone to holiness, for "this is the will of God: your sanctification." [27] After Second Vatican Council especially, we can say that both the Church universal and particular Churches have a greater duty than ever to broadcast the message of holiness and its apostolic overflow.

In theory, one could argue that now that the Church has so publicly and formally proclaimed the core of that October 2 message there is no need for Opus Dei. But that would be at odds both with the facts and with history; indeed, the Council's proclamation of the universal call to holiness and the Church's embracing of that message confer a special responsibility on that part of the Church that is Opus Dei (and on everyone else who has worked to spread and broadcast this truth). If the entire *communio* is to be imbued with this truth, does it not make sense that there should be people who set an example and dedicate themselves to that mission? A truly ecclesiological outlook would readily appreciate that Opus Dei, given the universal nature of its aim, never addresses the Church from outside, but, rather, born as it is in its bosom, it speaks as a "little bit" of the Church itself. Nor does the Church look upon the Work as distinct from itself; it sees it as a development of itself. As with all true developments in the Church, here too the Holy Spirit is at work, promoting the Church's own God-given mission.

At any rate, what I want to stress is that Opus Dei's mission within the Church clearly highlights that its aim and mission are not something narrow or relevant just to a sector or two but rather affect the whole body. It addresses not one particular group, but everyone, with no limitations of gender, race, age, job, social background, civilian status, political views or secular creed. It seeks only to help to fan everyone's baptismal grace and channel it toward work and other duties—secular realities which will thereby take their rightful place in people's awareness and daily agenda as the scenario for their "obedience of faith." Ordinary life then becomes the setting where one responds to the baptismal call to holiness. From the very start this was Josemaría Escriva's apostolic horizon and task; initially he worked alone at the job God had given him—to do Opus Dei. He began to work with young people, and to suffer—two clear Christian traits. "From then on I began to have contact with souls of laymen, students and others, but all of them young people. And to bring groups together. I began to pray and get others to pray. And I began to suffer..." Afterwards he would get around to the "not so young." In 1930 he extended the

---

[27] 1 Thess 4: 3.

work to women. From the very beginning he sought out both college students and workers.[28]

It is noteworthy that Opus Dei's prophetic and institutional aspects, linked as they are, were especially so in the early years. They are "dimensions" of a single reality, of a divine event, perceived by St. Josemaría as one and the same thing and carried out, as we have said, in "obedience of faith."

In those days "spreading the message" and seeking men and women for the *pusillus grex* (little flock) God had charged him with forming and shepherding were almost indistinguishable aspects that overlapped and reinforced one another. In fact, even today (in Opus Dei members' experience, despite organizational advances) substantially the same cross-fertilization takes place. Then, however, the *pusillus grex* had scarcely any institutional form.[29]

Josemaría Escrivá saw with noonday clarity that, in the daily discharge of God's will, spreading the message was inseparably linked to "convoking" men and women who would make it their *raison d'être*, committing themselves to carry it to all nations. He also saw that the nascent institution was internally dominated by the "message"; the institution would be the instrument and echo chamber for the God-given message. Josemaría Escrivá well knew

---

[28] Biographies of Opus Dei's founder abound. For example, A. Vázquez de Prada, *El Fundador del Opus Dei* (Madrid, 1983); F. Gondrand, *At God's Pace* (London and New York, 1989); P. Berglar, *Opus Dei: Life and Works of Its Founder, Josemaría Escrivá* (Princeton, 1994); A. Sastre, *Tiempo de caminar. Semblanza di Mons. Josemaría Escrivá de Balaguer* (Madrid, 1989).

[29] "Spreading the message" and "seeking" were ordinarily called by the founder "apostolate" and "*proselitismo*," or "winning over new apostles." In his life and in Opus Dei's spirit, both facets spring from a single desire, which is Christian love for all based on the universality of the Redemption and which he expressed in the formula: "out of a hundred souls, one hundred matter." "You have to allow your heart to expand more and more with real hunger for the apostolate. Out of a hundred souls we are interested in a hundred": *Furrow*, no. 183. "Out of a hundred souls we are interested in a hundred. We discriminate against no one for we know for certain that Jesus has redeemed us all, and that he wishes to make use of a few of us, despite our personal nothingness, to make his salvation known to all": *Friends of God*, no. 9. By expanding the scope of following Christ to "the hundred," St. Josemaría, ablaze with the fire of Christ, realized that God was calling some to "pull the cart of Opus Dei," to shoulder this "beautiful but heavy burden." It was the moment for inviting others to become Opus Dei members. When he used the word *proselitismo*, firmly rooted in the Bible, its meaning could not be further from the pejorative, sectarian sense it soon acquired in the Anglo-American world and has since become more widespread. Such a spiritual and missionary synthesis of "apostolate" and "*proselitismo*" we find in this *pensée*: "Yours is only a small love if you are not zealous for the salvation of all souls [apostolate]. Yours is only a poor love if you are not eager to inflame other apostles with your madness [*proselitismo*]": *The Way*, no. 796.

that to spread the message and to do Opus Dei were but the two sides of a single divine will. For the "word of God" (the message) to resound the world over, God would have to bring to his Work many of the People of God. That is, Opus Dei, the institution desired by God, had to grow.

Word and realization of the word; announcement of God's mercy and bestowal of the grace conferring that mercy—this is, as said before, the ecclesial-sacramental structure of salvation. In this sense Opus Dei as an institution—"founding" and developing God's Work—seemed to Josemaría Escrivá to be the first step God wanted him to take in order to *carry out* the message. The Work, we could say, is the message itself understood and structured in terms of its ability to change people.

Consequently, from what we have already seen and aiming at a theological understanding of the phenomenon, we could offer the following summary:

a) The public to which Josemaría Escriva's message-mission is addressed is the vast and varied People of God—old and young; single, married and widowed; men and women of every race and social status.

b) These men and women, whom Opus Dei has come to remind that holiness is not an elitist privilege, are those very crowds of Christians already "convoked" in God's Church by baptism, regardless of how conscious of, and responsive to, this dignity they may be. Indeed, Josemaría Escriva's message only makes sense in the context of that convocation. His mission has a direct connection with it, seeks to serve and enliven it, to make it more evident and attractive, so that those called by baptism understand its sanctifying promise. In doing so, he had to highlight the indispensable role played by secular, everyday realities, the "home" of ordinary Christians, who in this regard do not differ from their fellow-citizens and even non-Christian colleagues.

c) To the extent it takes place, the transformation of Christian life in those who heed the message is brought about by Christ's grace; it is the salvific fruit of the Church's holy reality present and operative (*inest et operatur*) in the local Churches to which those people belong. Ultimately, this transformation is the life, personal and communitarian, of the universal Church.

d) The message, service to the universal "convocation" that is the Church, seen from the supernatural event of October 2, 1928, led directly to the founding of Opus Dei—constituting that "little bit" of the Church by a special convoking of those already convoked to the Church—for two related purposes (the first leading to the second). Firstly, they would commit themselves to developing in their lives the original, baptismal convocation in line with the requirements of the call to holiness as spelled out in the message of October 2, 1928. Secondly, those men and women would establish a lasting and stable institution dedicated to spreading as widely as possible the message God revealed to the founder.

e) Consequently, Opus Dei as an institution is both an implementation of, and a permanent service to, the message. Thus, by analyzing the October 2, 1928, event, we have seen how its two elements are necessarily linked and how that linkage implies an immanent order, an internal structure. The message is the first thing God is concerned about; the institution is something he desires insofar as it can spread it. The message, therefore, determines the institution's end, mission and structure; the institution is to be understood in view of the message, which thus becomes the theological criterion to direct and discern the way it develops, institutionally, apostolically or pastorally.

f) Finally, our analysis shows that between the "little bit" of the Church and the Church itself there is an innate similarity, as we discover when we look at the *coetus fidelium* that is Opus Dei and the *Populus Dei* that is the Church. The "little flock" that Josemaría Escrivá convoked and shepherded reflects the myriad people and situations found in the People of God. The explanation remains the same: by reason of Opus Dei's message-mission, so central to the Church's very mission, those "convoked" in Opus Dei—or, if one prefers, Opus Dei as a "little flock" or ecclesial community—can and in fact do reflect the same variety found among the ordinary faithful of God's People. They are "ordinary Christians" whom God has called to Opus Dei to serve their brothers and sisters, "ordinary Christians" like them. If we want to understand this analogy or innate similarity we must take another step in our theological reflections.

3. *The institution's structure*

Christ founded *one* Church, "his" Church, and the various institutions found therein derive their meaning and theological place from the salvific power and spiritual richness of Christ's Spouse, *circumdata varietate*.[30] This is the same as saying that a community

---

[30] This variety was dear to Opus Dei's founder, who wrote: "[We] shall love the marvellous unity and variety found in the Church; we shall venerate and contribute to others venerating the instruments of that unity. We shall understand the manifestations of Catholicity and interior richness, manifested by diverse spiritualities,

or institution is only justified in the Church to the extent that its aim and mission share in the aim and mission of the Church itself. Opus Dei's aim (from which its mission derives) is not, therefore, identical with the Church's aim, but rather shares in it. That is self-evident. If the aim of Opus Dei were the same as that of the Church, Opus Dei would be the Church or, to put it another way, Opus Dei would have no Christian *raison d'être*. On the contrary, Opus Dei's aim is a sharing in the Church's aim, a specific aim, as we have seen.

Yet that aim, though participative and specific, is not restricted or sectional. Opus Dei is not designed to do specific things in the field of charity or justice or education or catechetics or missions, etc. (practically all such ventures, however, can be "corporate" activities[31] or may be carried out by its members).[32] Rather, Opus Dei's pastoral task is to help spread and encourage response to the original call to holiness (the very core of the Gospel) among people of all walks of life. An "immense horizon," a "sea without shores," was how its founder described that task. Moreover, Opus Dei asks those who take this message to heart, or are called to Opus Dei, to dedicate to this aim and task, not a certain amount of "time" or energy, but their whole lives, each in his place. For only one's whole life—all of it—is of a magnitude adequate to the search for holiness. A person can aspire to holiness—in this case, through his or her occupation and ordinary life—only by being committed fully to it.[33] Here too, we can see, Opus Dei's aim is not a "sectional" one. While having its own aim (in a certain sense, a specific one) that aim partakes, very profoundly, of the aim of the Church itself

The same could be said of the people to whom Opus Dei's message is addressed. We have already said that, within the Church, the Work addresses not a special kind of person, but, rather, Christians at large. Though called by God in baptism, their sense of vocation often lies dormant or ineffectual, certainly separate or cut off from what most occupies them—their jobs and

---

associations, families, and activities, which, always and everywhere, give proofs of stemming from one and the same indivisible Spirit (cf. 1 Cor 12: 11)": letter, May 31, 1943, no. 30.

[31] Or "corporate apostolates." See in their regard *Conversations*, no. 18.

[32] "You know very well, my children, that our apostolic work has no specialized aim; rather, it embraces all specializations, because it takes root in all the diverse specialties of life itself. It ennobles and elevates to the supernatural order, thus converting them into authentic work for souls, all the services people provide for one another, in the give-and-take of human society": letter, Jan. 9, 1959, no. 14.

[33] This "unrestricted" aspect is dealt with at more length in chapter two.

families. Only religious (and, in general, members of institutes of consecrated life) would formally be excluded from this "convocation." Not, of course, because of any kind of discrimination. Religious have already been divinely called to holiness; theirs is a vocation long proclaimed and acknowledged; their contribution is a permanent one, as is their specific place within the Church. Besides, anyone with a lively *sensus Ecclesiae*—an appreciation for the Church as a joyful communion of brothers and sisters who offer one another the benefit of the gifts and charisms each has received—will see how the two callings complement each other. Opus Dei's message to "ordinary Christians" can stimulate desires for holiness within the monastery or convent, just as the latter's consecrated life will remind their brethren struggling on in the world of the why and wherefore of their efforts.

I offer these reflections on Opus Dei's own particular "but nonsectional" aim and apostolic horizon, because they seem to reflect the all-embracing sense of the mission of the Church that from early on God inspired in Josemaría Escrivá. This shaped his apostolic endeavors and the steps he actually took to establish the institution God was asking him to establish. I think we can say this: the ecclesial community Josemaría Escrivá was establishing from October 2, 1928 gradually came to reflect the broad variety of persons who make up the People of God. There came to Opus Dei, convoked by Josemaría Escrivá, men and women, priests and lay people, married or not, all with the same vocation. The founder tended to this small flock, and all of them—led by "the Father," as he was called—began to play their part in this mission directed towards their fellow "ordinary Christians."

At this point in our inquiry into the theological nature of the new "space" in the Church being created by Fr. Escrivá, let us turn to a key feature, that of the presence in the Work of both priests and laity. Opus Dei is well known to be a largely lay organization. For many, to speak of Opus Dei is to refer to lay people and their role in the Church. Speaking of the "vein" into which Opus Dei's spirituality and action flow, the founder said it is "the active, theological process leading lay people fully to assume their ecclesial responsibilities, in keeping with their specific way of participating in the mission of Christ and his Church."[34] One reason why the founder used such terms was his desire to avoid Opus Dei's being

[34] The text continues: "This is and has been, over the Work's nearly 40 years, the constant restlessness—serene but powerful—with which God has sought to channel, in my soul and in those of my children, the desire to serve him": *Conversations*, no. 20.

seen as a new, "modern," "updated" phase of the centuries-long evolution of the Church's "states of perfection"; Opus Dei belongs in that other "vein," one of more recent origin[35] and extraordinary richness. Yet, although it is something genuinely lay in character, the Work has never been just a lay association or movement or grouping whose members pool their ecclesial contributions and, when they deem necessary, ask ecclesiastical authorities to provide "chaplains" for particular functions (in some cases the provision of chaplains is the initiative of the authorities themselves). The "organic and ministerial" presence of priests has always been essential to Opus Dei.

Indeed, from October 1928 onwards, Opus Dei comes into being as the action of a priest (the founder), opening apostolic horizons for the lay, secular life of ordinary people.[36] In close union with that priest, these lay people begin to achieve all that secular apostles can achieve with their word and example, up to the point which St. Josemaría called "the sacramental wall." [37] At that point a priest's specifically ministerial presence and action are required by the very nature of the economy of salvation. Led by his thorough *ecclesial* appreciation of the lay apostolate and its role in renewing the Church, Fr. Escrivá saw that, to "do Opus Dei" as God wanted it done, the cooperation of priests and lay people was "essential." That was how he acted from the start. His early pastoral experience soon showed him that this wide-ranging apostolate could only be fully carried out by lay people and priests who were vitally and institutionally identified with the original inspiration; in other words, Opus Dei's priests must come from the ranks of lay members. The year 1944 saw the first ordinations.

As far as our study is concerned, the conclusion to be drawn is this: Opus Dei has never been a "branch of the laity" aided by clerics from outside, or a grouping of laity and priests who associate simply as *christifideles* (faithful). Rather, from day one, Opus Dei has seen itself as an ecclesial institution essentially and organically made up of *lay people and priests*. This fact gives rise to important consequences when trying to understand how Opus Dei fits into the structure of the Church. In a certain sense, almost everything

---

[35] More recent only as a historical development, because in fact the "vein" is found in the life of the earliest Christian communities, as seen in the New Testament.

[36] See Fuenmayor, Gómez Iglesias, Illanes, *El itinerario jurídico*, p. 44.

[37] "Without priests the work initiated by the lay members of Opus Dei would be incomplete, since they can't go beyond what I usually call the *sacramental wall*, administering the sacraments reserved to priests": letter, Feb. 14, 1944, no. 9.

we shall go on to discuss is contained in what we have just said. That is why we must first examine the fundamental structure of the Church in some detail and its relationship to Christ's priesthood. We will return then to Opus Dei to see how it fits into that structure.

(II)

THE FUNDAMENTAL STRUCTURE OF THE CHURCH [38]

At the deepest level, the Church is a mystery of communion; she is the *mysterium communionis hominum cum Deo et inter se per Christum in Spiritu Sancto* ("the mystery of men's communion with God and among themselves through Christ in the Holy Spirit").[39] Yet as long as she is a pilgrim in history, the Church is also the *sacrament* of that communion. On the one hand (as a sign), this expression indicates the "structural moment" taken by the mystery of communion in its earthly phase (the *"compages socialis"* of *Lumen gentium*, 8). On the other (as an instrument), it expresses the *way* salvation *works* in and through the Church. In effect, it is part of its very mystery that the Church is, here on earth and since its origin, both *communio* and *sacramentum*—spiritual community with a social structure or institution.

These are basic concepts used in general ecclesiology; we need to understand them to deal with the subject in hand—Opus Dei's true nature and theological characteristics.

1. *Community and structure in the Church's origin* [40]

The Church as a society is made up of its members, Christian women and men who belong to Christ's Body, citizens of the People of God. But the Church is no mere aggregate or ensemble

[38] For this section, see my "El concepto de estructura fundamental de la iglesia," in *Veritati Catholicae*, Festschrift für Leo Scheffczyk zum 65. Geburtstag, herausgegeben von A. Ziegenaus, F. Courth, Ph. Schaefer (Aschaffenburg, 1985), pp. 237–46; also my "Sacerdocio ministerial y sacerdocio común en la estructura de la Iglesia," in *Romana* 3 (1987) 162–76.

[39] This is the formula I use to condense the Church's essential description. See my *Iglesias particulares*, p. 142.

[40] With the expression "structure of the Church," we designate the constitutive way of arranging the elements and functions of which the Church is composed insofar as "constituted and organized as a society in the present world": *Lumen gentium*, no. 8/b.

of people who, sharing ideas, come together at some early point in time, only later to define for themselves, and impose upon themselves, an institutional framework. (Such an organization by its very nature would alter in line with social change; about the only permanent thing would be its abiding generic need for some sort of social order.) Nor is the Church a community of wholly intangible links that, through a historical process of assimilating cultural forms, acquires a certain social structure. In both cases we would have a concept of Church that separates the community of persons from its respective social structure; in both scenarios, the community would be the "true" Church, and its organization simply a "superstructure."

Rather, the mystery of the Church, at least in its earthly phase, embraces at once both community and social structure (institution). This excludes not only chronological priority (first, communion, then its institutional arrangement), but also the mere juxtaposition of both elements (the institution or structure alongside the community). On the contrary, the simultaneity we refer to includes communion and structure as dimensions of a single reality that is the sacrament of the Church. The pilgrim Church is always a community of people and, to that extent, is always a community endowed with a social framework. Never is the former present without the latter, while the latter exists only in the former. That is tantamount to saying that both dimensions stem from God and are facets of a single reality—not self-standing, autonomous things.

The Church is always—not just in her historical origin—a convocation-congregation that God brings about through Christ in the Holy Spirit. Its members are called and congregated to form a communion with a definite structure that is equally divine in its origin. It is God who calls and gathers mankind, and he likewise establishes once for all the appropriate arrangement for this convocation-congregation. This proper, permanent, and transcendent arrangement is found in the Church's structure, which is always incarnated in concrete people yet always transcends those called and congregated. This permanent and transcendent character of the Church's structure with respect to its members, while not being distinct from them, is what allows us to speak of the Church as an institution.

God's enduring activity of calling and congregating people in Christ through the action of the Holy Spirit takes place precisely in the sacramental and prophetic institution of the Church. The Church is continuously being recreated by trinitarian action which avails itself of "the ministry of the word and the sacraments." The word that convokes and gathers, and the sacraments that bring about what is thus proclaimed, are radically divine actions. They have for subject Christ himself as man; he, through the mission of the Spirit, associates persons to the Church *sacramentaliter* (that is, the Church acting as both sign and instrument), so as to bring about in an ongoing way the convocation-congregation that is the Church.

To help us understand the Church's structure, the following outline scheme may be useful: Christ sends his Spirit in the word and sacraments and thereby brings the Church into being, both her members and sacramental structure;[41] and this structure (the *compages socialis*, the Church as institution) is used by the Spirit of Christ for the celebration-administration of the sacraments. In this way, by building up the members of his Body and assigning them functions, Christ maintains the Church in its structure. Man's response to the trinitarian and ecclesial action of preaching and sacraments is faith, and, along with faith, those same sacraments (of faith) insofar as they call for man's collaboration. Men and women "live" in the Church through the sacraments, at the same time "situating" themselves in the Church's structure. And, through those same sacramental actions, the Church continuously constitutes herself as Church and thereby maintains itself as Church.

2. The Church-sacrament as a structural dimension of "communion"

(a) *The internal dimension of the Church's structure: "faithful" and "sacred ministers" as primary elements* The inseparability and simultaneity of the two dimensions of the Church on earth (community of persons and sacred structure) are affirmed by Vatican Council II in a dense expression: "the sacred nature and organic structure of the priestly community."[42] The structure, therefore, is not "superstructure," but rather the very substance of the Christian community. And this is so (there is no harm in repeating), because the structure is not "added on to" an already existing

---

[41] "Ecclesia fabricata per sacramenta": St. Thomas Aquinas, *Summa Theologiae*, III, q. 64, a. 2, ad 3.

[42] "Indoles sacra et organice exstructa communitatis sacerdotalis": *Lumen gentium*, no. 11/a. "Ecclesia non exsistit nisi ut Ecclesia structura praedita": Commissio Theologica Internationalis, *Themata selecta de Ecclesiologia* (Città del Vaticano, 1985), p. 42. Relevant, even fundamental, to our subject is all of chapter 7: "De sacerdotio communi in sua relatione ad sacerdotium ministeriale."

community, but rather is the *sacramental* dimension of the communion: it is that by which the communion, already inchoate in history and present to the community, is at the same time the sacrament of full, eschatological communion. The *sacraments* themselves, drawing us as they do into communion with God and the brethren, bring forth (in its unity and its differentiation) *the sacrament*, the Church-community insofar as it is endowed with its fundamental structure.

It is clear from what has been said that this structuring action is principally brought about by the actions of those sacraments that "imprint" character—baptism (and confirmation), on the one hand, and holy orders, on the other. There thus arise the two most primary elements of the fundamental structure of the Church, which we respectively call *"christifideles"* and "sacred ministry."

Baptism creates the state of being a "member of God's People" (it makes a person a Christian, a *christifidelis*), and it presents the Church-community in its most primary and naked condition—the assembly or congregation of the Christian faithful (*congregatio fidelium*). Prior to any division of functions and duties, of distinct states and conditions, we have in the Church the radical equality of all *christifideles*, which arises from God's baptismal call; we are on the elementary and eschatological level of the *communion of the faithful*, of *Christian fraternity*.[43]

In the bosom of God's People, however, Jesus calls some members for a particular ministry, a "sacred ministry." In the words of the last Council: "The Lord also appointed certain men as ministers, in order that they might be united in one body in which 'all the members do not have the same function' (Rom 12:4). These men were to hold in the community *of the faithful* the *sacred power of Order*, that of offering sacrifice and forgiving sins, and were to exercise the *priestly office* publicly on behalf of men and women in the name of Christ."[44] By means of the sacrament of Orders, which enables them to act *in persona Christi*,[45] Christ configures the hierarchical dimension of the Church's fundamental structure. This "sacred ministry" embraces all deacons, priests, and bishops, including the office of the bishop who succeeds Peter in the Roman see (but there is no need for us here to examine the internal features of the "sacred ministry"). This new element of its structure is what

---

[43] See on this subject J. Ratzinger, *La fraternidad cristiana* (Madrid, 1960).

[44] *Presbyterorum ordinis*, no. 2/b (my italics).

[45] L. Scheffczyk, *Schwerpunkte des Glaubens. Gesammelte Schriften zur Theologie* (Einsiedeln, 1977), pp. 367–86 (Die Christusrepräsentation als Wesensmoment des Priesteramtes).

makes the communion of the Church not only a *communion of the faithful* but also and simultaneously a *hierarchical communion*.

It is important to note that the sacraments that give rise to the first dimension of the structure are those that confer a participation in Christ's priesthood. That serves to highlight how the first level of the Church's fundamental structure evidences the various elements and functions of the ecclesial society structuring itself into something radically priestly—so much so that, evoking the conciliar formula, the Church, all of it, is called a "priestly community." Let us explore this feature.

(b) *The priestly nature of the Church's structure*   As much in its structure as in its deepest being (communion), the Church is to be understood from the mystery of the Incarnate Word—not only because it was founded by him, but also because in itself the Church is a mystery of "christification" in the Spirit whereby it becomes Christ's Body. But Christ, in his humanity, by the Spirit's anointing (the hypostatic union itself), is essentially the one Mediator between God and mankind, the eternal priest of the New Covenant, whose fruit is the Church.

The Second Vatican Council linked Christ's saving mission to his messianic identity as priest, prophet, and king. Likewise it saw the Church's structure as a sacramental participation in his three-fold ministry (*munus*) designed to make the Lord's salvific mission present to the world. The "worship" the Church offers the Father, the "word" of salvation proclaimed in it, and the *exousía* [46] or sacred power directing and governing it are three functions that should not be separated from one another. Rather, they form an "organic complex" [47] rooted in Christ's unity. Since its ontological center is found in the only Mediator, its core is Christ's (ontological) priesthood, which is displayed in the priestly, prophetic, and kingly dimensions of his salvific activity. Analogically, the same can be said of the Church, a priestly community by reason of its consecrated, priestly structure which unifies the whole. In the Church the radically priestly reality (in its threefold priestly, prophetic, and kingly forms) derives, as we said, from baptism, confirmation, and holy orders.

The dimensions of "faithful" and "sacred ministry," born of Christ's *sacramental* gift of the Spirit, are operatively qualified to collaborate with Christ's salvific action, which is why the Church calls them "common priesthood" and "ministerial priesthood." In

[46] "All power [*exousía*] in heaven and on earth has been given me" (Mt 28:18).
[47] K. Wojtyla, *La renovación en sus fuentes* (Madrid, 1982), p. 178.

this regard, we should note that, even though the Council did not say so expressly, it follows from the ecclesiology of Vatican II that the essential distinction (not merely one of degree) between the "common priesthood of the faithful" and the "ministerial priesthood" also holds good, when the Church participates in Christ's two other *munera*—the kingly and prophetic. Thus both the Church's "redeemed life" (Christian life), which will reach its plenitude in the consummated kingdom, and the redemptive structure proper to her pilgrim phase are historical expressions of that radical transformation in Christ. This work of the Spirit ensures that, through Christ, with him, and in him, all honor and glory be given to the Father.

(c) *The external dimension of the Church's structure—universal Church and particular Churches* [48]   The two elements of *christifideles* and sacred ministry certainly do not exhaust the Holy Spirit's "structuring" action in the Church. Two further dimensions of that action deserve mention. On the one hand, the Spirit's action continues to express itself in charisms (this subsequent and ongoing action presupposes the primary structural nucleus). On the other, as our analysis of the fundamental structure also shows, Christ's one Church on earth is found in the forms of "universal Church" and "particular Churches." We will not concern ourselves here with the charismatic aspect of the Church's structure (part of its *internal* dimension). Staying at the more radical and primary level, we should inquire into the relevance to our subject of the second binomial—"universal Church/particular Churches."

The *"christifideles*/sacred ministers" binomial affects the basic, aboriginal sacramental structure of the Church founded by Christ, making of it an "organically structured priestly community." And it also pertains to the Church's mystery that this organic priestly community--People of God and Body of Christ—manifests itself in human history under the dual form of "universal Church and particular Churches."

The mystery of the Church is indeed the mystery of the unity of communion of all the faithful under Christ's *exousía* activated in

---

[48] On this subject see a crucial document: Congregation for the Doctrine of the Faith, *Communionis notio* (letter), to the Bishops of the Catholic Church on some aspects of the Church as communion, Rome, May 28, 1992. Permit me to cite my commentary: "La comunión en la Iglesia," in *Scripta Theologica* 24 (1992) 559–68. Likewise that of R. Lanzetti, "La Iglesia como comunión," in *Palabra*, July 1992, pp. 66–68. On the theme's theological background, see my *Iglesias particulares*, pp. 140–84, and J. R. Villar, *Teología de la Iglesia particular* (Pamplona, 1990), passim.

Spiritu Sancto through a life of faith and through the supreme ministry of the Pope and the episcopal college. This is the ecumenical "congregation of believers," the mysterious *ekklesía*—dispersed the world over and always congregated in the Lord—of those who "devoted themselves to the apostles' teaching and fellowship (*koinonía*), to the breaking of bread and the prayers."[49] The article of the Apostles' Creed "I believe in the catholic Church" is the definitive witness to this identity-setting.[50] When Vatican II relates "Christ the only Mediator" to the "only Church of Christ,"[51] it is only reflecting this fundamental dimension of the redemptive work of the Word made flesh.

But the Second Vatican Council made a further decisive contribution to the theological understanding of the Church's mystery and its fundamental structure. According to *Lumen gentium*, the Church is not only the universal "congregation of the faithful," but also the "body of the Churches." That is, the Church founded by Christ not only assembles the ecumenical multitude of the faithful under the supreme authority of the Pope and the episcopal college; these faithful are convoked and congregated in particular Churches, each headed by its bishop. The communion of all these Churches constitutes Christ's Church. So teaches *Lumen gentium*, 23, where we find this passage: ". . . the whole Mystical Body, which . . . is a corporate body of Churches."[52] Thus the "mystery" of the particular Church within the framework of the universal Church consists in the fact that while it is "particular" or "part," "in it is truly present and operative (*inest et operatur*) Christ's Church: one, holy, catholic and apostolic."[53]

Gérard Philips, secretary for the conciliar commission that drafted the Constitution on the Church, holds the view, with conclusive arguments from tradition (from the New Testament to

---

[49] Acts 2:42.

[50] Cf. J. Ratzinger, *Introducción al Cristianismo* (Salamanca, 1971), pp. 291-307.

[51] *Lumen gentium*, no. 8/a–b.

[52] The Church, which at the ontological level is a *communio cum Deo et hominibus*, is at the structural level of its constitution a *communio ecclesiarum*": E. Corecco, "Sinodalità": in *Nuevo Dizionarino di Teologia* (Rome, 1972), p. 1484. This is so because the *communio ecclesiarum* has its own structural elements at the service of communion—the Pope and the college. Concretely, the "proper, ordinary and immediate" power wherewith bishops rule their particular Churches has an internal relationship with the Church's supreme authority, whose role it is to moderate its exercise and circumscribe it within certain limits, "*intuitu utilitatis Ecclesiae vel fidelium*" (*Lumen gentium*, no. 27/a). See Congregation for the Doctrine of the Faith, *Communionis notio* (letter), chapter 3, nos. 11–14

[53] Vatican Council II, *Christus Dominus*, no. 11/a.

Vatican II) that the particular Church, in its theological content, belongs to the *ius divinum* of the Church founded by Christ.[54] Consequently, we can say that the mutual implication or "mutual interiority" of universal Church and particular Churches is a constitutive dimension of the mystery of the Church here on earth. To put it another way: it pertains to the mystery of the Church that this double dimension never be an alternative (universal Church *or* particular Church), nor therefore can it be resolved by excluding one of the terms. Both must be affirmed simultaneously. So, according to the Catholic faith, the Church, which is one and unique, is at the same time a "body of Churches," or, if you wish, "the body of the Churches."[55]

If we look at what we have called the institutional dimension of the fundamental structure ("universal Church/particular Churches") in relation to that other, radical, and self-standing dimension ("*christifideles*/sacred ministry"), it is easy to see that the latter binomial effectively lends its structure to the former's double manifestation of Christ's Church. Both the universal Church and the particular Churches are Christ's Church because they are "structurally" constituted by the institutional articulation of both *christifideles* and sacred ministers. The Christian community, in its most basic form, is always structured in this way.

Speaking now at this second level, we ought to stress that the "sacred ministry," in turn, has an internal, sacramental articulation. The ministerial priesthood finds its fullest expression in the bishops, who, under the Holy Spirit, tend to God's Church[56] and ordinarily head the particular Churches. As successor to St. Peter, the bishop of the Church in Rome is the head of the episcopal college and presides over the universal Church and the communion of all the Churches. The episcopal college and the Pope, who as head presides over the college, are thus the two particular moments of the "sacred ministry" dimension at the level proper to the universal Church. For their part, priests, "prudent cooperators of the episcopal college," says Vatican II,[57] at both the universal and the particular levels, form around the bishops the great priestly

---

[54] "Particulares vero Ecclesiae, saltem episcopales seu dioecesanae, in quibus praesens et activa adest Ecclesia universalis, et quae suo modo catholicitatem et universalismum Ecclesiae manifestant, secundum traditionem pertinent ad institutionem iuris divini": G. Philips, "Utrum Ecclesiae particulares sint iuris divini an non," in *Periodica de re morali, liturgica et canonica* 58 (1969) 143–54.

[55] See my *Iglesias particulares*, p. 152.

[56] Acts 20: 28.

[57] *Lumen gentium*, no. 8.

and ministerial body that most of the faithful "experience" in daily life as expression of the structural element we have called "sacred ministry." The "Christian community" (both the total Church and the smaller, local one) thus appears as a group of Christian faithful presided over by a bishop, who shepherds them with the help of priests (and deacons). As ever, we have before us the Church as a community structured by the ministerial priesthood and the common priesthood of the faithful.

The time has come to transcribe the Vatican II text of greatest theological relevance to our purpose. According to the decree *Christus Dominus*, "a section of the People of God [is] entrusted (*concreditur*) to a bishop to be guided by him with the assistance of his clergy, so that, loyal (*adhaerens*) to its pastor and formed (*congregata*) by him into one community in the Holy Spirit through the Gospel and the Eucharist, it constitutes one particular Church in which the one, holy, catholic and apostolic Church of Christ is truly present (*inest*) and active (*operatur*)." [58] These words speak clearly of the "mystery" of the particular Church, though previously the Council pointed out no less clearly the three elements that form the organic reality of the particular Church—a portion of God's People, the bishop who brings unity to it, and the clergy collaborating with the bishop. To be rigorously theological, without all three there is no particular Church.

3. The Church-sacrament as an "operative" moment of communion

We will now look at the purpose of this *priestly* structure, whether of the universal or particular Church. The Church has been so constituted—that is, with a dual structural element (universal and local) and with a dual way of participating in Christ's priesthood—to serve the Lord's salvific action in history. That is simply another way of saying that the Church's mission is carried out and fulfilled by the workings of the *sacramentum salutis*. Now, the most basic stratum of this ecclesial activity is one whose dynamism stems from the relationship between the common priesthood of the faithful and the priestly ministry. We ought, therefore, to return— not now in a structural, but in an operative "mode"—to the priestly community that is the Church, to study that dynamism. *Lumen gentium*, number 10, is relevant here: "Though they differ essentially and not only in degree (*essentia et non gradu tantum*), the

[58] No. 11/a.

common priesthood of the faithful and the ministerial or hierarchical priesthood are none the less ordered one to another; each in its own proper way (*suo peculiari modo*) shares in the one priesthood of Christ. The ministerial priest, by the sacred power that he has, forms and rules the priestly people; in the person of Christ he effects the eucharistic sacrifice and offers it to God in the name of all the people. The faithful indeed, by virtue of their royal priesthood, participate in the offering of the eucharist. They exercise that priesthood, too, by the reception of the sacraments, prayer and thanksgiving, the witness of a holy life, abnegation and active charity." Let us see how these priesthoods differ and, then, how they are ordered to each other. This analysis will point to "structural" consequences.

(a) *Two ecclesial forms of participating in Christ's priesthood: their difference*   First Pius XII[59] and then Vatican II expressed a unanimous conviction of Catholic faith by affirming that the two forms of participating in Christ's priesthood differ essentially and not merely in degree. The terminology has given rise to much debate, mainly in an effort to explain metaphysically the meaning here of *essence* and *participation*.[60] That does not concern us now. As I see it, the Council itself interprets the expression "in essence and not merely in degree" when it says that this is so *because* each priesthood participates in Christ's single priesthood *suo peculiari modo*.[61] I take this to mean that:

1. As participations in Christ's priesthood, both are inalienable: one cannot be derived from or reduced to the other. Only through the activity proper to both priesthoods (or both forms of participation) does Christ's unique priesthood fully display its salvific power in history: what in Christ is one is found in the Church under two forms.

2. They are essentially complementary; thus the text, "one is ordered to the other," has more than a moral or legal meaning (it does not simply mean, for example, "helpful to ecclesial life"). Rather; it expresses the profound "why" for that essential differen-

---

[59] Pius XII, *Address to the Cardinals*, Nov. 2, 1954, in *AAS* 46 (1954) 669.
[60] Cf. A. Fernáandez, "Nota teológica sobre la explicación conceptual de una fórmula difícil: la diferencia entre el sacerdocio común y el sacerdocio ministerial," in *Revista Española de Teología* 36 (1976) 329–47; and A. Vanhoye, "Sacerdoce commun et sacerdoce ministériel. Distinctions et rapports," in *Nouvelle Revue Théologique* 97 (1975) 193–207.
[61] Cf. A. Aranda, "El sacerdocio de Jesucristo en los ministros y en los fieles. Estudio teológico sobre la distinción 'essentia et non grado tantum'" in *La formación de los sacerdotes en las circunstancias actuales* (Pamplona, 1990), pp. 207–46.

tiation—the theological mode of the priestly being of the Church as a whole, as a priestly community.

This essential difference and mutual correlation express the mystery of the Church as (priestly) body of Christ (the priest). Let us explore the essential difference by delving into the content of each form. With the concrete and historical acts of his life culminating in the paschal mystery, Christ is the priest and victim eternally pleasing to the Father. He alone, the Son of God made man, "the man Christ Jesus," is the "one Mediator between God and men," as we read in the First Letter to Timothy (2: 5). The common priesthood of the faithful means participating in the priesthood bestowed on his own by Christ. Believers are thereby enabled to offer their lives—"their bodies," says St. Paul (Rom 15: 1)—as living, holy hosts, pleasing to God:[62] the common priesthood of the faithful is an "existential" priesthood. Opus Dei's founder was perfectly correct when he said that Christians are made by God "priests of our own lives."[63] The exercise of the common priesthood consists primarily in the daily hallowing of real, concrete life: what are transformed into the "spiritual hosts" St. Peter refers to (1 Pet 2: 5) are the particular deeds of a Christian person, deeds that display the consecration of a Christian's whole being, of his "body" in the Pauline sense. Through the common priesthood, Christ associates Christians to his sacrifice and praise of the Father.

A. Feuillet concluded his research into this subject as follows: "The spiritual sacrifices spoken of in 1 Peter 2: 5, seen within the context of other passages mentioned, ought, above all, to be interpreted as a voluntary imitation by Christians of the sacrificial offering of Christ, the suffering Servant."[64] The practice of the faithful's common priesthood is, then, nothing other than Christian life in action. Accordingly, every Christian can say of himself, in words of St. Josemaría, that his is radically a "priestly soul," one that imbues everything he does.[65]

---

[62] The biblical roots for the common priesthood of the faithful have been rigorously studied by A. Feuillet, "Les 'sacrifices spirituels' du sacerdoce royal des baptisés (1 Pet 2: 5) et leur préparation dans l'ancien Testament," in *Nouvelle Revue Théologique* 96 (1974) 704–28 and his "Les chrétiens prêtres et rois d'après l'Apocalypse," in *Revue Thomiste* 75 (1975) 40–66.

[63] "Through baptism all of us have been made priests of our lives, 'to offer spiritual sacrifices acceptable to God through Jesus Christ.' Everything we do can be an expression of our obedience to God's will and so perpetuate the mission of the God-man" (*Christ Is Passing By*, no. 96).

[64] A. Feuillet, *Jésus et sa mère* (Paris, 1974), p. 237.

[65] Cf. letter, March 11, 1940, no. 11; letter, March 28, 1955, no. 3.

The common priesthood of the faithful, then, is something priestly, prophetic, and kingly practiced in the concrete circumstances of life in the midst of the world—something that cannot be reduced to, although it includes, liturgical actions.[66] The joyful offering of one's life to God as continual praise in the Holy Spirit is something that belongs to the essence of the common priesthood. In this sense, its exercise will never disappear, but rather will reach eternal culmination in the consummated Church (*Ecclesia in patria*). But it is also praise *per Filium*: so, here on earth it relates essentially to the eucharistic sacrifice. As Feuillet remarks: "The baptized are, in similarity to Christ, priests and victims of the sacrifice they offer, but this sacrifice becomes possible through the one sacrifice of Christ."[67]

This last statement brings us to discuss what is proper and specific to the "ministerial or hierarchical priesthood," the undeniable need for it, and its irreducibility to the common priesthood. Despite the accuracy of everything we have said about the priesthood of all the baptized, it is still a central truth of our faith that there is no priest but Christ and no sacrifice more pleasing to God than the gift Christ makes of his very existence. The *congregatio fidelium* does not bestow on itself the salvation it witnesses to, nor does it generate the saving word and sacrament, for it is Christ alone who saves. Therefore, Christians can be living hosts only by "receiving" from Christ here and now the power of his word and sacrifice. The ministerial priesthood, in the economy of grace, is, so to say, the divine "invention" whereby Christ, exalted at the Father's right hand, delivers *today* to mankind his word, pardon, and grace. This is the *raison d'être* of the ecclesiastical ministry—to serve as the infallible and efficacious sign and instrument, of Christ's presence, head with the body, *amidst the faithful*. As Bishop del Portillo put it: "Christ is present to his Church not only insofar as he attracts to himself all the faithful so that with and in him they all might form one Body; he is present, and eminently so, as Head and Pastor who instructs, redeems, and ever watches over his People. And it is this presence of Jesus Christ the Head that is brought about through the ministerial priesthood he instituted in the bosom of the Church."[68] "The central meaning of priestly

---

[66] Cf. F. Ocáriz, "La partecipazione dei laici alla missione della Chiesa," in *Annales Theologici* I (1987) 7–26.

[67] *Jésus et sa mère*, p. 245.

[68] A. del Portillo, *Escritos sobre el sacerdocio*, 6th ed. (Madrid, 1990), pp. 98–99. An earlier edition of this work was translated into English with the title *On Priesthood* (Chicago, 1974).

ministry in the Church is the ministry of Jesus Christ himself, who, through the conferring of priestly ordination, continues to live in the Church's ministerial priesthood."[69]

The ministerial priesthood is, then, a "sacramental" priesthood, distinct from the "existential" priesthood common to all the faithful. It is sacramental, not by reason of its origin (both priesthoods derive from their respective sacraments), but rather because the specific purpose of the ministerial priesthood and its functions is to serve as a "sacramental" (re-presentative) channel of the presence of Christ, the mediator and head. As St. Josemaría wrote: "All of us Christians can and should be, not just *alter Christus*, but *ipse Christus*: other Christs: Christ himself! But in the priest this happens in a direct way, *in a sacramental way*."[70] The actions proper to the common priesthood, on the other hand, are not "sacramental" (re-presentative), but rather, as we have seen, "real," belonging to the *res* of sanctified Christian life. The ministerial priesthood, which seals *forever* those ordained, belongs nevertheless to the category of *medium salutis* characteristic of the Church's pilgrim phase; but the royal priesthood of the baptized belongs to the category of ends (*fructus salutis*), for it consists in the doxological communion with Christ, priest and victim, which is the very heart of Christian existence, and which will reach its fullness in eternal life.[71]

Let us now look at the mutual relations between the two priesthoods, something implied in the preceding considerations. Both forms of priesthood, with their practical expressions, need one another: each is "for" the other, but in different ways.

(b) *The ministerial serves the common priesthood: substantial priority of the "christifideles"*   "Our sacramental priesthood," wrote John Paul II in 1979 with respect to sacred ministers, "constitutes a particular *ministerium*: it is a service to the community of the faithful."[72] The ministry's orientation to the faithful should be

---

[69] *Schreiben der Bischöfe des deutschprachigen Raumes über das priesterliche Amt*, Nov. 11, 1969 (Trier, 1970), p. 98.

[70] *In Love with the Church*, p. 48.

[71] A. Feuillet, "Les sacrifices . . . , p. 276. The essential difference between the two forms of participation, according to the terms we have been using, highlights something obvious but of the greatest importance: the common priesthood retains its native content in those who receive the ministerial priesthood. It is neither "superseded" nor "subsumed" by the latter. The priesthood common to the faithful demands of the *christifidelis*-minister that his ministerial priesthood become "existential"—the dedicated existence of a priest.

[72] Letter *Novo incipiente*, in *AAS* 71 (1979) 399.

seen in this perspective. The first and most radical relation between ministry and faithful is the service of ministering to the "congregation of the Christian faithful." Here is how *Lumen gentium* solemnly affirms it: "The office . . . the Lord committed to the pastors of his people is, in the strict sense of the term, a service, which is called very expressively in holy Scripture a *diakonía* or ministry (cf. Acts 1:17, 25; 21:19; Rom 11:13; 1 Tim 1:12.)" [73]

The formal reason of this service, as we saw, is the "re-presentation of Christ." To exercise it, priestly ministers are endowed with "sacred power," as the Council declares: "The bishops, as vicars and legates of Christ, govern the particular Churches assigned to them by their counsels, exhortations, and example, but over and above that also by the authority and sacred power (*auctoritate et sacra potestate*) which indeed they exercise exclusively for the spiritual development of their flock in truth and holiness, keeping in mind that he who is greater should become as the lesser, and he who is the leader as the servant." [74] "For the exercise of this ministry, as for the rest of the priests' functions, a spiritual power is given them, a power whose purpose is to build up the Church." [75]

Thus, to say that ordination, the orientation of the priest to the faithful, is essentially *diakonía* or service is equivalent to saying that the "ontology" of Church structure indicates the *substantial* priority of the "Christian condition" (the common priesthood). "With you I am a Christian; for you I am the bishop," said Augustine of Hippo. [76] With respect to the common priesthood, the "priestly ministry" element has a *relative* character, theologically subordinate: "Christ instituted the hierarchical priesthood for the benefit of the common priesthood." [77]

This priority is "substantial," which does not mean that the ministerial priesthood is derived from the common priesthood (a position formally at odds with Catholic faith). [78] Both forms of priesthood are "basic and aboriginal," as we have sufficiently seen, and "essentially" distinct.

[73] No. 24/a.

[74] *Lumen gentium*, no. 27/a.

[75] *Presbyterorum ordinis*, no. 6/a.

[76] "Ubi me terret quod vobis sum, ibi me consolatur quod vobiscum sum. *Vobis enim episcopus, vobiscum christianus*. Illud est nomen officii, hoc gratiae; illud periculi est, hoc salutis": *Sermo* 340, 1; PL 38:1482—quoted in *Lumen gentium*, no. 32/d.

[77] K. Wojtyla, *La renovación* . . . , p. 183.

[78] Cf. Congregation for the Doctrine of the Faith, letter, August 6, 1983, II, 2, in *AAS* 75 (1983) 1001–1009.

Having skirted error, we nonetheless ought to affirm this substantial priority. To understand and affirm it with all its consequences pertains to the essence of the Catholic conception of the
Church.[79] Given the common priesthood's priority, we can clearly
see why the ministerial priesthood's power to represent Christ does
not mean that clerics are more Christian than others or that they
contribute more to the Church's mission, as if the faithful could be
reduced to mere recipients of clerical ministrations.

We here witness one of the greatest developments brought
about by Vatican II's theology of the Church, one that paradoxi-
cally reveals something most ancient and primordial in its structure. It shows that it is all God's priestly People, *organice exstructus*,
that bears the message of salvation to the world, and that what
really matters and abides forever is the substantive condition of
"christifideles," of "being a Christian." Consequently, ministry is
something structurally relative—relative to Christ and to the
"congregation of Christians." The cleric relates to Christ insofar as
his service to the Lord consists in being a sign and instrument of
Christ's saving gift to the community. And he relates to the congregation insofar as, through his priestly ministry, he enriches the
congregatio fidelium with godly gifts. Thus the latter are spurred to
practice *their* priesthood (the "priestly soul" St. Josemaría refers to)
by living the substance of that faith and by their in-worldly worship of God, the charity that Christ himself, not his ministers, has
granted them in the Spirit. This smacks of Scripture, even of Old
Testament Scripture: "The role of the *kohanim* (*hiereis*) is essentially that of keeping the people aware of their priestly character
and spurring them to live in such a way as to glorify God by
everything they do." [80]

This ecclesiological twist produced by Vatican II is found in its
definition of the particular Church: no longer is it a territory or
jurisdiction, but rather a portion of God's People. The above-
quoted conciliar text succinctly puts forth the theology of the
interaction of twofold participation in Christ's priesthood. In

[79] The ecumenical transcendence of this teaching is evident. Rigorously pointing
to the *substantial* priority we recognize in the "faithful" and their baptismal priesthood are the following: (a) the radicality and permanent exercise *in Patria* of the
christifidelis' condition transformed into that of *comprehensor*; at this is all of Christianity aimed *simpliciter*; this level, as St. Augustine said, is the *nomen gratiae*; (b) the
character of service to the *congregatio fidelium* that defines sacred ministers and is the
raison d'être for the priestly ministry; whence its name: *nomen officii*.

[80] J. Colson, *Ministre de Jésus-Christ ou le sacerdoce de L'Évangile* (Paris, 1966), p.
185; quoted by J. Ratzinger, *La Iglesia, una comunidad siempre en camino* (Madrid,
1992), p. 76.

defining the Church, the substantive element is the community, the *portio*, the ensemble of Christian faithful, which is the focus of the dual ministerial element that composes it and structures it as Church—the bishop, "visible source and foundation of unity," [81] and the priests, "prudent cooperators of the episcopal college and its support and mouthpiece." [82] By the ministerial action of the bishop with the clergy (exercising the "ministerial priesthood": preaching and sacraments, above all the eucharist), the particular Church, the portion, is and lives as Church: there *the* Church of Christ as such *inest et operatur*. But having said that much, we are already pointing to the "functional" priority of the sacred ministry.

(c) *How the common priesthood relates to the ministerial: the latter's "functional" priority*   It is now time we looked from the other side at the mystery of participation in Christ's priesthood in the Church, both in its communion and in its structure. To affirm the *substantive* priority of the "Christian condition" with respect to the ministry only fully makes sense when admitting the latter's *functional* priority. This priority stems from the *ordinatio* the faithful have to the ministry of the clergy. *Christifideles* and ministry are ordered to one another (*ad invicem ordinantur*). In the light of what we have seen, their mutual relations should be easy to grasp.

Christian "substance" (what Augustine calls *nomen gratiae*) is radically found in the faithful: all baptized persons in the Church are on the way to salvation and holiness by reason of their status as Christians. But the *congregatio fidelium* does not bestow this substantive condition on itself; rather it is a fruit of the Spirit, whom Christ sends in the word and the sacraments. So, the specific *service* rendered the community by the ministers of the word and the sacraments is no mere "option"; it is indispensable to Christian life. In the economy of salvation established by Christ, availing themselves of this ministry is essential if the "congregation of the faithful" are to develop as Christians. In this sense ministers, because they represent Christ the head, enjoy *functional* priority within the Church structure; this testifies to Christ's being the head and savior of his Body.

From this can be seen the common priesthood's special *ordinatio* to the ministerial. While the relationship of ministerial to common priesthood is that of service, not so the relationship of common to ministerial. If anything, it is a relationship expressing the need *to be*

[81] *Lumen gentium*, no. 23/a.

[82] "Ordinis episcopalis providi cooperatores eiusque adiutorium et organum" (*Lumen gentium*, no. 28/b).

served. The faithful need the sacramental, prophetic, and pastoral services of ministers in order to be and live as Christians. They require the ministerial priesthood's specific actions if they are to exercise those pertaining to the common priesthood. Without the "help" of the priestly ministry, they could not be what they are, in the words of John Paul II, who bases himself on Vatican II: "Beloved brothers, the sacrament of Order, specific to us, fruit of the grace particular to our vocation and basis for our identity, by virtue of its very nature and everything it produces in our life and activity—all this helps the faithful to be aware of their common priesthood and to actualize it (cf. Eph 4: 11ff.). It reminds them that they are God's People and equips them to 'offer spiritual sacrifices' (cf. 1 Pet 2:5) through which Christ himself makes us an everlasting gift to the Father (cf. 1 Pet 3:18). This happens, above all, when the priest, 'by the sacred power he has . . . effects the eucharistic sacrifice and offers it to God in the name of all the people' (*Lumen gentium*, 10)." [83]

This functional priority of the sacred ministry has led some theologians to speak of it as the "structuring" ministry of the community.[84] Indeed, if the Church's fundamental structure arises from Christ's convoking the congregation through word and sacraments, thereby giving himself to the faithful, the role belonging to ministers is that of instruments which Christ the head uses to maintain the Church as Church, that is, endowed with the fundamental structure that enables it to perform its mission. That is the reason why ministers, despite being essentially servants, ought to be loved and honored by the Christian community, as St. Paul asked the Thessalonians: "But we beseech you, brethren, to respect those who labor among you and are over you in the Lord and admonish you, and to esteem them very highly in love because of their work" (1 Thess 5:12–13). The reason for their dignity is "structural," to do with the "work" they carry out; it is not something "personal."

4. *The foundational dynamics of the Church's structure*

We have just considered the "faithful/ministers" binomial, with their mutual relations (substantive priority of the former, functional-structuring priority of the latter). That helps us to appreciate better the unity-totality of the Church's basic structure, which, through both elements, is configured in its most primary

---

[83] Letter *Novo incipiente*, in *AAS* 71 (1979) 399.
[84] Cf. J. G. Pagé, *Qui est l'Église. III: Le Peuple de Dieu* (Montreal, 1979), p. 263.

dimensions. Here on earth, the Church, "organically structured" (*organice extructa*), is not just the faithful, or just the ministers; rather it is the priestly community consecrated by the Spirit, whom Christ sends from the Father, a community endowed with a structure wherein the common and ministerial priesthoods operate ineffably to make the Church Christ's Body.

This structure is basic and aboriginal inasmuch as its two component elements represent the most radical structural positions, though not the only ones, found in the Church. From this perspective we can understand theologically the historical entities in which this structure expresses itself, both at the universal as well as at the particular level. And this essential articulation, in turn, distinguishes those entities from other forms of Christian community where only one of the elements comes into theological play.

To sum up: the structure of the Church, as disclosed by divine revelation, is this: priestly ministers, by dedication to their ministry, serve their brethren (the "faithful"), so as to enable the latter, exercising their existential priesthood, to serve God and the world. The priestly ministry exists for "the growth of the Christian community to the point where it is enabled to radiate faith and love in civil society."[85] The dynamics of this twofold, stepped, service are eschatological—the mission, the building up of Christ's Body. In this context the Pope's title of "Servant of the Servants of God" acquires its full strength and meaning. By divine institution he presides and unites all the ecclesiastical "ministry." This title synthesizes all the theology of the ministerial priesthood and, with it, the true sense of the twin priority—substantive and functional—we have examined.

(III)

OPUS DEI'S INSTITUTIONAL STRUCTURE

As is known, Opus Dei has undergone a complex evolution within the forms of ecclesial institutions. A very detailed monograph on this subject has been published entitled *El itinerario jurídico del Opus Dei*,[86] on which we will rely in part. The subtitle of that work, "History and defense of a charism," alludes to what lies behind that evolution—the founder's effort to ensure that the Work's "true

[85] A. del Portillo, *Escritos . . .* , p. 60.
[86] A. de Fuenmayor, V. Gómez Iglesias, and J. L. Illanes, *El itinerario jurídico del Opus Dei. Historia y defensa de un carisma*, 4th ed. (Pamplona, 1990).

nature and theological characteristics," as the papal constitution *Ut sit* put it, be guided, at times against wind and countercurrent, to reach port unharmed. On the other hand, a safe harbor—to the extent that there is such a thing *dum peregrinamur a Domino*[87]—is only found when the "true nature and theological characteristics" are safe from every storm. And that eventually happened when Pope John Paul II established Opus Dei as a *praelatura personalis ad peculiaria opera pastoralia perficienda*.

Opus Dei's "true nature and theological characteristics" embrace more questions (spiritual, pastoral, and so on) than what concerns us here—the ecclesiology of Opus Dei. What, in theological terms, is the ecclesial structure of Opus Dei that has braved so many seas and made it necessary to put in at such different ports?

1. *The ecclesiological nature of Opus Dei*

In the previous section we went into the theology of the Church at some length, highlighting the primary elements of the Church's fundamental structure, while keeping in mind what we had said about Opus Dei earlier on. This leads us to suggest that Opus Dei—the Christian community formed by Josemaría Escrivá and his followers—in its native reality does seem to be an ecclesial body whose initial structure is "analogous," we might say, to those self-structuring forms (particular Churches) that arose originally in the Church. If that is so, it is quite paradoxical, because it would situate Opus Dei (which in some ways represents no little novelty in the Church) into an organizational framework similar to the oldest forms of communion and service known to the Church. Maybe that is what led its founder to call Opus Dei's message as "old as the Gospel and like the Gospel new." [88] But let us not get distracted.

We only said an "analogous" institution. As we saw earlier, the basic and aboriginal forms of Christ's Church are those of "universal Church" and "particular Churches." Opus Dei is moreover something born "inside" the Church. It is not "the" (particular) Church, though it is still Church. This affirmation, so obvious that it is in a certain sense the very basis of everything Christian, is, nonetheless, the route to understanding the institutional analogy

---

[87] 2 Cor 5: 6.

[88] "Jesus our Lord wants us to proclaim today in a thousand tongues—and with gift of tongues, so that all may apply it to their own lives—to every corner of the world, that message, as old as the Gospel and like the Gospel new" (letter, Jan. 9, 1932, no. 91).

we have made. It in turn sends us again to a further consideration of the Church's fundamental structure.[89]

(a) *How the Spirit and history affect the Church's structure*   To reflect on the "structure" of the Church is always to consider the Church as a sacrament in time and history. We see how Christ, by means of the sacramentum salutis, brings about the definitive and eschatological "communion of men with God and with one another." Now, in this history of the *sacramentum salutis* we must distinguish between the "basic, aboriginal structure" of the Church as sacrament, endowed with the dimensions and elements we have described, and the "historical forms" in which that basic structure manifests itself. Without the former (the basic structure), the Church is not Church (or at best it is an impaired Church: this is a hotly debated ecumenical subject). Therefore, the one Church, the *catholica*, to use St. Augustine's word, always has that structure and therefore is effectively and fully Church; it is *the* Church. The structure we are talking about is, consequently, what grounds the identity of the *sacramentum salutis* throughout the centuries. From the tiny group in the Cenacle at Jerusalem to the great, worldwide body on the eve of the third millennium, Christ's Church is always identical.

But the so-structured Church, with its in-built orientation to the salvific mission received from the Redeemer, is in the Holy Spirit's hands. The Spirit is like its soul, and he sends upon it his charisms to enrich and "restructure" it. By the very nature of history, assumed already by Christ in the incarnational mystery, the Church ever meditates on the Lord's word, while symbiotically relating to the ways and culture of each age. All these factors combine in the historical development of the Church's basic structure. "From the start the Church's history is, from this point of view, the history of organizational developments and of pastoral adaptation of divinely instituted elements to the growth of the People of God. The Church must always be responding to apostolic and spiritual needs encountered throughout the ages as it goes about its saving mission, while rightly leaving inviolate its essential elements." [90]

We can furthermore say that the Church's "basic structure" never appears in a "chemically pure state," so to speak. It always

---

[89] On this subject see my *Iglesias particulares*, pp. 159–61, and my "La identidad teológica del laico" in *La misión del laico en la iglesia y en el mundo*, Actas del VIII Simposio Internacional de Teología (Pamplona, 1987), pp. 84–91.

[90] My *Iglesias particulares*, pp. 159–60.

adopts some particular form of historical organization. In each age one finds a concrete "historical structure," which evidences a particular degree of development of its fundamental elements, and which remains open to further change. The International Theological Commission, in a 1985 document, called these two levels the "*essentialis Ecclesiae structura*" and its "*Ecclesia definita et mutabilis forma*" (or "*Ecclesiae organizatio*").[91]

Earlier I pointed out that this development and "articulation" of the "basic structure" are due to the Spirit's graces and charisms, to the Church's own reflection and meditation, and to its connections with the culture in which it lives. We need not examine each of these aspects. It suffices to note that it is in this developmental context where we ought to look for Opus Dei's novelty.

(b) *Opus Dei's novelty and the Church's structure*   The foundational charism which Josemaría Escrivá received, let us not forget, found him as a "sacred minister," one of Christ's priests.[92] Seen from the perspective of the Church's historical structure, this God-given grace led him to promote within the Church a Christian community whose members—lay faithful and priests—began to relate to

[91] "Distinguimus etiam inter essentialem Ecclesiae structuram eiusque definitam et mutabilem formam (vel eius organizationem). Structura essentialis complectitur omnia quae in Ecclesia ex eius a Deo institutione (iure divino), mediante eius a Iesu Christo fundatione et Spiritus Sancti dono, proveniunt. Ipsa structura nonnisi unica et durabilis esse potest. Attamen, ista essentialis et permanens structura semper aliquam definitam formam atque organizationem (iure ecclesiastico) induit, ex contingentibus et mutabilibus, sive historicis vel culturalibus, sive geographicis vel ad rem publicam spectantibus, elementis constitutam. Ex hoc sequitur quod definita Ecclesiae forma mutationibus subiecta est; in ipsa apparent legitimae et etiam necessariae differentiae. Tamen, institutionum diversitas ad structurae unitatem refertur. Inter essentialem structuram et definitam Ecclesiae formam (vel organizationem) discernere non est disiungere. Essentialis Ecclesiae structura in quadam definita forma semper implicata est, extra quam subsistere non potest": Commissio Theologica Internationalis, *Themata selecta ecclesiologiae occasione XX anniversarii conclusionis Concilii Oecumenici Vaticani II* (Città del Vaticano, 1985), pp. 30–31.

[92] Opus Dei's founder, when referring to the time of "inklings" (presentiments that God was asking of him something not yet revealed), explained his priestly vocation as a way to "prepare himself" for whatever was to come. In his case the ministerial priesthood was to be a form of "readiness" (RHF, no. 20164, p. 801). This could seem paradoxical when what God wanted St. Josemaría for was to launch an organization, not for priests, but almost entirely for lay people. Looking at matters both historically and ecclesially, the founder's condition as priest no longer seems preparatory but rather essential to his founding and presiding over the organization born on Oct. 2, 1928. In fact, Josemaría Escrivá knew himself to be Opus Dei's founder precisely as a priest. See the biographies cited above, note 28.

each other just as they had before coming to the Work, as "faithful" or "sacred ministers." They did so in order to attain the goal God had assigned to Opus Dei—to proclaim and practice the universal call to holiness. Thus, it will be those same ecclesial positions that determine the structure of the new "organization," Opus Dei.

On the other hand, the Church in its wisdom, "taught by the Holy Spirit," [93] has grasped that the basic form of a Christian community, and therefore of Christian mission (how *christifideles* and sacred ministry relate) can also articulate communities that are not particular Churches but institutions of the universal Church. Among the myriad ecclesial forms that have developed over time, the Church has discerned Christian groupings that can best express their message and serve communion and mission as institutions of the universal Church. This is what John Paul II has done with respect to Opus Dei through the Constitution *Ut sit*. This discernment, coming as it does from the head of the Communion of the Churches, [94] deserves close attention. First, however, we should note that in carrying out this theological assessment of Opus Dei, the Pope availed himself of a previous discernment, that of Vatican II. Its *Presbyterorum Ordinis* (no. 10), adumbrated a type of institution called *praelaturae personales ad peculiaria opera pastoralia*. [95] Let us turn to the text of John Paul II.

The Pope says that Opus Dei has become present in the Church's life "as an apostolic organism made up of priests and lay people, both men and women, that is at the same time organic and undivided, that is to say, as an institution endowed with a unity of spirit, of aims, of government and of formation." [96] This is a very

[93] *Lumen gentium*, no. 53.

[94] On this subject, see J. Hervada, "Aspectos de la estructura juridica del Opus Dei," in *Lex Nova* 1 (1991) 301–22.

[95] Let us note that shortly thereafter, in 1969, Fr. Josemaría wrote to the Holy See, manifesting Opus Dei's gratitude and hope for the institutional possibilities opened to the Work by the Council: "Il Congresso ha preso finalmente atto, con vivo senso di gratitudine e di speranza, che dopo il Concilio Ecumenico Vaticano II possono esistere in seno all'ordinamento della Chiesa, altre forme canoniche, con regime a carattere universale, che non richiedono la professione dei consigli evangelici, da parte dei componenti la persona morale (cfr. *Presbyterorum Ordinis*, 10, and *Ecclesiae Sanctae*, 4)." This was an official letter from Monsignor Escrivá as President General of Opus Dei to Hildebrando Cardinal Antoniutti, prefect of the relevant congregation of the Roman Curia. The complete text is found in *El itinerario jurídico*, p. 583.

[96] "Quasi apostolica compages quae sacerdotibus et laicis sive viris sive mulieribus constabat eratque simul organica et indivisa, una simul spiritu, fine, regimine et spirituali institutione": *Ut sit*, Nov. 28, 1982, introduction.

accurate way of summarizing the existential and operative reality of Opus Dei. The Christian community launched by St. Josemaría Escrivá and now spread throughout the Church universal displays these fundamental features—(a) a structured social community (*compages*); (b) galvanized by its mission (*apostolica*); (c) consisting of clergy, and laity of both sexes; (d) whose internal structure is "organic and undivided"; and (e) endowed with a unity of aim, spirit, organization, and training.

This important document tersely but clearly identifies the kind of social body that Opus Dei is and, therefore, the position the Work occupies in the Church—how it functions within the larger body. There are other kinds of social arrangements among the faithful. The Church's richness, as a recinct of freedom in Christ, knows many forms of gathering and community, diverse ways for Christians to relate to one another. For instance, there are many forms of associative life, in which the *christifideles* component of the Church's structure expresses its Christian initiative and responsibility. These associations gather in their ranks both lay people and clerics, precisely under the structural dimension of *christifideles*. There are also associations for priests with various purposes, particularly those devoted to improving their spiritual and apostolic life. Then, finally, we have the immense ecclesial phenomenon of institutions which are "forms of consecrated life." Modeled on religious Orders, their social arrangement is structurally determined not by the "*christifideles*/sacred ministers" relationship (though the entity may contain both), but by the profession of the evangelical counsels insofar as these configure a way of life. How the faithful deploy their social nature is a classical and rich vein within canon law, not to mention theology.

Now, the theological reality according to which Opus Dei is structured is none of the above, but rather the one to which John Paul II refers in the Constitution. Opus Dei's social arrangement as a "Christian community" stems from what we have called the "internal dimension of the Church's structure". That is, it is born of mutual relations of *christifideles* and "sacred minister," or, if you prefer, it derives from the two forms of participating in Christ's priesthood. That is also why Opus Dei as a social reality in the Church is organic and undivided. Its lay faithful (men and women) and the priests who act as its clergy complement each other in exemplary adherence to the basic aboriginal relationship obtaining in the Church between *christifideles*—called to live out the requirements and implications of their baptism—and sacred ministers, who bring in, besides, the "ministerial" consequences of the sacrament of Order. As the Work's Statutes (no. 1) put it: "Opus Dei is a prelature embracing in its bosom (*simul complectens*) clerics and lay people." Three numbers later this statement is developed: "The ministerial priesthood of the clergy and the common priesthood of the lay people are so intimately linked that both, in unity of vocation and government, require and complement each other (*ad invicem*) in striving for the end proper to the prelature."[97]

Thus, to the question, What is the ecclesiological nature of Opus Dei? one could reply: "It is an institution whose internal structure replicates the basic ecclesial articulation between the common priesthood of the faithful, possessed by virtue of baptism, and the ministerial or hierarchical priesthood, possessed by the clerics incardinated in it."

So, what we find in Opus Dei, different yet complementing one another, are the two ecclesial forms of participating in Christ's priesthood. We find both the "substantial" priority of Opus Dei's lay faithful, at whose service is the priestly ministry, and the "functional" priority of the sacred ministry, in whose head (the prelate) resides the *sacra potestas* that governs the prelature. The clergy's "functional" priority was described by the founder when he said that the ministerial priesthood "impregnates with its spirit our personal life and all our apostolic work."[98] Opus Dei's Statutes put it more technically: "Under the prelate's authority, the clergy, by means of their priestly ministry, enliven and inform all of Opus Dei."[99] But if these terms—inform, enliven—point to a "functional priority," they also clearly manifest the "substantial priority" of Opus Dei's lay faithful. Graphically, the founder told the Work's priests that their task is to be a "carpet" for others. He wrote: "In Opus Dei we're all equal. There's only a practical difference: priests are more bound to *place their hearts on the floor like a carpet, so that their brothers and sisters may tread softly*."[100]

---

[97] *Statuta*, no. 4 § 2.

[98] Here is the complete passage: "If exalted is the dignity of the priesthood and great its importance for all the People of God, great also is its value among us (who form a part of the holy Church), because the priesthood, venerated by all of Opus Dei's members, impregnates with its spirit our personal life and all our apostolic work" (letter, Feb. 2, 1945, no. 4).

[99] No. 4 § 1.

[100] Letter, August 8, 1956, no. 7. "All of you, my children, ought to serve one another as required by our fraternal spirit, but priests cannot permit their lay brethren to treat them preferentially. We priests in the Work are slaves of the others and, following the Lord's example (who came not to be served, but to serve: *non venit ministrari, sed ministrare*: Mt 20:28), we have to place our hearts on the floor, so that the others may tread softly. Therefore, to let yourselves be served by your lay

Among other things, this means that the life of the institution, the way it is Church, its projection towards its God-given mission, in a word, the dynamics of its structure, theologically relate to what we said above concerning sacramentality as an *operative* moment of the Church.[101] A Holy See document, studying Opus Dei's Statutes, lucidly described this dynamic, calling it "reduplicatively pastoral."

"In effect," we read, "the prelate and his clergy carry out a 'particular pastoral work' in favor of the prelature's laity... and all the prelature, clergy and laity, carry out a specific apostolate at the service of the universal Church and the particular Churches. There are, therefore, two fundamental aspects of the prelature's aim and structure that explain its reason for being and its natural and specific insertion within the global pastoral and evangelizing activity of the Church—(a) the 'particular pastoral work' the prelate and his clergy develop to sustain and tend to the lay faithful incorporated to Opus Dei in the fulfillment of the specific commitments (ascetical, formative, and apostolic) they have undertaken and that are particularly demanding; and (b) the apostolate that the prelature's clergy and laity, inseparably united, perform with the aim of spreading in all social sectors a profound awareness of the universal call to holiness and apostolate and, more concretely, of the sanctifying value of ordinary professional work." [102]

The double purpose (or double apostolic step) expressed by this document fits in very well with the double moment of the Church's dynamics developed by St. Paul in a celebrated passage of his Letter to the Ephesians:[103] "And his gifts (*edôken*) were that some

---

brothers and sisters without necessity goes against Opus Dei's spirit" (letter, Feb. 2, 1945, no. 20). This awareness of the substantial priority of the Work's lay faithful led the founder to write even the following: "In our path to holiness, owing to its lay nature, the priesthood—while it is a sacrament that also imprints a character—is for us, so to speak, a circumstance that in no way alters our God-given vocation. Our calling is the same for all, each one responding to it in his own state in life" (letter, March 28, 1955, no. 44). Regarding the oneness of vocation in Opus Dei, again I refer readers to chapter two, section IV.

[101] Section II, 3 and 4.

[102] Note of the Congregation for Bishops dated Nov. 14, 1981; cited by J. L. Gutiérrez, "Unità organica e norma giuridica nella Costituzione Apostolica *Ut sit*," in *Romana* 2 (1986) 345.

[103] Eph 4: 11–12. Syntactically, this passage is made complex by a chain of prepositions: *pros ... eis ... eis*. We follow the reading of R. Penna, *Lettera agli Efesini* (Bologna, 1988), pp. 189–94. Also see H. Schlier, *Der Brief an die Efheser. Ein Kommentar* (Düsseldorf, 1962; Italian translation: Brescia 1965, pp. 238–43), with the developments contained in his later work, "La eclesiologia del Nuevo Testamento," in *Mysterium salutis*, vol. 4.1, *La Iglesia* (Madrid, 1973), pp. 171ff.

should be apostles, some prophets, some evangelists, some pastors and teachers, for the equipment of the saints (*pros ton katartismon tôn hagiôn*) for the work of ministry (*eis ergon diakonias*), for building up the body of Christ (*eis oikodomén tou sômatos tou Christou*)." Synthesizing, we can say that the first verse of this passage describes the Church's ministerial dimension *ad intra*—beginning with the apostles' fontlike and all-embracing ministry—which is presented to the Ephesians as a "gift" from Christ to his Church, for the Church that they are. Note the "objective" character of the gift ("structural," we should say in the language we are using), to be related to the preceding verse 8, which speaks of how the exalted Christ "gave gifts to men." St. Paul does not look directly to the persons of the ministers—who are called to be apostles and so forth—but rather to the community, the Church, enriched by the roles that these persons carry out or, if you prefer, enriched by those persons, who by virtue of their roles are gifts for the Church.[104]

The sacred ministers do not exist for themselves, but for the faithful, to serve the "saints," as the following verse says. The ministers exist "*pros ton katartismon tôn hagiôn*." Their first and fundamental task (here we have the first apostolic step) is "for the equipment of the saints," as the Greek expression is translated, which is much denser and richer than to "perfect": to capacitate them, organize them; that is, to prepare and ready them[105]—the original word suggests all of these. In theological language it means to serve one's brethren, to provide them the service that only they can provide, the service of the word and sacraments.

That is why St. Paul goes on to describe the second step, that is, the purpose of this supernatural outfitting: to equip them, he says, "for a work of ministry," to minister, we could say, to *all* the Church. Structured in this way, the "saints" are able to offer the Church and world the work God himself has entrusted to them and that St. Paul expresses christologically, when he says its aim is "building up the body of Christ." So, it is not only the ministers, but rather the whole Christian community, organically structured of laity and sacred ministers, that achieves the Church's mission, the building up of Christ's body in the midst of the world.

This double step, which expresses the Church's basic apostolic dynamism, is well reflected in the following text of Opus Dei's

---

[104] Cf. in R. Penna, *Lettera*, pp. 189–91, the study of these figures and their ministries.

[105] The Neo-Vulgate translates: "ad *instructionem* sanctorum." In the New Testament *katartismos* is a hapaxlegomenon.

founder: "It is in the practice of that ministry—*ministerium verbi et sacramentorum*—that they are to show themselves to be God's ministers and servants of all souls, especially those of their brothers and sisters. . . . Servants, I say, because, forgetting themselves, they should concern themselves primarily—subordinating everything else, however important it may appear—with the holiness of their brethren [first step] and active cooperation with them in all the apostolates proper to our spirit [second step]."[106] It is the same teaching with which *Lumen gentium* begins its treatment of the Church's sacred ministry: "The holders of office, who are invested with a sacred power, are, in fact, dedicated to promoting the interests of their brethren, so that all who belong to the People of God, and are consequently endowed with true Christian dignity, may, through their free and well-ordered efforts towards a common goal, attain to salvation."[107]

(c) *The theological reason for Opus Dei's institutional form* What we have just described is the structure and dynamism of Opus Dei seen from an ecclesiological perspective. This is how it was first perceived by its founder in the light of the foundational charism. Later it was fleshed out by dint of his prayer and ecclesial experience, illuminated by studying and meditating on God's word, submitted constantly to the Church's authority and, finally, recognized and promulgated by the Church. The question about its ecclesiological nature now takes a new turn. Why does Opus Dei have this structure and not another? Why does the Work claim that its establishment by John Paul II as a personal prelature is the "definitive juridical solution" to its long evolution?

---

[106] Letter, Feb. 2, 1945, no. 25. The brackets contain my commentary. Note that in the "second step," it is not the laity who "cooperate" with the priests, but rather the latter who collaborate in the laity's apostolates. This nuance serves to affirm again the substantial priority of the faithful. This primacy is stressed even more in another text, where, speaking of the clergy's ministerial priesthood, he says that priests "will be support and sap for the endeavors of their secular brothers, in whom they will foster a 'healthy anticlericalism.' Opus Dei's lay people are not trained to be sacristans, but rather, with the greatest fidelity to the holy Church and the Pope, they operate on their own initiative in a spirit of freedom and responsibility" (ibid., no. 28). Ephesians' double step is reflected in other texts: "Let our priests realize that the fruitfulness of their endeavors is measured by the efficacy they contribute to the others' apostolic work [2nd step] and—above all, since it is an indispensable condition—to the spiritual life of their brothers and sisters" [1st step] (ibid.). "Priests ought not to forget that they are especially ordained (let me never tire of repeating it) to tend to their brothers and sisters [1st step] and to work in our apostolic undertakings [2nd step]" (letter, August 8, 1956, no. 9).

[107] No. 18.

First, a clarification. "Definitive" here means the last of a series of solutions perceived as inadequate to its "true nature and theological characteristics." St. Josemaría knew this full well throughout the canonical vicissitudes. While he waited for better times and did his best to bring them about, he spoke, not without a touch of irony, of finding the "least inadequate possible" formula. God did not grant him to see the "definitive solution" he longed for. Definitive therefore means appropriate, the juridical solution thanks to which the structure's various elements and functions fit together (*mutua compositio*), making the legal norms conform perfectly to the foundational charism.

It is common knowledge that the reason the founder wanted Opus Dei to become a personal prelature had to do with two main concerns. On the one hand, this framework fully expresses the secularity of Opus Dei members, both clergy and laity.[108] And on the other, this canonical status assures the Work's unity: all its members, men and women, priests and lay people, with but one vocation,[109] constitute a single jurisdictional unity governed by its prelate and pastor. In the light of the foundational charism, both aspects seem truly central to Opus Dei's ability to provide the Church with the service God has called it to offer—the proclamation and practice of the universal call to holiness through work and life's ordinary situations, and that with its own specific spirituality. In a certain way it can be said that Opus Dei either stands or falls on the Work's secularity and unity. The precariousness (or juridical exceptionality) of both features in the previous phases of its evolution have been duly studied by specialists.[110]

Now let us see how these two essential features acquire, with the "definitive solution" sanctioned by John Paul II in *Ut sit*, the greatest clarity and protection. The "personal prelature" formula, appropriating as it does an institution that expresses the *internal* dimension of the Church's basic structure, locates Opus Dei within the order of ecclesial realities prior to the historically verified tensions between canonically secular and religious persons or institutions within the Church, with their legal and social consequences. A personal prelature simply indicates that in Opus Dei there is no consecration other than that of character-imprinting sacraments, which alone, as we have said repeatedly, structure this kind of institution. Opus Dei, as an institution, enjoys the secularity proper to the Church's hierarchical institutions. Consequently,

---

[108] Chapter three, below, is devoted to this theme.

[109] This is the central theme of chapter two.

[110] Cf. *El itinerario jurídico*, passim.

all the members of Opus Dei are secular: the lay faithful are ordinary faithful who live their Christian life from the lay or secular status characteristic of all lay people; and the priests incardinated in the Work are simply secular priests, who find their place in the prelature—and therefore in the Church—through the "ministeriality" that structurally defines sacred ministers.[111] In a certain sense it can be said that Opus Dei's establishment as a personal prelature simply leaves its previous juridical problem behind: it is now irrelevant.

The same can be said, *congrua congruis referendo*, about the vocational and institutional unity of the Work. Those who incorporate themselves into the personal prelature of Opus Dei are lay faithful (men and women, single, married, or widowed), all of whom have, in different forms, the same vocation. (In chapter two, the rich subject of unity and variety will be amply discussed.)[112] Once they become members of Opus Dei, the one vocation is found in the different structural roles proper to the lay faithful/sacred ministers binomial, since some of the laymen are later ordained as priests. On the other hand, a personal prelature, as a hierarchical institution, ensures in the simplest way governmental unity among men and women, laity and clergy. Men and women are structurally envisioned for what they are—"lay faithful," the prelature's faithful. There are not two institutions, one for men and another for women, nor one for priests and another for lay people, but rather a single one, the prelature of Opus Dei, where each plays his own structural part under the prelate.[113]

Considering the historical-institutional process leading to *Ut sit*, one can also reach another conclusion. If this configuration of Opus Dei as a personal prelature (an ecclesial institution responding exclusively to the *christifideles*/sacred ministry dimension) resolves the problems and dissipates the threats or precariousness seen by the founder, it does so because this "ecclesial form" does indeed correspond to the "mission" laid on Opus Dei by its foundational charism.

---

[111] See my "La identidad . . . ," 84–91.

[112] It is no harm to mention in advance, though it is probably obvious, that the vocational unity Opus Dei's founder insisted on takes place on a plane diverse from that of the differentiation of structural positions in the Church (faithful/ministers), which, as we are seeing, is also to be found in the Work.

[113] There is one branch for women and another for men, each with its own apostolates, but with a full institutional unity: "In utraque pariter Operis Dei Sectione, virorum scilicet ac mulierum, eadem est unitas vocationis, spiritus, finis et regiminis, etsi unaquaeque Sectio proprios habeat apostolatus": *Statuta*, no 4 § 3. On the subject also see *Statuta*, nos. 133 § 3, 145–47, 157, 159, 170.

We devoted the first section of this chapter to discussing how "mission" determines institution." That seemed the best way to an ecclesiological understanding of Opus Dei. What we said there about the Work's charismatic origin, reappears here at the level of theological reflection. The first facet of that 1928 "illumination," we said, was the renewed message of the universal call to holiness and apostolate of all Christians—not just a few, but the general mass of ordinary lay faithful. But this "prophetic" dimension was inseparably interwoven with God's call to Josemaría Escrivá to "incarnate" the message. It is at that point that we find what theologians call "foundational charism" in the strict sense—a charism that gives rise to a form of Christian community and institution in the Church. Referring to the historical experience of Opus Dei (the theological analysis of which led to his making it a personal prelature), John Paul II notes: "From its very beginnings this Institution has in fact striven not only to *illuminate* with new lights the mission of the laity in the Church and in society, but also to *put it into practice*." [114] By the prophetic dimension of that charism, St. Josemaría and his followers endeavored to remind everyone in the Church of that call to apostolic holiness amid everyday life *in mundo et in Ecclesia*. The institutional dimension also had to respond in its ecclesial structure to those ordinary circumstances; otherwise the institution's social arrangement would negate, or at least weaken, the pristine power of the prophetic message that it proclaims and claims to carry out. In this sense, only an institution organized in line with the *internal* dimension of the Church's structure (*christifideles*/sacred ministry) appears adequate to manifest the ordinary ecclesial circumstances of the multitudes God has called, via baptism, to holiness and apostolate, however unaware of it these lay people may be. Therefore, Opus Dei's establishment as a personal prelature, an institution reflecting the Church's ordinary constitutional structure, simultaneously consolidates these two important institutional dimensions of Opus Dei—its members' secularity and their vocational and institutional unity.

2. *Analogous to the particular Church*

(a) *Opus Dei's organizational form*   At times particular Churches, personal prelatures, etc. are described as "hierarchical" institutions or "belonging to the hierarchical structure of the Church."

---

[114] *Ut sit*, introduction.

In itself this expression is correct and sanctioned by Vatican II;[115] but it needs to be properly understood. It does not refer to institutions that autonomously organize the Church's ministerial or hierarchical element, but rather to Christian communities whose social form is the one we have been discussing. In these latter, the ministerial or hierarchical element is an element internal to the social arrangement, though not the only one; they are institutions where not only the *communio fidelium* but also the *communio hierarchica* configure the whole social arrangement from within.

As we saw in the second section, particular Churches—"principally dioceses," says the Code of Canon Law[116]—are the communities where, by divine law and in an eminent way, what we have just said is realized. On the other hand, the particular Church, precisely since it is an element of the "Church's essential structure," to quote the International Theological Commission, historically takes a variety of forms *de iure ecclesiastico* (those described by canon 368: diocese, territorial prelatures, and so forth). These forms pertain to the Church's *definita et mutabilis forma*, and the communion of all of them in the universal Church makes up the *Corpus Ecclesiarum* of Vatican II.

The "eminent" character of the particular Church makes of it a natural analogue for understanding theologically those other institutions that, without being particular Churches, do respond to the structural element *"christifideles/*sacred ministry." [117] These other forms of Christian community are structurally canonical creations (*de iure ecclesiastico*) that thus represent an historical development of the oft-cited structural dimension of the Church (*"christifideles/*sacred ministry"). As we have seen, this dimension is certainly primary, basic, aboriginal (*de iure divino*). I called the former "canonical creations," but I added "structurally," to signify that the community in itself can be of charismatic origin, as is manifest in the case of the convocation wrought by St. Josemaría. When this is so, the granting of the legal form by Church authority implies that the Church has discerned the foundational charism and the social arrangement immanent in the Christian community born of that charism.

Opus Dei's organizational form reflects the *internal* dimension of the fundamental structure of the Church. We can see this from

---

[115] *Lumen gentium*, chapter 3, for example.

[116] See my *Iglesias particulares*, pp. 168–83.

[117] Some canon lawyers have begun to speak (appropriately) of "particular Churches and complementary structures." See J. Hervada, *Elementos de Derecho constitucional canónico* (Pamplona, 1987), pp. 293ff.

its Statutes, which spell out the prelature's organization by articulating the consequences of that dimension. Let us take a brief look at these Statutes. The document has five titles. Title I, first chapter, deals with Opus Dei's nature. Here, in concentrated and synthesized form, it says (as we have partially seen) that the Work is in fact organized in line with the structural dimension under discussion. The following three chapters describe in some detail the structural element of "faithful." The Catholic faithful incorporated in Opus Dei and their structural role in the prelature by reason of their bond correspond to what in our general analysis of the Church's structure we have called its "substantive element." In its regard, everything else in the structure is "relative": it concerns service," "function." The Statutes here describe the Work's lay faithful, diverse but with one vocation, since they make up the vast majority of the prelature's members. However, with theological rigor, the Statutes also include "sacred ministers" within the term "faithful of the prelature," since, as we saw above, they do not renounce their baptismal condition or the common priesthood of the faithful, when ordained.

Paraphrasing Vatican II,[118] we could say: in order to coalesce its members into a single body, God has chosen some, from among Opus Dei's faithful, to be ministers. . . .[119] This is, in effect, the link between titles I and II of the Statutes, where the element of "sacred ministry" is formally treated—how the prelature's presbyterium is constituted; how Opus Dei's faithful accede to it; how one receives canonical mission; and so forth. Express mention is made of how the prelate and his vicars strive to foster among the prelature's priests a spirit of communion with all the other priests of the local Churches in which the former are at work.[120] In this context we find the norms governing the "Priestly Society of the Holy Cross."[121]

---

[118] "Idem vero Dominus, inter fideles, ut in unum coalescerent corpus . . . quosdam instituit ministros": *Presbyterorum ordinis*, no. 2/b.

[119] A text from the founder to accompany this train of thought: "The specific vocation with which, among your brothers, you have been called and to which you have freely responded obliges you to serve them in everything that refers to God. First, to offer the holy sacrifice; then, to administer the sacraments and to preach the divine word, 'as ministers of Christ and dispensers of God's mysteries' (*ut ministros Christi: et dispensatores mysteriorum Dei*: 1 Cor 4: 1). And this greatness, my children, is carried out, if we are faithful to grace, on the foundation of our weakness: *quoniam et ipse circumdatus est infirmitate* (Heb 5: 2): because the priest himself is beset with weakness": letter, August 8, 1956, no. 1.

[120] Cf. *Statuta*, no. 56

[121] See later in this chapter, section IV, 5.

Having covered the double structural element that sustains the institution, title III describes the "dynamics" of the *compages apostolica* that is Opus Dei—"Life, Training, and Apostolate of the Prelature's Faithful." Then, title IV is devoted to how the prelature is governed; its direction pertains to the prelate, who governs this organic body of clergy and laity with the help of his vicars and councils.[122]

Opus Dei, in sum, has a tripartite structure in keeping with the ecclesial bodies we have been speaking of—the prelate, his clergy, and the faithful people whom he guides. Later we will have more to say about this threefold element in Opus Dei. But now we should return to our theme and consider more closely the analogy with the particular Church—a comparison that has emerged naturally from our analysis of Opus Dei's internal ecclesiological nature.

(b) *Content and scope of the analogy*   To say that one thing is analogous to another presupposes differences and similarities. As we have said above, Opus Dei is not a particular Church, but it has in common with the particular Church a certain level of "theological substance." So, it will be the simultaneous understanding of how they differ and how they overlap that will disclose in what the analogy consists and therefore Opus Dei's role within the Church. Ultimately, the question has to do with the difference between particular Churches and personal prelatures. I explored the subject in a book with that title,[123] but it might be worthwhile to look at it from the concrete and vital perspective of Opus Dei.

Internally structured in the "*christifideles*/sacred ministry" form, the Church manifests itself in history under the double form of "universal Church/particular Churches," what we earlier called the "external dimension of the Church's structure."[124] To dwell on Opus Dei's relationship with both of the Church's basic forms of configuration is the best way to identify ecclesiologically the difference between Opus Dei and particular Churches, because Opus Dei is an institution of the universal Church; it is not a particular Church.

We can say that the ground for the analogy between Opus Dei and the particular Church is the common "theological substance"

---

[122] Title V is very brief and contains five articles concerning the "stability and obligatoriness of this Code." There are two final norms. The full text of the Statutes is included as an appendix to the present volume.

[123] *Iglesias particulares*, pp. 210ff.

[124] See above, section II, 2, c.

of ecclesial bodies structurally organized according to the basic "common priesthood/ministerial priesthood" relationship[125]—the fact that both have the substantial elements of the *internal* dimension of the Church's structure. But that co-possession can involve different meanings and purposes as far as the Church's saving mission is concerned. These give rise to different roles in the Church's structure, when seen against what we call the "external" dimension of that structure (the "universal Church/particular Churches" binomial). Let us look at it more carefully.

The triple substantial element (head, clergy, faithful) of that internal dimension is found in the particular Church in ways adequate to the expression and realization of its "mystery," that is, of the mysterious emergence in it (*adest, inest, operatur*) of the one, holy, catholic and apostolic Church. Hence the need that its head be an ordained bishop and for the relationship between both priesthoods to be expressed in the celebration of all the sacraments and in openness to all charisms. Indeed, particular Churches are the universal Church fulfilling itself, concentrating itself existentially in a particular moment; each Church represents the whole in the part, the sacramental "plenitude" in the *portio*. It is this concentration of the universal Church's saving reality in the particular Church that permits each particular Church to have *all* the virtualities, both existential and institutional, of the one Church. Thus the particular Church has the potential to integrate in its life *all* the qualitative variety of charisms and ministries. Therein, not otherwise, consists its sacramental mystery. Therefore the particular Church is in the image (*ad imaginem*) of the universal Church.

As a personal prelature, however, Opus Dei is not, by its theological structure, *ad imaginem* of the universal Church. Rather, personal prelatures, and therefore Opus Dei, are designed for particular pastoral tasks (*ad peculiaria opera pastoralia*). The universal Church's end and mission—all aspects of which are, in concentrated form, found at least potentially in each particular Church—acquires in the prelature a *particular* dimension, albeit one which is as radical and "non-sectional" as that which configures Opus Dei. That dimension is what determines the jurisdictional scope of Opus Dei's prelate, the ways in which the ministerial priesthood is exercised in it, the presence among its faithful of lay people and not of religious, and so forth. But that particular mission and task are carried out in Opus Dei, as in the particular Church, from a common theological substance; that is, from the "prelate/clergy/

---

[125] See my *Iglesias particulares*, pp. 200f.

faithful" relationship and from the two kinds of social arrangements we have called *communio fidelium* and *communio hierarchica*.

How the *internal* dimension of the Church's structure works in Opus Dei determines in turn, as we have said, its different role in the Church's structure, now looked at *externally*. Opus Dei is not a particular Church, but an institution of the universal Church. It pays to understand this. The document of the Congregation for the Doctrine of the Faith already cited, referring to the "institutions and communities established by the Apostolic Authority *ad peculiaria opera pastoralia*," [126] says of them that "as such, they pertain to the universal Church, although their members are also members of the particular Churches where they live and work." [127] Since it is one of those institutions and communities, Opus Dei, therefore, belongs, as such, to the universal Church.

Translated to the ecclesiological categories we have been using, that "as such" means "at the level proper to the external dimension of the Church's structure." [128] And applied to our subject: Opus Dei, as a Christian community, is not a particular Church, but rather a transdiocesan, universal convocation of the faithful that transcends particular Churches (even though it has in common with them, as we have pointed out, the *internal* dimension of their structure). But that "as such" also means that Opus Dei's ecclesial reality does not entirely consist in being an institution of the universal Church. Being what it is, it is inserted in the mystery of the "mutual interiority" [129] or "mutual immanence" [130] of the universal Church/particular Churches binomial. Therefore, though structurally Opus Dei belongs to the universal Church, its existential reality—the reality of its members' Christian life—belongs to the richness of the particular Churches, to the real communion of each diocese. In other words: since the universal *communio fidelium* that is the universal Church is historically realized (*exsistit, inest, operatur*) in the *portiones Populi Dei* which the particular Churches are, members of Opus Dei (a Christian community that "belongs to the universal Church") are also members of the particular Churches where they live and work. It could not be any other way, for that is the ecclesial structure of salvation. Personal prelatures

---

[126] *Communionis notio*, no. 16. The document largely deals with personal prelatures and military ordinariates; see F. Ocáriz, "Unità e diversità nella comunione ecclesiale," in *L'Osservatore Romano*, June 21, 1992, p. 11.

[127] *Communionis notio*, no. 16.

[128] See above, section II, 2, c.

[129] *Communionis notio*, no. 9.

[130] My *Iglesias particulares*, p. 161.

and, therefore, Opus Dei "are institutions of the universal Church in the dimension of particularity" [131] or, as Ocáriz says, "particular expressions of the universal Church in the particular Churches, not exclusively reducible to one or the other." [132]

From what has been said and speaking in scholastic terms, a particular Church (say, a diocese) and a personal prelature are not distinguished by an "adequate" distinction, *sicut aliud et aliud*: like two different things. That distinction does apply between two dioceses or between a diocese and a territorial prelature, but not between a particular Church (diocese, territorial prelature, and the like) and a personal prelature, since they are "inadequately distinct" entities.

(iv)

Some Particular Matters Related to Opus Dei's Structure

The preceding thoughts about Opus Dei's nature and structure help us to see it as an "apostolic organism" endowed with the unity of which John Paul II speaks in his introduction to *Ut sit*. This manifold unity is due to Opus Dei's having the structure we have been analyzing; that is, it corresponds to the *internal* dimension (*christifideles*/sacred ministry) of the Church's structure.[133] It is expressed moreover by the social arrangement suited to that dimension—the dual form of communion that we call *communio fidelium* and *communio hierarchica*. That having been established, let us now turn to some details of its structure that help to sketch the ecclesiological profile of Opus Dei, beginning with the subject of incorporation into the prelature.

1. *The incorporation of christifideles into the prelature*

How do the lay faithful become linked to Opus Dei? What is the nature of the act whereby a person becomes a member of the prelature? [134] In its first number the Statutes say that members join

[131] Ibid., pp. 213f.

[132] F. Ocáriz, "Unità ...," p. 11.

[133] See section II, 2, above, for our analysis.

[134] The norms governing this theme are spelled out in Title II of the Statutes, whose third chapter is entitled "De fidelium admissione et incorporatione in Praelaturam" and which consists of nos. 17–27. See especially no. 27 and also nos. 1 and 6.

"in response to a divine vocation," [135] and from the act of incorporation a "legal bond" arises whereby they are incorporated to the prelature.[136] Again according to the Statutes, the act is a "formal declaration," before two witnesses, by the prelature, on the one hand, and the Christian, on the other, of the mutual rights and duties[137] succinctly enumerated therein.[138] The bond with Opus Dei arises in the person as a form of exercising his or her *lay options as such* and consequently its theological and legal nature differs from *sacra ligamina* (vows, oaths, promises, and the like) proper to institutes of consecrated life.[139] We have already discussed this; it was one of the reasons that led St. Josemaria and Opus Dei to ask for it to be made a personal prelature. This step certainly ensures the *secular* character of the bond, but it still does not disclose the ecclesiological nature of the act of incorporation. For that we must investigate further.

Since the incorporation embodies an exchange of declared wills (obliging in justice on both parties) we can speak of an agreement or contract, as do both *Ut sit* and the Code of Canon Law.[140] Nonetheless, the term "agreement" or "contract" by itself cannot express all the ecclesiological meaning of that "formal declaration," which Opus Dei's founder from the early days used to call a "commitment of love and service." [141] We say this because the relationship which incorporation establishes between Opus Dei's faithful and the prelature is not in the strict sense a contractual relationship, inasmuch as there is no longer a "bilaterality" (prelature/faithful): bilaterality would make the relationship between the parties an "extrinsic" one. The effect proper to this "contract" is incorporation," the "legal bond of incorporation"; the original bilaterality ceases once a *christifidelis* becomes a "member" of Opus Dei, that is, joins Opus Dei itself. What this means is that

---

[135] "By the same [*eadem*] divine vocation," says no. 6 of the Statutes.

[136] "Laicatus Praelaturae ab iis fidelibus efformatur qui, vocatione divina moti, vinculo iuridico incorporationis speciali ratione Praelaturae devinciuntur" (*Statuta*, no. 1 § 2).

[137] "Pro incorporatione temporanea vel definitiva alicuius christifidelis, fiat a Praelatura et ab eo cuius intersit formalis declaratio coram duobus testibus circa mutua officia et iura" (*Statuta*, no. 1 § 2).

[138] Cf. *Statuta*, no. 27 § 2–3.

[139] Cf. *Lumen gentium*, no. 44, and Code of Canon Law, canon 573 § 2.

[140] *Ut sit*, norm III; canon 296.

[141] Among many other texts: "We are convinced that this commitment of love for God and of service to his Church is not a garment to be doffed and donned, because it embraces all our life. And we desire that, with God's grace, it embrace our life for ever": letter, March 2, 1940, no. 10.

for a member of the Work his relationship with the prelature takes place "within" the prelature itself, not in the *vis-à-vis* style characteristic of a contract.

The canonist Javier Hervada aptly says that here "the commitment or agreement acts as the *cause* of the incorporation and of its continuation." [142] Opus Dei in effect is not the ecclesiological "product" of a successive series of contracts (which would make it a structure with contractual bonds); rather, it is something organic, having an ecclesial structure prior to the "contract" it makes with each of its faithful. That ecclesial structure stems from the basic structural roles of *christifideles*/sacred ministry," with its internal communitarian linkage of the *communio fidelium* and the *communio hierarchica*. In sum: by the formal declaration under discussion a person is incorporated into the prelature's particular *communio*, and the prelature recognizes him or her as a legally full member thereof.

But with this we have not said everything about the ecclesial nature of the act of incorporation. The *communio* that structures Opus Dei is, as we have already said, analogous with, not identical to, that which structures a particular Church. We found that the difference between them stems mainly from Opus Dei's having a *specific* purpose within the *general* aim of the Church. That specific *purpose* and the consequent *opera peculiaria* define the area and the modes of the *communio* that obtains in Opus Dei. This communion is the same, certainly, as that arising from baptism-*communio fidelium* and *communio hierarchica*—that is, the same as that found in particular Churches to which Opus Dei's faithful belong, but it is *qualified* in the prelature by the *vocational commitment* all its members make to practice their *baptismal commitments* in keeping with the aim, spirit, and administration of Opus Dei; this involves "serious and qualified obligations." [143] At the same time, the aim proper to Opus Dei configures the act of incorporation, which is a "declaration" and "commitment" subsequent to baptism whereby one gains entry to that particular communion. What we have here is a declaration of will by the future member that does not make Opus Dei an associative entity; rather, that *mutua declaratio* results in a person's incorporation into a structure that corresponds, as we have now seen sufficiently, to the Church's constitutional *communio*.

[142] "Aspectos de la estructura juridica del Opus Dei," in *Lex Nova* 1 (1991) 315.

[143] This expression is from the declaration *Praelaturae personales*, of the Congregation for Bishops, regarding the Prelature of the Holy Cross and Opus Dei, August 23, 1982, I, c (*AAS*, 75 [1983] 465).

2. The prelate and his pastoral task

Opus Dei is a prelature because it has a prelate directing it, possessed of *sacra potestas*. And, of course, because it has clergy and laity—its faithful people. But a gathering of priests and lay people does not produce the "organic unity" of a "personal prelature" unless it has a head, who brings unity to that grouping and makes it the *compages apostolica* identified and regulated by John Paul II in *Ut sit*. In other words, that "little bit" of the Church of which Monsignor Escrivá spoke is a personal prelature because the Church's supreme authority has entrusted its pastoral care (*cura pastoralis*) to a prelate. Within Opus Dei we find the constitutional dimension of the *communio hierarchica*, because we find a prelate who belongs to the Church's hierarchy and is the hierarchical head of the prelature.

His jurisdiction extends to all members of the prelature, priests as well as lay people, but it is circumscribed by the specific aim and the apostolic mission that the Church has recognized and approved for Opus Dei. In a stricter sense one could say that the prelate's power has the scope and content determined in the Statutes as approved by the Holy Father in *Ut sit*. To the prelate's jurisdictional power corresponds the obedience owed him by the prelature's members, both priests and lay people.[144] Here too we meet another aspect of the analogy with the particular Church. Like the faithful with regard to their diocesan bishops, Opus Dei's faithful obey the prelate (on matters to do with the prelature's special mission) under the same and only title--the power of jurisdiction invested in its prelate. There is no other basis for accepting mandates and obeying in Opus Dei.

Moreover, there is no collision of jurisdictions or jurisdictional parallelism with regard to particular Churches, because Church and prelature have different areas of competence. In what has to do with the ordinary pastoral care of the faithful, the diocesan bishop alone is competent; in what concerns the specific formative, pastoral and apostolic tasks of Opus Dei, its prelate is competent.

Opus Dei's prelate, we said earlier, is endowed with the *sacra potestas* that underpins the prelature; he directs it, as *Ut sit* puts it, as its own ordinary and pastor.[145] This is a clear legal norm, developed throughout title IV of Opus Dei's Statutes. Ecclesiological

[144] "Omnes fideles tenentur praeterea humiliter Praelato ceterisque Praelaturae auctoritatibus in omnibus oboedire, quad ad finem peculiarem Operis Dei pertinent": *Statuta*, no. 88 § 2.
[145] *Ut Sit*, Norm IV.

reflection needs to use this as the basis for discovering the origin, foundation, and meaning of this power, within the context of the sacred power wherewith the Church is endowed.[146]

Before all else let us say that Christ's *exousía-diakonía*, whereby he has been constituted as priest, prophet, and king, is present in the Church and doubly participated in—through the power of the Spirit (common priesthood of the faithful, personal holiness, charisms, ecclesial initiatives on the part of the faithful, since the "soul" is in "all" the body) and through the *sacra potestas* of the apostles,[147] who "shepherd the Church *sub ductu Domini ministrando*," that is, fulfilling their pastoral office through the power of the Spirit sent by Christ. What concerns us now is this second power, given in the Church by apostolic succession and transmitted by the effusion of the Spirit in episcopal ordination and therefore found in the bishops, successors to the apostles.[148] We can thus say that the sacred power whereby Christ's Church is governed, both at the universal and particular or local level, is of an *episcopal* nature.[149]

In the universal Church the structure of this sacred power—both in its original apostolic moment as in successive ones—is a *hierarchical communion*, with a double manifestation, primatial and collegial.[150] The Pope and the episcopal college are the supreme, constitutional, hierarchical dimensions whereby Christ, sending his Spirit, exercises his saving *exousía*. The universal Church, in its internal and external growth, in the development of its mission, is "hierarchically" structured by its Lord and head by means of the ministerial power of the Pope and the episcopal college. These dimensions of *exousía-diakonía*, wherein acts the Spirit of Jesus, make of the ecumenical multitude of believers "the" Church convoked by Christ, the "only" Church, "the" very Body of the Lord.

But the *exousía-potestas* also extends to the local Church in its mystery. The bishop is source and foundation of the unity of the

---

[146] I examined the subject at length in my *Iglesias particulares*, pp. 139–237, whose central ideas I am now trying to summarize.

[147] *Lumen gentium*, no. 19: "*suae* participes potestatis."

[148] Ibid., no. 21.

[149] "Vere episcopalis," says Vatican Council I (*Pastor Aeternus*, chap. 3; DS, 3060), speaking of the Pope's power of jurisdiction.

[150] "The Roman Pontiff, by reason of his office [*vi muneris sui*] as Vicar of Christ, namely, and as pastor of the entire Church, has full, supreme, and universal power over the whole Church, a power he can always exercise unhindered." And in turn "the *ordo episcoporum*, together with their head, the Supreme Pontiff, and never apart from him, have supreme and full power over the universal Church": *Lumen gentium*, no. 22.

Church entrusted to his pastoral ministry.[151] The Supreme Authority certainly entrusts to him the local Church he governs, but the power wherewith he serves it comes radically neither from the Pope nor the episcopal college, but from Christ himself by means of episcopal ordination.[152] That is why *Lumen gentium* says that bishops of particular Churches discharge their mission as "vicars and legates of Christ."[153]

This doctrinal background helps to illustrate better the origin, foundation, and meaning of the prelate's power in Opus Dei. The power whereby bishops of particular Churches govern their *portiones Populi Dei* is of a sacramental origin, since episcopal ordination confers the fullness of the priesthood. Opus Dei's prelate, however, governs the prelature entrusted to him with a power conferred by a *juridical* act (that has no sacramental nature) of the Church's Supreme Authority. If the origin is diverse, so too is the basis of this power: we said above that personal prelatures, and therefore Opus Dei, are institutions of the universal Church in the dimension of particularity;[154] in the light of *exousía-potestas*, the theme reappears in Opus Dei's prelate, whose power is manifested as a particularized moment of the structural *exousía* of the *universal* Church, where it finds its basis and support. The power conferred by the Pope on whoever presides over Opus Dei is, in fact, sustained by the (episcopal) *exousía* belonging to the Supreme Authority and appears as development and participation—for *particular*, *concrete* pastoral tasks—in its universal *sacra potestas*.

This should not be construed to mean that the prelate's power is vicarious, in the *canonical* sense, of the Supreme Authority. We already saw that the prelate is the rightful ordinary and pastor of Opus Dei. But, nonetheless, his is an authority whose *theological* formal reason is found in the universal dimension of the *sacra potestas*. It falls within the purpose and content of the Church's universal hierarchical dimension, which is to serve the particular Churches by means of the particular tasks entrusted to it. Therefore, the prelate's power has an intrinsic *theological* dependence on the Supreme Authority. And this not only or principally because the prelate need not be a bishop, but rather because the power he receives participates in the native character of service to the

---

[151] *Lumen gentium*, no. 23.
[152] On this subject see Vatican II's *Nota praevia* to the Constitution *Lumen gentium*, second observation; and my "Sobre un punto de la 'nota praevia'" in *Paolo VI e i problemi ecclesiologici al Concilio* (Brescia, 1989), pp. 426–27.
[153] *Lumen gentium*, no. 27.
[154] My *Iglesias particulares*, pp. 213–14.

mission and communion of the Churches that is proper to the Supreme Authority. From this perspective, the constitutive theological dependence could be understood as a form of theological vicariousness in the broad sense.[155]

The power of Opus Dei's prelate, having this origin and basis, has a jurisdictional content of an episcopal nature (even when the prelate is not a bishop). This is so, because the object of that power radically consists in moderating and regulating the constitutional "faithful/sacred ministry" relation, which is the nucleus of the internal dynamism of the Church[156] and of the "pastoral" function of bishops. Opus Dei's prelate carries out this function with regard to his faithful and clergy in order to serve the *communio Ecclesiarum* entrusted to the prelature. We already said that the power in question can have this content, because it is supported and grounded in the episcopal authority of the Pope and participates in it. It is not, therefore, "the mere immanent unfurling of the 'clerical' possibilities of the ordination received," as Villar so aptly remarks.[157] Rather, on the basis of priestly ordination, when a priest is made prelate of Opus Dei, functions are conferred on him *in Ecclesia* that in themselves are episcopal, theologically sustained in the Supreme Authority, and specified by his canonical mission and the prelature's Statutes. Therefore, even if he be only a priest, his power is of an "episcopal" nature, that is, he is canonically capacitated "as if he were a bishop" (*ad instar episcopi*).

The kind of power its prelate has is explained by the theological nature of Opus Dei. He does not "need" the fullness of the priesthood as a bishop does, since his role, unlike that of the bishops presiding over local Churches, is not one of making the universal Church's sacramental fullness present in a particular place (local Church). Rather, his role is to gather faithful and priests in Opus Dei in order to carry out its own particular apostolic mission, which is one of a universal scope. But, at the same time, it is very appropriate that Opus Dei's prelate, since he has episcopal powers, should also have episcopal ordination.[158] However, even if the

---

[155] See what I add in my *Iglesias particulares*, p. 183. Also, F. Ocáriz, "La consacrazione episcopale del prelato dell'Opus Dei" in *Studi Cattolici* 36 (1991) 23.

[156] See above, section II, 4.

[157] J. R. Villar, "La capitalidad de las estructuras jerárquicas de la Iglesia," in *Scripta Theologica* 23 (1991) 961–82; also quotation on p. 972. This research is very relevant to our subject.

[158] Opus Dei's first prelate, Alvaro del Portillo, was ordained a bishop by Pope John Paul II in Saint Peter's on Jan. 6, 1991. Besides the cited comment of F. Ocáriz, see V. Gómez Iglesias, "L'ordinazione episcopale del Prelato dell'Opus Dei," in *Ius Ecclesiae* 3 (1991) 251–65.

prelate is ordained a bishop that in no way modifies the theological and legal nature of the *coetus Populi Dei* of the prelature, or its relation with particular Churches, or the statute of his authority,[159] which continues to be a canonical development of the power-service of the *universal* Authority in the Church—not a form of presiding over a *local* Church. But episcopal ordination does give whoever heads up Opus Dei a new sacramental title to exercise the ministry he discharged. Thus his ministry moves from being a priestly way of cooperating with the *Corpus episcoporum* (though, as we have seen, with some powers of an episcopal nature) to an episcopal ministry of a member of the episcopal college and in collegial communion with all of them. In effect, if the sacred power that sustains the prelature as a hierarchical institution is concentrated in the prelate, in a certain way he also personifies the prelature's communion with the Pope and the episcopal college, and represents the *sollicitudo* of the Pope and episcopal college to serve the communion of the particular Churches, within the scope of the pastoral task entrusted to the prelature. His episcopal ordination then acquires a profound theological meaning, because it brings the prelate into a sacramental relation of *communio* with the diocesan bishops of the particular Churches, and the prelature itself is seen more clearly as a structure at the service of the *communio Ecclesiarum*.[160]

3. *Opus Dei's family structure*

Any prelate's *munus pastorale* includes the "power of jurisdiction" under discussion, but the endeavors and concerns of a pastor do not end there. Moreover, looking at things in an existentially Christian fashion, we ought to say that in Opus Dei's institutional life and in its members' relations with their prelate, what is decisive is neither his "jurisdiction" nor their obedience. Rather, what truly defines Opus Dei's prelate is his "fatherhood," his role as a pastor who is a father to all the prelature's faithful. That is why in Opus Dei he is usually called "Father."[161] The prelate's role in the life of Opus Dei deeply configures the prelature. Therefore it is important to consider it when determining the ecclesial profile of the social arrangement lived therein.

Holy Scripture, not to mention its echoes in Vatican II,[162] uses

[159] See F. Ocáriz, "La consacrazione episcopale . . . ," p. 29.
[160] See my *Iglesias particulares*, pp. 215–17.
[161] "Praelatus, qui interne dicitur Pater . . .": *Statuta*, no. 130 § 1.
[162] *Lumen gentium*, nos. 5–7 and chap. 2.

many images to describe and explain the Church—People of God, Christ's body, spouse of Christ, temple of the Holy Spirit, and so forth. We could say that, in Opus Dei, the image or dimension of the Church's mystery that most stands out in its ecclesial experience is that of "family," the "Church as family of God." *Lumen gentium* alludes to this when it says that the Church is the "house of God where dwells his family."[163] In a beautiful historical perspective, *Gaudium et spes* puts it this way: "Proceeding from the love of the eternal Father, the Church was founded by Christ in time and gathered into one by the Holy Spirit. It has a saving and eschatological purpose which can be fully attained only in the next life. But it is now present here on earth and is composed of men; they, the members of the earthly city, are called to form the family of the children of God (*familiam filiorum Dei*) even in this present history of mankind and to increase it continually until the Lord comes."[164]

For its part, contemporary biblical exegesis has put forward the image of *familia Dei* as Christ's favorite image to describe the new People of God.[165] For Jesus, "the Father is God (Mt 23:9); Jesus is the master of the house and those who live with him are his own (Mt 10:25); the older women who listen to his word are his mothers; the men and youths are his brothers (Mk 3:34). And, at the same time, all are little ones, children, the *nepioi* of the family (Mt 11:25) in fact, whom Jesus addresses as children (Mk 10:24) even if they are grown-ups."[166]

The source of this experience of the "Church as family of God" in Opus Dei is not primarily ecclesiological reflection on the matter, but rather two spiritual events in the founder's life dating from 1931 whereby he mystically understood and overwhelmingly experienced God as Father and saw himself as God's son in Christ.[167]

---

[163] "Domus Dei in qua nempe habitat eius *familia*" (emphasis in original): *Lumen gentium*, no. 5.

[164] No. 40/b.

[165] The Protestant exegete J. Jeremias writes: "Jesus is constantly speaking, with a multitude of images, of a new people of God, of a new people congregated by him. . . . Jesus' favourite image, to signify God's new people, is the comparison of the saving community with the eschatological *familia Dei*" (here the author cites J. Schniewind, *Das Evangelium nach Markus*, 10th ed. [Göttingen, 1963], in his commentary on Mk 3:31ff.): *Teologia del Nuevo Testamento*, vol. 1, *La predicación de Jesús* (Salamanca, 1985), pp. 200ff.

[166] Ibid., p. 201.

[167] These occurred on Sept. 22 and Oct. 17, 1931. Fr. Escrivá himself describes them in his "Apuntes íntimos," nos. 296 and 334. The texts appear in *El itinerario jurídico*, pp. 31f.

Besides, Josemaría Escrivá understood these experiences as "having to do with the foundation," that is, a gift from God designed to shape Opus Dei, which God himself had shown him barely two years earlier. From then on, speaking or writing about "awareness" of divine filiation would be a constant theme of St. Josemaría's life, right to the very end. As seen in the first regulations he composed, divine filiation would be, in the strict sense, a "fundamental" or foundational norm for the Work: "The solid foundation on which everything rests in Opus Dei, and the fruitful root that enlivens everything else, is humble and sincere awareness of divine filiation in Christ Jesus, whereby we believe in and relish the paternal charity with which God loves us." [168]

From the perspective of Opus Dei's structure and nascent life, these spiritual experiences were definitive also in another sense (although more research would be required to prove a genetic relationship). Josemaría Escrivá, who knew himself called by God to shepherd that *pusillus grex* that was taking shape, also felt, from those early days, that God was expanding his heart to love those children of God (and all those to come later) as his own. Here we see the ecclesiological implication. If God wanted people in Opus Dei to live the Christian calling on that "foundation"—on the "sweet awareness" that forms its very core (divine filiation in Christ)—its pastor's role, precisely owing to the Church's *sacramental* structure, had to be radically that of a father, who would be a kind of "living sign" of the love God the Father has for us in the Son. That is how Fr. Escrivá lived, as the college students and workers at his side were discovering. The ecclesial experience which they initiated had its root and richness in the joyful practice of divine filiation in Christ,[169] whose ecclesial dimensions were the brotherhood of all (including the secular aspects of Christian life)

---

[168] "Fundamentum solidum, quo omnia in Opere Dei constant, radixque fecunda singular vivificans, est sensus humilis ac sincerus filiationis divinae in Christo Iesu, ex quo dulciter creditur caritati paternae quam habet Deus in nobis": *Statuta*, no. 80 § 1. The text continues: "[E]t Christus Dominus, Deus homo, ut frater primogenitus ineffabili sua bonitate sentitur a Praelaturae fidelibus, qui Spiritus Sancti gratia Iesum imitari conantur, in memoriam praesertim revocantes mirum exemplum et fecunditatem operosae eius vitae in Nazareth." See F. Ocáriz, "La filiación divina, realidad central en la vida y en la enseñanas de Mons. Escrivá de Balaguer," in *Mons. Josemaría Escrivá . . .*, pp. 173–214.

[169] " 'Father, I was thinking about what you told me,' said that big lad, a good student at the Central [the University of Madrid was called 'the Central' at the time this was written] (I wonder what ever became of him), '. . . that I'm a son of God! And I found myself walking along the street, head up and chin out, a feeling of pride within me . . . a son of God!' With a clear conscience I advised him to foster that 'pride' ": *The Way*, no. 274.

and the fatherhood of that priest, of that pastor, who loved them with God's love, who took care of them and guided them with a "fatherhood" that partook of the Father "from whom every family in heaven and on earth is named." [170] For them, Fr. Josemaría was simply "Father"; and their group a family within the great *familia Dei* of the Church. [171]

This spiritual experience was no mere "spiritual incident"; rather, as said above, it had indeed "foundational" implications. This experience of the Church and of Opus Dei as "family" is a real and permanent gift in that "little bit" of the Church under study. Looking at the Work, the founder saw an extraordinary reality of brotherhood and unity ... a family of supernatural bonds, where Jesus' words are fulfilled: *ecce mater mea et fratres mei; quicumque enim fecerit voluntatem Patris mei qui in caelis est, ipse meus frater et soror et mater est* (Mt 12:49–50): behold my mother and brethren, because whoever does the will of my Father who is in heaven is my brother and my sister and my mother." [172] Opus Dei's Statutes, what is more, given the fatherhood practiced by St. Josemaría (which is likewise a gift to and a duty for his successors), handsomely describe the prelate as father: "For all the prelature's faithful he is to be teacher and Father, who truly loves everyone in the heart of Christ, who in pouring out charity takes care of and teaches everyone, who cheerfully spends and outdoes himself for the sake of all." [173]

From what has been said, one can see how the biblical categories of family, father, brethren, rooted in Christ's own preaching express (in the scriptural language St. Josemaría used so much) what we have earlier described in ecclesiological terms—structure, sacred ministry, Christian faithful. In a single brush stroke the

---

[170] Eph 3:15. Commenting on this verse, H. Schlier writes: (for Paul) "earthly paternity is not only the analogy whereby we understand God's paternity, but rather the other way around: from God's paternity we derive the name of earthly paternity and its true realization": *La eclesiología* pp. 171ff.

[171] Possibly amid their urgent apostolic activities they lacked time to think that what they were living day by day at St. Josemaría's side was analogous to the doctrine that Ignatius of Antioch taught early in the second century to the ChristianS of Tralla: "The bishop is image of the Father" (*Trall.* 3, 1); and to those of Smyrna, who ought to follow the pastor, the bishop, "as Jesus Christ followed the Father" (*Smyrn.* 8, r); and to those of Magnesia, who ought to see in him "the Father of our Lord Jesus Christ, who is the bishop of all" (*Magn.* 3, 1). The true "pastoral" theology of the bishop-pastor is at bottom a theology of how effectively to "image forth" God's paternity before the faithful. See *Lumen gentium*, no. 27, where this teaching of St. Ignatius of Antioch is put forth.

[172] Letter, Sept. 29, 1957, no. 76.

[173] *Statuta*, 132 §3.

founder synthesized this experience of the Church: "In your apostolic undertaking don't fear the enemies 'outside,' however great their power. This is the enemy most to be feared: your lack of filial spirit [*communio hierarchica*] and your lack of fraternal spirit [*communio fidelium*]."[174]

This aspect of the Church's mystery is relevant to understanding the prelature's insertion into the universal Church and the particular Churches, how it sees and breathes the Church. In the eyes of Josemaría Escrivá and his followers, the Church is as the great family of God's children, and fatherhood the main feature of its pastors. From this ecclesiological perspective new light is shed on what will later be said about the "unity of vocation" of Opus Dei members;[175] and on the attitude of the prelature's members toward the Pope and the bishops of the local Churches ("filial union" with the Pope, "filial love" for the bishops);[175a] and their joyful openness to the catholic communion of the universal Church, pastors, and faithful very united to the Holy Father. They thus rise above any provincialism, making Chrysostom's phrase a daily and familiar reality: "He who dwells in Rome knows that the Indians are his brethren."[176]

In Opus Dei the dynamics of this twofold "apostolic step" described above are shot through with this sense of "family": "The prelature's faithful carry out their personal apostolate primarily among their peers, on the basis mainly of a relationship of friendship and mutual trust. We are all friends (*vos autem dixi amicos*: Jn 15:15); still more, we are children of the same Father and therefore *una simul* brothers in and of Christ."[177]

---

[174] *The Way*, no. 955.

[175] "Within the Work we are all equal; there are no categories that distinguish and separate priests and lay people into two classes. This marvellous feature of our family's unity leads us to live as the Apostle teaches: *multi unum Corpus sumus in Christo, singuli autem alter alterius membra* (Rom 12: 5): we, being many, are only one body in Christ, but each member is at the service of the other members": letter, Feb. 2, 1945, no. 20. The subject is amply covered in chapter two, section IV.

[175a] See section V later in this chapter.

[176] St. John Chrysostom, *In Io. hom.*, 65, 1; PG 59:361; cited by *Lumen gentium*, no. 13/b.

[177] "Praelaturae fideles qui ad apostolatum efficaciorem reddendum, exemplum christianum in exercitio proprii uniuscuiusque laboris professionalis, necnon in proprio ambitu familiari, culturali et sociali, dare conabuntur, suum personalem apostolatum exercent praesertim inter pares, ope praecipue amicitiae et mutuae fiduciae. Omnes nos amici sumus—'vos autem dixi amicos' (Ioann. 15: 15)—immo eiusdem Patris filii ac proinde in Christo et Christi una simul fratres": *Statuta*, no. 117.

Opus Dei's "familial" structure, carrying as it does this *theological* and *ecclesiological* imprint, derives (following Jesus' word and style) from the *anthropological* experience of the social arrangements proper to a family. In other words: the family of Opus Dei, being supernatural in its origin and bond, is completely imbued with Christian "secularity."[178] Indeed, the vast majority of Opus Dei members live with their own families and their call is to hallow the family and its human context. Moreover, Opus Dei centers, where some members reside, have a lifestyle (the founder called it "family life") which simply reflects the style of a Christian family.[179]

An important aspect of the presence of women in the prelature has to do with this human and supernatural context of Opus Dei as a family. Because it is a part of the Church, what St. Paul calls for holds good in Opus Dei: "There is neither Jew nor Greek, there is neither slave nor free, there is neither male nor female, because you are all one in Christ Jesus.[180] The man/woman distinction is, in effect, irrelevant from the point of view of Christian substance. The men and women God calls to Opus Dei are simply its "faithful," just as they continue to be "faithful" of the dioceses to which they belong. The apostolic horizon of sanctification in the midst of the world is common to all men and women of the prelature, in "unity of vocation," with great professional, social, etc., diversity.

Nevertheless, women in Opus Dei have a special responsibility, with respect to the entire prelature—to make *all* the Work a "family." They are responsible for the material care and housekeeping of the prelature's centers; for many of them this is their professional work, the very *place* that defines them socially and where they thus encounter Christ. In Opus Dei, as in most normal families, feminine hands make its houses truly homes of a Christian family.[181] And all that with the "distance" that separates the centers and apostolic tasks of the men from those of the women (despite the closest unity of spirit and direction).

If here I anticipate this aspect of Opus Dei (to be covered amply in the following chapter),[182] it is because it is a structural dimension

[178] See how the question is developed in chapter three, section III, 5.

[179] "You must combine intense professional work with care for your home—all our houses are homes—with the loving requirements of our family life, with the apostolic assignments you are given, with due care for your brothers or sisters": letter, Oct. 15, 1948, no. 10.

[180] Gal 3: 28.

[181] Speaking of Opus Del's centers, the founder wrote: "They're not institutions, nor schools, nor barracks, nor offices . . . they're homes": letter, June 6, 1945, no. 22.

[182] Especially see section IV, 2, of chapter two.

of the Work, as the founder saw and understood it. Without it, all the men and women who make up Opus Dei would hardly experience life in the Work as *the life of a family*, with that warmth (human as well as supernatural) of filiation and brotherhood which they all try to practice as God's children in Christ. But let us take up our broken thread.

Opus Dei's structure, on the one hand, is that of a *corpus ecclesiale*, fully and legally defined and analogous to a particular Church; but it is also that of a Christian family, a "large and highly varied" family, in St. Josemaría's words, where a "spirit of personal freedom" is the order of the day.[183] One can thus see why the founder called Opus Dei an "organized unorganization." Here is how he explained this paradoxical definition: "I mean that in our apostolate we give primary and fundamental importance to the *spontaneity of the individual*, to free and responsible initiative guided by the action of the Spirit, and not to organizational structures, commands and tactics imposed from above, from the seat of government."[184] One can thus see that, amid this "blessed unorganization,"[185] the prelature's prelate and pastor does not govern mainly by "jurisdictional" acts, but, rather, through fatherhood, which certainly includes and embraces such authoritative acts, but which transcends them from the viewpoint of *"caritas pastoralis."* So affirm the Statutes, with words similar to those found in *Lumen gentium* when it describes the *munus regendi* of bishops: "His pastoral solicitude ought to manifest itself in counsels and suggestions and also in laws, precepts and instructions,"[186] and "principally in the concern that all those entrusted to him, priests and laity, are abundantly supplied with the spiritual and intellectual means and assistance necessary to nourish

---

[183] "My children, we are a large and diverse family that grows and develops *in libertatem gloriae filiorum Dei* (Rom 8: 21), *qua libertate Christus nos liberavit* (Gal 4: 31), in the glorious freedom wherewith Jesus Christ has acquired us, redeeming us from all slavery. Our spirit is based on personal freedom": letter, May 31, 1954, no. 24.

[184] *Conversations*, no. 19. The entire passage, extraordinarily important to grasp in depth Escrivá's thought and Opus Dei's apostolic "dynamism," concludes: "The logical result is that we have a multicoloured and varied mosaic of activities, a mosaic which is *organizedly unorganized.*"

[185] "Naturally, as each one autonomously makes decisions in his secular life, in the temporal realities in which he moves, there will often be different options, criteria and ways of acting. We have, in a word, that blessed unorganization, that just and necessary pluralism which is an essential characteristic of good spirit in Opus Dei, and which has always seemed to me the only just and orderly way to conceive the apostolate of the laity": *Conversations*, no. 19.

[186] *Statuta*, no. 54 § 5.

and foster their spiritual life and to carry out their apostolic aims." [187]

4. How clergy and laity participate in directing Opus Dei

As an ecclesial body belonging to the Church's hierarchical structure, Opus Dei has both priests and lay people participating in its pastoral governance, in keeping with the basic theology immanent to their respective Church roles. In both cases their roles are of course colored by Opus Dei's specific aim and spirit. Lest we get ahead of ourselves, however, we must not forget that it was to the prelate that the Pope entrusted the pastoral government of the Work. But in the very act of doing so, he also approved the Statutes whereby it is directed. In making the first prelate, Alvaro del Portillo, a sharer in his episcopal status, he granted him *sacra potestas* to be exercised "according to the Statutes." [188] They read: "The prelature's administration or government is entrusted to the prelate, who is helped (*qui adiuvatur*) by his Vicars and Councils, in keeping with the norms of general law and of this Code." [189] The sacred power that sustains the prelature thus resides in the prelate, who is its own ordinary and pastor. Opus Dei members help him in the exercise of that power in a twofold way—"vicariously" and by "collegial cooperation."

By the very nature of *sacra potestas* and in accordance with canon law, only priests serve as vicars, [190] once named by the prelate for overall or regional government of the prelature. As their name indicates, they possess "vicarious power." At central headquarters (Rome) they are: the Auxiliary Vicar (if there is one), [191] the Vicar General and the Central Vicar Priest Secretary. [192] At the regional level, they are: the Regional Vicar, the Regional Vicar Priest Secretary, and whatever Delegate Vicars are needed. [193] As vicars, these priests *personally* represent the prelate *ex officio* and, within established limits, exercise the power that he has conferred on them.

---

[187] "Curet praesertim ut sacerdotibus ac laicis sibi commissis assidue et abundanter praebeantur media et auxilia spiritualia atque intellectualia, quae necessaria sunt ad eorum vitam spiritualem alendam ac fovendam eorumque peculiarem finem apostolicum exsequendum": *Statuta*, no. 132 § 4.

[188] "Praelati potestas, sive in clericos sive in laicos, ad normam iuris universalis et huius codicis exercetur": *Statuta*, no. 125 § 3.

[189] *Statuta*, no. 125 § 1.

[190] Speaking of the prelate's vicars for worldwide governance, the Statutes' no. 138 § 2 says: "semper inter sacerdotes nominentur."

[191] On this position see the Statutes, nos. 134–37.

[192] His attributes are described in nos. 144–45.

"Collegial cooperation," on the other hand, pertains to the various "Councils." Collegial style of government is one of the main features of Opus Dei's administration, as practiced and taught by the founder, who insisted that government always be so.[194] This collegial cooperation takes place in the bodies that assist the prelate in his work—two Councils at the central level in Rome and two more in each region or major circumscription of the prelature (one each for men and women). To these respective Councils belong as members the priest vicars named above and other prelature members, almost all lay people.[195] We now take a closer look at this cooperation of clergy and laity.

At first glance the role of the prelature's priests in its administration comes as no surprise. The fact that *sacra potestas* is possessed by a priest (presbyter or bishop) who is the prelate and that those (except for the prelate himself) who are ordinaries in the prelature[196] are always priests acting as his vicars—this raises no question; it is simply a requirement of the Church's constitutional structure. But, as we have seen, these priests are few in number. The vast majority of priests in Opus Dei do not serve as directors. A "sociological" glance at Opus Dei's institutional life clearly discloses that lay people are in charge. The founder's word and the Work's experience leave no doubt: "As a rule, priests are not there to govern." [197]

What lies behind that statement, that experience? To my way of thinking, the answer really has to do with St. Josemaría's appreciation and practice of the ministerial priesthood and the "sacred ministry/lay faithful" relationship.[198] The priest, for him, was a servant of others, whom he does not order around. He wanted to

---

[193] See nos. 150–61.

[194] "As you well know, there is no possible tyranny within our spiritual family. We have taken a number of precautions to skirt that danger and to make sure direction is collegial": letter, March 2, 1940, no. 27.

[195] "In the General Council there are normally only four priests; all the rest, many in fact, are lay people. In the Regional Commissions the only priests directing are the Counsellor and the Priest Secretary; all the rest are also lay people": letter, August 8, 1956, no. 7. The Statutes say that the members of the Councils who assist the regional vicars can be up to twelve (no. 151 § 1). The members of the General Council—called "counsellors"—are currently in the neighborhood of forty. A similar number make up the prelate's central council for Opus Dei's women, called the Central Advisory.

[196] See *Statuta*, no. 125 § 4.

[197] Letter, August 8, 1956, no. 7.

[198] "Although all of this makes the apostolic work carried out with the calling proper to Opus Dei . . . eminently lay, it's also evident that, to carry it out fully, priests have to be called upon": letter, Feb. 14, 1944, no. 9.

avoid "among us any trace of *clericalism*, with all that this implies of *caste, exclusivity and dominion*." [199] In matters of government, the founder felt the need to be helped by the "collegial" collaboration of priests and, above all, of lay people, to avoid any hint of despotism.[200] He realized that, in the *munus pastorale*, more radical than the power of jurisdiction is the "fatherhood" of sacramental origin, which leads to guiding, serving, and directing the souls of those who approach the priest.

Hence it can be said, in more strictly theological terms, that for St. Josemaría the typical exercise of the *munus pastorale* in Opus Dei's priests is "spiritual guidance," which is channeled through the other two *munera*—the ministry of the word and of the sacraments: the "authority" and "power" of Christ's priests stem from having God's word on their 1ips[201] and having Jesus Christ's saving power and Jesus Christ himself in their sacramental actions. To be a priest in Opus Dei's clergy is to enter, by ordination, into the "sacramental brotherhood" of the *Ordo presbyterorum* and thereby be equipped to attend as a priest to Opus Dei's other members. The canonical mission conferred by the prelate defines a *coetus fidelium* within the prelature that a priest is to care for as a *priest*, that is, by serving them in their spiritual life and in their apostolic undertakings, by preaching and administering the sacraments. This is how the prelature's clergy exercise the mission assigned by St. Paul to sacred ministers—to live and work "*pros ton katartismon tôn hagiôn*" (for the equipment of the saints), to prepare and help their brethren in their apostolic service of the world.

[199] Letter, Feb. 2, 1945, no. 13 (the italics are mine). In another document, after enumerating the various tasks for which priests are needed in Opus Dei, he concludes that they are needed also for a "fundamental point of the Work's very constitution: to occupy some positions of government. I have left this point deliberately for the last, because, while strictly necessary for the legal figure that corresponds to us, I understand it only as an indispensable service of love. We cannot forget that the Work's principal aim is to train its members, so that each of them can, in his milieu and by means of his occupation, undertake personally the apostolate God is asking of us": letter, Feb. 14, 1944, no. 9.

[200] In a 1968 gathering, when asked what it was like to be the Work's president general, he said: "I see myself as a son of God, a poor man whom God has chosen to be the head, because I'm no tyrant. I greatly trust God and my children, and I do no more than take part in a collegial government with people from many different countries. I am just another vote": RHF, no. 20157, pp. 19–29. (In the personal prelature, of course, the only repository of the *sacra potestas* is the prelate and not the council; the council *helps* the prelate: see *Statuta*, no. 151 § 1.)

[201] It is pertinent to note that one of the tasks Opus Dei's founder assigns to the prelature's priests is to give "a deep theological instruction" to the other members: letter, Feb. 14, 1944, no. 9.

As we continue to explore the nature of the prelature, of maximum interest is the way the lay people cooperate with the prelate. From the ecclesiological point of view, what does it mean for a lay person to be a member of Opus Dei's General Council or Regional Council? The point of departure has already been established: Opus Dei's prelate is a member of the Church's hierarchy, and the prelature is a *corpus ecclesiale* of its constitutional structure. Canon 228 says: "Lay people who are found to be suitable are capable of being admitted by the sacred Pastors to those ecclesiastical offices and functions [*munera*] which, in accordance with the provisions of law, they can discharge. Lay people who are outstanding in the requisite knowledge, prudence and integrity, are capable of being experts or advisors, even in councils in accordance with the law, in order to *provide assistance* to the Pastors of the Church" (our italics). It is interesting, moreover, to note that this is a perfectly lay option, which the Code of Canon Law regulates in fact under the title "Obligations and rights of the lay faithful."

But Church law says even more. Not only may certain *officia* or *munera* be performed by the laity, but also in canon 129 § 2 of the Code we read: "Lay members of Christ's faithful can *cooperate* in the *exercise* of this same power [of jurisdiction] in accordance with the law" (our italics). Thus there is room for lay persons in the very exercise of the power of jurisdiction.[202] This is precisely what we are discussing: it applies to that form of *cooperation* whereby some of the prelature's lay faithful play a part in the *exercise* of the jurisdictional power the Holy Father has conferred on the prelate. Indeed, the prelature's lay people who make up these councils have been called to cooperate in the prelate's pastoral role, and they discharge this ecclesial ministry, as the canon says, "in accordance with the law," which in this case is the prelature's Code or Statutes in the first instance. This ministry, moreover, involves considerable responsibility, since it implies no more and no less than working on councils whose ecclesial task is not just to "advise" the prelate, but also to cooperate formally in the exercise of his *sacra potestas*.[203]

In the perspective of Opus Dei as family, all this theological-canonical reality (since it is a true ecclesial ministry of cooperating with the hierarchy) can be expressed very simply—to help the Father and pastor of this large family shoulder the weighty burden

---

[202] It is clear from the first paragraph of this canon that only those in holy orders are "capable subjects" of this power.

[203] This cooperation, in certain cases, can entail a deliberative vote, as in the case, for example, of naming Regional Vicars (cf. *Statuta*, no. 151 § 1): "quem [Vicarium] nominat Praelatus cum voto deliberativo sui Consilii."

of directing Opus Dei; to occupy oneself, in direct cooperation with him, in serving one's brothers and sisters.

Congrua congruis referendo, something similar applies to the lay persons who direct Opus Dei's numerous centers the world over. Theirs is an "apostolic assignment," a ministry in the prelature's structure, one of the *munera* mentioned above in canon 228 § 1. It is an office entrusted to them by the prelate or his vicars, with their respective councils. These local directors serve as channels whereby the directives and encouragement from above reach all the prelature's members, whom they also "direct" on a daily basis in their spiritual and apostolic life.

The ecclesiological difference between this ecclesial *munus* and that of the members of council we have been discussing hitherto is not only the "local" scope these directors have. The main difference lies in the fact that their participation in the prelate's pastoral *munus* involves formal cooperation in the exercise of his jurisdictional power only in those specific acts for which they receive express delegation from the vicars with their councils.[104] Using categories spelled out above, we could say that these ecclesial ministries within the Opus Dei prelature involve, above all, participating in the prelature's pastoral *munus*; they are to perform this task, as the founder would say, *ad mentem Patris*, in keeping with the prelate's "fatherhood," described earlier. Since the Work is a family, the directors of Opus Dei centers, along with the prelature's priests who exercise their priestly mission therein, are like older brothers who tend to their siblings in the father's absence. Their role is to enliven, energize, and "demand" of the others daily faithfulness to their God-given vocation and apostolic duties.

The apostolic assignment of council members, as of those who direct the prelature's centers, is always for a period only. Nevertheless, it calls for considerable investment of time, which usually is compatible with continuing in one's occupation; only in a few cases does it become full-time. Be that as it may, Opus Dei's founder often explained and stressed that this service is to be discharged with a truly professional outlook. Not only because directors are called to invest in these assignments their specific professional, social, and apostolic experience, but also because they are to bring to this cooperation with the prelate a professional, secular style

---

[104] Apparently this can be deduced from the Statutes, no. 125 § 1, which is the central norm regarding the prelature's governance. As we have already noted, the prelate exercises jurisdictional power abetted by the vicars and councils described in the following numbers.

that implies vigor, seriousness, dedication, deliberativeness, and enthusiasm.

In both cases (part-time and full-time) these lay people are perfectly up to this work by virtue of their being "faithful" of the prelature. The strictly ecclesial nature of these tasks and ministries in no way means—neither in the Church in general nor more particularly in Opus Dei—any kind of clericalization, as is also true in the case of a lay person who participates in a diocesan pastoral council, teaches catechism, or reads the Lesson in liturgical celebrations. We have already seen St. Josemaría's attitude on this matter; clericalism is nowhere in sight. The idea of "clericalization" could occur only to someone who thought that the Church and its tasks were only for clerics.

Lay people are perfectly capable of carrying out this work, I have said. But it would be a serious mistake (one that has in fact wrought confusion and havoc in the Church's pastoral work) to imagine that the laity's participation in the Church's life and apostolate consisted in "collaborating in the mission that belongs to the hierarchy." In Opus Dei, starting with those the prelate calls to work with him as council members or local directors, all are conversant with the truth that the essence of secularity (*indoles saecularis*), the substance of the laity's life and apostolate, in the Church and therefore in the prelature, does not consist in "cooperating in the *munus* of pastors." Rather, their role is to redeem the ordinary situations of life by drawing on the divine gifts conferred by baptism and confirmation (*conditio fidelis*)[205] and seeing Christ's gift of the world and worldly affairs as their own "place" in the Church (*conditio laicalis*).

First Vatican II[206] and then the 1987 Synod of Bishops[207] have left the subject unequivocally clear at the level of the magisterium. In Opus Dei doctrinal and practical clarity on this point dates from October 2, 1928: this "foundational" feature is found in the very essence of Opus Dei and its mission in the Church. Thus in Opus Dei no one would think that, because he holds some "position" in the prelature, he is "more" Opus Dei, or "more" Church, or more "lay" (assuming the person in question is lay). The vast majority of Opus Dei members, just like their fellow lay Catholics, live their call to apostolic holiness and their duties in regard to the prelature

---

[205] "Apostolatus autem laicorum eat participatio ipsius salvificae missionis Ecclesiae, ad quem apostolatum omnes ab ipso Domino per baptismum et confirmationem deputantur" (*Lumen gentium*, no. 33).

[206] Ibid., and *Apostolicam actuositatem*, passim.

[207] John Paul II, *Christifideles laici* (post-synodal apostolic exhortation), chap. 1.

exclusively through their professional, social, and familial lives (I mean, with no "position" in the prelature). In Opus Dei one always accedes to a "position" passively: the prelate does the calling. And in the daily life of the "family" that is Opus Dei an assignment from the prelate is seen as a sacrifice, especially when it entails curtailing or postponing one's career (the natural habitat of the lay person). But at the same time it proves a savory and joyful sacrifice, because in a "family" to help the parent is always an honor and joy for the children.[208]

On this basis one can easily understand how the apostolic dynamism of this particular family (the prelature of Opus Dei) is that of an *"organized unorganization"* or the *"blessed unorganization"* Josemaría Escrivá spoke of In Opus Dei, he explained in an interview, there is a minimum of organization, but there *is* organization. Opus Dei is something quite different from a "powerful organization, spread out like a vast network to the farthest corners of the world. Rather, imagine an *unorganized organization* in which the principal work of the directors is to ensure that all the members receive the genuine spirit of the Gospels (a spirit of charity, harmony, understanding, all of which are absolutely foreign to extremism) by means of a solid and appropriate theological and apostolic training. Beyond this each member acts with complete personal freedom. He forms his conscience autonomously. And he tries to seek Christian perfection and Christianize his environment by sanctifying his own work, be it intellectual or manual, in all the circumstances of his life and in his own home."[209]

This spirit of the founder, which influences all the structural dimensions of Opus Dei, is like a secular "exegesis" of the double "apostolic step or articulation" (seen above) that St. Paul proposed to the Ephesians. On Opus Dei's "first step" work is done not only by the ordained ministers, but also by the prelate and those who *help* him (priests and lay persons) to guide, serve, teach, prepare, equip ("for building up the saints" in Pauline words): here we have the "organization," the "minimum of organization" to quote Monsignor Escrivá. The "second step" is the "deeds of the saints in building up the Body of Christ": it is here that we find the plurality

---

[208] Vatican II spoke unambiguously of these tasks: "Praeter hunc apostolatum, quad omnes omnino christifideles spectat, laici insuper diversis modis ad cooperationem magis immediatam cum apostolatu Hierarchiae vocari possunt, ad modum illorum virorum ac mulierum, qui Paulum apostolum in Evangelio *adiuvabant*, multum in Domino laborantes (cf. Phil 4: 3; Rom 16: 3ff.)": *Lumen gentium*, no. 33/ c. I put the word "adiuvare" in italics, for the same word is employed in Opus Dei's Statutes to designate this task (*Statuta*, no. 125 § 1, transcribed above).

[209] *Conversations*, no. 35; also germane is no. 19.

of charisms and services the Spirit evokes in the Christian community, "*the apostolic spontaneity of the individual,* his free and responsible initiative," the "unorganization" that Monsignor Escrivá called "blessed," because he saw it "guided by the action of the Spirit." [210]

5. *The Priestly Society of the Holy Cross*

Our structural description of Opus Dei would not be complete if, after dealing with the prelature as such, we did not at least outline the ecclesiological framework of another important institutional dimension of Opus Dei—the *Priestly Society of the Holy Cross.* Founded by Monsignor Escrivá on February 14, 1943, it is according to Opus Dei's Statutes "an association of clerics that is proper and intrinsic to the prelature," inseparable from it, since together they constitute *aliquid unum.*[211] It is regulated, as we said, by the second title of the Statutes (*De Praelaturae Presbyterio deque Societate Sacerdotali Sanctae Crucis*).

It may be useful first to restate somewhat technically what we already know: namely, that the prelature's clergy consists in those Opus Dei faithful who are ordained, become incardinated in it, and dedicate themselves to its service.[212] These clerics, by being ordained, belong *ipso facto* to the Priestly Society of the Holy Cross.[213] Priests and deacons incardinated in particular Churches can also join this Society,[214] whose president is the prelate of ꞏOpus Dei.[215] The association's purpose is "priestly sanctification . . . according to the spirit and ascetical praxis of Opus Dei." [216] It is one of the associations that Vatican II said are to be fostered in the Church and held in great esteem—namely, approved groups that, through assistance in spirituality and fraternal help, promote priestly holiness in and through the ministry and offer a service to the entire *Ordo presbyterorum.*[217]

---

[210] Ibid.

[211] "Associatio clericalis Praelaturae propria ac intrinseca, unde cum ea aliquid unum constituit et ab ea seiungi non potest": *Statuta,* no. 36 § 2.

[212] "Praelaturae presbyterium ab illis clericis constituitur, qui, ad sacros Ordines a Praelato promoti ad normam nn. 44–51, Praelaturae incardinantur eiusque servitio devoventur": *Statuta,* no. 36 § 1.

[213] *Statuta,* no. 36 § 2.

[214] See *Statuta,* no. 57.

[215] "Praelatus Operis Dei est Praeses Generalis Societatis Sacerdotalis Sanctae Crucis": *Statuta,* no. 36 § 2.

[216] *Statuta,* no. 7.

[217] Cf. *Presbyterorum ordinis,* no. 8/c.

The Priestly Society grew out of Monsignor Escrivá's deep love for priests (in the thirties and forties he devoted a considerable part of his pastoral endeavors to preaching to the secular clergy). The Society is made up of priests who had been laymen in Opus Dei and of diocesan clergy whom God calls to Opus Dei. Its profile, as regulated by the Statutes and therefore in the ecclesiological context of the personal prelature, is of great interest. Number 57 describes the Society as an institutional "self-opening" in favor of priestly holiness and brotherhood by the prelature's clergy to their colleagues and brothers from all dioceses. The prelature's clergy (which as such has with its prelate relations of dependence and hierarchical communion stemming from incardination) *constituitur in Associationem*, becomes an Association; at this point the relations of incardination disappear, so that diocesan clerics can be called to Opus Dei through an appropriate ecclesial channel, leaving untouched and intact their native and permanent incardination in the dioceses to which they belong.

We find, then, in the Priestly Society priests (and deacons) incardinated in many different presbyterates, among them, that of the Opus Dei prelature, which is as it were the matrix of the Association. All these clerics strictly depend on their bishops or prelates. Moreover, by the very nature of the ministerial priesthood and of the holiness to which God calls these priests, the spiritual dynamic of the Priestly Society consists in fostering and reinforcing their confreres' obedience to their respective bishops. That obedience and filial dedication is an *element internal* to the practice of the priestly ministry, which is the path to and means of sanctification.[218] So crucial is this feature that the Statutes lay down as a condition for joining the Society that priests and deacons "above all have the desire of fulfilling perfectly the *munus pastorale* conferred on them by their own bishop and the clearest awareness that only to the Ordinary of the place may they report on its fulfillment."[219] So, the Association is not situated in the sphere of relations of *communio hierarchica* (for no jurisdictional power operates in it), but rather in that of mutual spiritual help and brotherhood. And for this, a few simple regulations suffice.[220]

---

[218] See *Statuta*, no. 58 § 1, and in general all of title II.

[219] "Imprimis studium perfecte adimplendi munus pastorale a proprio Episcopo concreditum, sciente unoquoque se soli Ordinario loci rationem reddere debere de huiusmodi muneris adimpletione": *Statuta*, no. 61.

[220] "Nulla enim viget oboedientia interna, sed solummodo normalis illa disciplina in qualibet Societate exsistens, quae provenit ex obligatione colendi ac servandi proprias ordinationes; quae ordinationes, hoc in casu, ad vitam spiritualem exclusive referuntur": *Statuta*, no. 58 § 2).

The Priestly Society's openness to all secular priests called by God to Opus Dei[221] has its radical foundation in the founder's conviction that the October 2 "message" (sanctifying work and ordinary life with certain specific features of spirituality) also includes secular priests—those of the prelature, owing to their essential involvement in Opus Dei's very structure, and diocesan priests in general, owing to their secular way of living the ministry, which characterizes the ecclesial role of the priest.[222] Whence St. Josemaría could say to priests that the priestly ministry is "professional work."[223] He *analogically* employed this term central to Opus Dei's spirituality, knowing that, in the strict sense, "professional work" is something belonging to the order of creation. With those two words he emphasized that a priest's holiness consists in taking his priestly ministry seriously, and at the same time he projected on to it all the spiritual richness God had helped him to understand.

The "self-opening" under discussion is an expression of the tendency toward ecclesial *communio* immanent in Opus Dei and its spirituality; it takes a familial form (friendship, familiar dealings with colleagues, joint prayer, material and spiritual concern for others, and so on) and in the case of priests it has an additional ecclesiological foundation—the conviction that priestly brotherliness does not end with the prelature's clergy, but rather is constitutively open to the fraternity of the whole *Ordo presbyterorum*, which is essentially *universal*. That *Ordo*, as Vatican II said,[224] is a *sacramental* brotherhood, based on ordination and not only on incardination.

---

[221] The Statutes say that the priests who come to the Priestly Society do so "peculiari superaddita vocatione": *Statuta*, no. 58 § 1)—added, that is, to their prior calling by God to the ministerial priesthood.

[222] See earlier in this chapter: section II, 3b.

[223] Alluding to some prelature members who had just received priestly ordination, he said apropos of the priestly ministry: "If I can put it this way, I would say that this is their new professional work. To it they should devote their whole day and find that they still have not enough time to do all that has to be done. They should always be studying theology; they should give spiritual guidance to very many souls, hear many confessions, preach tirelessly and pray very, very much; their heart should always be focused on the tabernacle, where He is really present who has chosen us to be His. Their life is a wonderful, joyful dedication, though like everyone they will meet setbacks": *In Love with the Church*, p. 38.

[224] "Presbyteri, per Ordinationem in Ordine presbyteratus constituti, omnes inter se intima *fraternitate sacramentali* nectuntur; specialiter autem in dioecesi cuius servitio sub Episcopo proprio addicuntur unum Presbyterium efformant": *Presbyterorum ordinis*, no. 8/a; the italics are mine. See also A. García Suárez, "La unidad de los presbíteros," in *Los presbíteros: ministeria y vida* (Madrid, 1969), pp. 229–52.

For its part, the Priestly Society with its international reach offers priests belonging to it (or those who take part in it without joining) a special experience of the universality of the *Ordo* of priests. A local Church's clergy, by its service to the local Church, is the ministerial instrument—ever united to the bishop as head—for effecting the mystery of the particular Church through the word and sacraments. And that mystery, as we well know, is the mysterious presence in it of the universal Church. But, thanks to the mysterious character of that presence, the *experiences* of the universal Church at all levels, for both faithful and priests, are a considerable help to "live the mystery" and overcome the temptation to "provincialism" (sociologically, the other side of the coin) which always dogs the local Church. In this sense, the life and activities of an international, interdiocesan association offer members of the various local clergies an experience of priestly friendship and fraternity that strengthens and stimulates the local clergy's openness to other presbyterates and, ultimately, to the entire *Ordo presbyterorum*. From the perspective of the Church's catholicity, priests are a worldwide reality linked and proportioned to the *Ordo episcoporum*.

(v)

AT THE SERVICE OF THE "COMMUNIO ECCLESIARUM."

As seen throughout this chapter, Opus Dei is an institution of the universal Church; that is the same as saying that it is a body at the service of the mission and communion of the Churches. So, it does not act in their regard as a distinct *portio*, but rather, by its formal reason of origin and its pastoral reality, it lives and actualizes itself in the particular Churches, in the bosom of their sacramental mystery, in fullest communion with the bishops presiding over them. This means that Opus Dei and the particular Churches are theologically, constitutionally, linked, as are the universal Church and particular Churches. This mutual involvement expresses itself in the concrete coordination determined by the Apostolic See (as guarantor of the *communio*) in Opus Dei's Statutes.

The Statutes devote a chapter to this subject, entitled "Relations with diocesan bishops." [225] In fact its content is wider than the title indicates, since the first three articles refer mainly to the prelature's

---

[225] Chapter 5 of title IV: "De relationibus cum Episcopis dioecesanis," consisting of nos. 171–80.

relations with the Pope. This is theologically very appropriate, since its relations with bishops can be understood only within the whole framework of the *communio*, headed by the successor of Peter. What is prescribed in the Statutes is dominated by the idea of "service," echoing the foundational charism.[226] Within the rigor of legal terms, so too are the two numbers which, as I see it, "govern" this chapter. The first refers to relations with the Apostolic See: "The prelature of Opus Dei depends directly and immediately on the Holy See, which approved its purpose and spirit and also reinforces and fosters its governance and discipline *in bonum Ecclesiae universae*."[227] The second looks to relations with the bishops of particular Churches: "The sum of the apostolic labors that, in keeping with its own nature and end the prelature carries out contributes *ad bonum singularum Ecclesiarum localium*, and the prelature always cultivates propitious relations with the territorial ecclesiastical Authority."[228] It is clear that the service rendered by the prelature of Opus Dei to the Church (universal and local) conforms to its own ecclesial identity, that is, in line with its nature and purpose.[229] Faithful to its role in the *communio*, the Apostolic See fosters this identity, which is manifest in the sum of the apostolate (*universus labor*) carried out in the local Churches, where *adest* the universal Church.

It is interesting to see a legal text spelling out these relations in language more akin to charity than to law. But that seems appro-

---

[226] So did things start out: "We come to sanctify every honest human toil: ordinary work, very much in the world, done in lay, secular fashion, in the service of the holy Church, the Pope, and all souls": letter, Jan. 9, 1932, no. 2. "The only ambition, the one desire of Opus Dei and of each of its children is to serve the Church, as she wants to be served, within the specific call the Lord has made to us. *Nos sumus servi Dei caeli et terrae* (1 Ezra 5: 11): we are servants of the God of heaven and earth": letter, May 31, 1943, no. 1. And two years before he died, he wrote: "We have no aim other than serving the Lord, his holy Church, the Roman Pontiff, all souls. Were the Work to stint this service, I would have no time for it; it would have lost its way. So too would the Church be denatured, were the impossible to happen: namely, that it didn't ultimately save souls, leading them to paradise, which Christ himself has gained for us by dying on the cross": letter, June 17, 1973, no. 11.

[227] *Statuta*, no. 171.

[228] *Statuta*, no. 174 § 1.

[229] The ecclesial identity of each one, within the Church's unity, seemed to the founder, not as self-affirmation, but the contrary: as a condition for possible communion itself, as respect and esteem for the variety of vocations in the Church. A text among others: "Unity, therefore, asks of us love for our divine call and faithfulness thereto, because that is the way for us to work, to be useful to all the Church, which desires for us God's will; also because it is the practical way to make known and loved all the vocations, the highly varied gifts that the Holy Spirit communicates to Christians": letter, May 31, 1943, no. 57.

priate, dealing as the text does with the relations of *communio*. Indeed, speaking of how the prelature's faithful relate to the Pope, it says that all of them are bound (*tenentur*) humbly to obey the Pope in everything (*in omnibus*). And to drain the expression *tenentur* of any hint of mere duty, the text adds, in words of love, that this duty is really, for one and all, a "sweet and strong bond" (*forti ac dulci vinculo*).[230] And a little later: "Opus Dei's spirit cultivates *maximo amore* a filial union with the Roman Pontiff."[231] Not for nothing was St. Josemaría's motto to inspire its steps from day one: *Omnes cum Petro ad Jesum per Mariam.*[232]

Similar language describes its relations with bishops. First, a fundamental principle is affirmed: the prelature's faithful, in keeping with the Church's universal law and their own Statutes, come under (*subiiciuntur*) diocesan bishops, just the same (*eadem ratione*) as the other Catholics.[233] We have repeatedly said that by virtue of the ecclesiological foundations of Opus Dei, its faithful are "ordinary Christians" in the dioceses to which they belong and therefore enjoy the same ordinary, structural relationship with the bishops presiding over them. That is true, in strictly legal terms. But in the vital reality of the *communio*, charity informs law and transcends it. As when dealing with the Pope, now, speaking of bishops, the *subiiciuntur* is transformed by love: the directives coming from bishops, say the Statutes,[234] are carried out by Opus Dei's faithful in a spirit of filial charity (*amore filiali*).

That is the spirit of the founder, who began one of his letters: "At the start of these considerations, there comes to mind *the heavy burden weighing on the Pope and the bishops*, and I feel urged to remind you of the veneration, the affection and the help you should give them through your prayer and dedication. The members of the Mystical Body are very diverse, but all can reduce their mission to serving God, the entire Mystical Body and all souls."[235]

---

[230] *Statuta*, no. 172 § 1.

[231] *Statuta*, no. 173 § 2.

[232] "United to Christ and his blessed Mother (who is ours too: *refugium peccatorum*), faithfully adhering to the Pope, Christ's vicar on earth—*il dolce Cristo in terra*—we are fired with the ambition of bringing to all peoples the means of salvation possessed by the Church, making a reality of that aspiration I have been saying since the day of the Holy Guardian Angels in 1928: *Omnes cum Petro ad Iesum per Mariam!*": letter, Jan. 9, 1932, no. 82.

[233] "Ordinariis quoque locorum subiiciuntur ad normam iuris universalis, eadem ratione ac ceteri catholici in propria dioecesi, iuxta praescripta huius Codicis": *Statuta*, no. 172 § 2.

[234] Cf. ibid., no. 174 § 2.

[235] Letter, May 31, 1943, no. 4; in this case the italics are mine.

Towards the Pope and bishops, then, Opus Dei's spirit and norm tell its faithful to have a filial attitude. This is something that infuses Opus Dei and its members, and something they try to share with all Catholics. On the other hand, its ecclesiological *humus*, as we saw earlier, is an awareness of the Church as *familia Dei*. Besides daily prayer for the Pope and the bishop, "all the faithful of the Work show them the greatest reverence and love, and they strive zealously to foster the same among others." [236] The "vital" and "apostolic" feature of this love translates into two norms. First, the prelate makes sure that all Opus Dei members are very familiar with the documents of papal magisterium that refer to the universal Church and that they spread this teaching. [237] Also the prelature's regional authorities strive to make sure that the faithful are fully acquainted with the pastoral directives from the local bishops and episcopal conferences, "so that each, within his personal, family, and working circumstances, may carry them out and cooperate in them." [238] Opus Dei's authorities—the prelate with the Pope and

---

[236] "Praeter orationes quas pro Romano Pontifice et Episcopo dioecesano eorumque intentionibus quotidie Praelaturae fideles recitare tenentur, maximam eis reverentiam et amorem demonstrabunt, quae etiam impense apud omnes fovere contendant": *Statuta*, no. 175.

[237] "Ipse Praelatus curabit, etiam quia spiritus Operis Dei maximo amore filialem unionem cum Romano Pontifice, Christi Vicario, colit, ut eiusdem Magisterii documenta et acta universam Ecclesiam respicientia ab omnibus Praelaturae fidelibus accurate cognoscantur, utque eorum doctrinam ipsi diffundant": *Statuta*, no. 173 § 2. "As regards theology, we accept everything the Church proposes as objects of faith. And with the same submission, we are ready to accept everything laid down by the Roman Pontiff, though our fidelity not be understood by those who ignore or despise the Church's magisterium": letter, Jan. 9, 1951, no. 21. "In Opus Dei, beloved sons and daughters of mine, always and in all things we try to agree with Christ's Church (*sentire cum Ecclesia*), our Mother. Corporately we have no other doctrine than that taught by the Holy See's magisterium": letter, Feb. 14, 1964, no. 1. And all that as a condition for freedom: "We can recall that old saying: *in necessariis, unitas; in dubius, libertas; in omnibus, caritas*: unity in essentials, freedom in what is doubtful; in everything, charity. And let's ask our Lord that we Christians today, keeping ourselves united in faith and obedience to the Church's magisterium, know how to respect different opinions, temperaments, and cultures, living the spirit of charity. *Omnia vestra in caritate fiant* (1 Cor 16: 14), advised the apostle Paul to the Corinthians. And to the Galatians: 'Let us have no self-conceit, no provoking of one another, no envy of one another' (Gal 5: 26)": letter, Oct. 24, 1965, no. 52.

[238] "Singulis in circumscriptionibus, auctoritates Praelaturae curent ut eiusdem fideles bene cognoscant normas directivas pastorales a competenti ecclesiastica Auctoritate territoriali, nempe a Conferentia Episcopali, ab Episcopo dioecesano, etc., statutas, ut unusquisque, iuxta propria adiuncta personalia, familiaria et professionalia, eas ad effectum deducere et in ipsis cooperari valeat": *Statuta*, no. 176.

his collaborators, the vicars with diocesan bishops—must also maintain this dialogue, characterized too with filial love, "accepting the bishops' indications" and getting the prelature's faithful to carry them out.[239]

Obviously, diocesan bishops are supposed to respect the Christian and ecclesial identity Opus Dei has within the universal communion, since the prelature and its members can truly serve the Church only by working from that identity. For the bishops, this is a requirement of the office they have received and of the very nature of the *communio* they serve. Their office makes them well aware that the local Church's life is *ad imaginem Ecclesiae universalis* and therefore reflects (as it must) the pluralism of the universal Church. Pope John Paul II has noted that it is this diversity that gives the Church its character of *communio*, of "unity in communion."[240] According to the Letter *Communionis notio*, this pluralism has to do, among other things, with "the diversity of ministries, charisms, forms of life, and apostolate within each particular Church." Therefore, the pastoral and apostolic task that these *corpora ecclesialia* and their members, from their ecclesial identity, carry out in the Church "not only does not harm the unity of the particular Church grounded in the bishop, but, on the contrary, helps to give to that unity the interior diversification that is proper to communion."[241]

Opus Dei's founder wrote: "As in heaven, so too in the holy Church, God's dwelling-place on earth, there's room for everyone, for all forms of apostolic endeavors, each with its own features: *unusquisque proprium donum habet ex Deo: alius quidem sic; alius vero sic* (1 Cor 7:7): each has from God his own gift, one of this kind, another of that."[242] But St. Josemaría knew very well that such variety only makes sense within unity, a unity (he

---

[239] According to the Statutes it is a duty of the prelate to make sure the prelature's regional officials "frequenter colloquatur cum illis Episcopis locorum in quibus Opus Dei Centra erecta habet, necnon cum iis qui muneribus directivis funguntur in respectiva Conferentia Episcopali, ad illas indicationes ab iisdem Episcopis suscipiendas, quas Praelaturae fideles filiorum animo in praxim deducant (cf. no. 176)": *Statuta*, no. 174 § 2.

[240] "The universality of the Church, on the one hand, entails the firmest unity and, on the other, *a pluralism and diversity* that do not hinder unity, but rather confer on it the character of 'communion'": General Audience, Sept. 27, 1989, no. 2, cited by Congregation for the Doctrine of the Faith, letter *Communionis notio*, no. 15. See in my "La comunión . . . ," p. 564, the distinction between "unity of communion" and "unity of unification."

[241] No. 16.

[242] Letter, August 15, 1953, no. 15.

wrote) that only the Pope confers on the entire Church; and the bishop, in communion with the Holy See, on the particular Church.[243]

---

[243] "*Ut omnes unum sint.* . . . Such is the prayer Jesus raises to God the Father for us, and this is also the prayer that, united to Jesus Christ, all God's children in Opus Dei have said since the Work's outset: *pro unitate apostolatus*, for the unity that only the Pope confers on the whole Church, and the bishop, in communion with the Holy See, on his diocese": letter, May 31, 1943, no. 31.

CHAPTER II.

VOCATION TO OPUS DEI
AS A VOCATION IN
THE CHURCH

FERNANDO OCÁRIZ

Given the ecclesiological context of this book, a theological reflection on vocation to Opus Dei is appropriate in the light of the previous chapter; which revolves around one basic fact: Opus Dei is an institution belonging to the ordinary structure of the Church which presupposes in anyone who joins it a special vocation.

St. Josemaría Escrivá constantly referred to one's needing a *special* divine election/vocation to be in Opus Dei. For him, the light he received on October 2, 1928, meant a personal call and a foundational mission; it also showed him that life in Opus Dei would involve a personal calling for all those who, over the years, would form part of that institution God caused to be born within the Church on that day. This deep conviction he expressed in words that stressed the divine initiative of the calling, on the one hand, and its personal nature, on the other. For example, he wrote in 1934: "In my conversations with you I have often emphasized that the undertaking which we are engaged in is not a human undertaking, but a great *supernatural undertaking*, which from the start could be called, without any presumption, the *Work of God*; and by a divine calling we form part of it." [1] Addressing himself again to members of Opus Dei, he wrote: "Our Work, my dear daughters and sons, has come to accomplish in the world and in the bosom of the Church a very definite purpose, a supernatural one. You and I are in Opus Dei not because we decided to carry

[1] Instruction, March 19, 1934, no. 1.

out some good, or even very noble, work. We are here because God called us, with a special and personal vocation." [2]

What we are dealing with here, therefore, is not an institution (its divine inspiration notwithstanding) that men and women join solely by a personal decision which, although certainly influenced by ordinary divine Providence (as every event is), does not arouse in them a sense of vocation. Admission to Opus Dei, and one's personal decision to join, presupposes a special election/vocation from God.

While he spoke of the existence of this vocation, the founder also made it clear quite forcefully from the very beginning, as we shall soon see, that it is a vocation that does not "take a person from his place": it does not call for a new consecration over and above baptismal consecration. While being a special divine vocation, it does not make the person who receives it any different from an ordinary member of the faithful. This statement and the previous one deserve some explanation; this, in turn, requires that we set our reflections within the wider framework of the theology of vocation.

(I)

VOCATION TO HOLINESS IN THE CHURCH

The concept of "vocation"—a very important one in the Old Testament as well as in the New—concerns a basic aspect of man's relationship with God; man is "called" into existence by God with a well-defined purpose that gives him meaning. This purpose is salvation, holiness, communion with God in Jesus Christ. However, vocation as a calling from God is not confined to revealing that terminus of every person's journey in time; it also points out the way he or she should take: everyone is called by God to a particular life, through a unique and personal vocation which is a specific mode of that general or common vocation to holiness, grace, and glory.

Everyone's vocation, aside from being personal, also involves the community: God calls within and through the Church by means of a word which, because it is divine, is not a mere external invitation but an interior grace as well—a light that reveals the ultimate meaning and the specific path God wants that person to follow, and an impulse that enables him or her to walk along that

[2] Letter, Feb. 14, 1944, no. 1.

path. It is the "grace" of vocation. In some cases the person has a psychological experience which convinces him that he is called by God. In others, the calling may not be psychologically perceptible but it is there, just the same. In any event a person's response to vocation is not only a free action but also in some way gives shape to that very vocation.

We shall now look at some aspects of vocation that seem particularly relevant to the main subject of this chapter.

1. *The universal salvific will of God and the vocation to holiness*

Man's calling to communion with God is at the heart of divine Revelation in history: "The invisible God, from the fullness of his love, addresses men as his friends and moves among them in order to invite and receive them into his own company."[3] This vocation, which is "the deepest source of man's dignity,"[4] expresses the universal salvific will: God "desires all men to be saved and to come to the knowledge of the truth."[5] In the language of the New Testament, coming "to the knowledge of the truth"[6] means "attaining personal union, through knowledge and love, with the Truth, who is the Way and the Life, that is, with Christ and, in him, with the Father and the Holy Spirit."[7] "We do not exist in order to pursue just any happiness. We have been called to enter the intimacy of God's own life, to know and love God the Father, God the Son, and God the Holy Spirit, and to love also—in that same love of the one God in three divine Persons—the angels and all men.

"This is the great boldness of the Christian faith—to proclaim the value and dignity of human nature and to affirm that we have been created to achieve the dignity of children of God, through the grace that raises us up to a supernatural level. An incredible boldness it would be, were it not founded on the promise of salvation given us by God the Father, confirmed by the blood of Christ, and reaffirmed and made possible by the constant action of the Holy Spirit."[8]

---

[3] Vatican Council II, *Dei Verbum*, no. 2.

[4] Idem, *Gaudium et Spes*, no. 19.

[5] 1 Tim 2:4. Cf. 2 Tim 2:25; Heb 10:26; Col 3:10.

[6] Cf. H. Zimmermann, "Conocer," and J. B. Bauer, "Verdad," in J. B. Bauer (ed.), *Diccionario de Teología Bíblica* (Barcelona, 1967), col. 201–209 and 1039–48, respectively.

[7] Cf. Jn 14:6.

[8] *Christ Is Passing By*, no. 133.

This communion with the Trinity is precisely what holiness is—the created person's sharing in the uncreated holiness of God.[9] Taken objectively, that is, setting aside semantic differences, salvation and holiness coincide: the universal call to holiness follows on from the universal salvific will of God. The universal salvific will is the eternal plan of God affecting each and every human being, who has been created—as has everything else—*in Christ and in view of Christ*.[10] Since God creates through the Word,[11] we can look at the existence itself of every human person, in all its aspects, as a call to holiness by God in Christ:[12] "one's whole life is a vocation."[13] In this sense, the universal salvific will of God is not simply a vocation to holiness: it is a specifically Christian vocation, that is, in Christ and from Christ: "in God's plan each human being is conceived and loved in Christ, that is, as a Christian. Man has no vocation other than to be a Christian."[14]

Vocation in turn presupposes and includes a *choice*: God has *chosen* us in Christ, "before the creation of the world, to be saints";[15] thus, "we can say that God *first* chooses man, in the eternal and consubstantial Son, to share in divine filiation, and only *later* decides to create the world to which man belongs."[16] As St. Clement of Rome put it: God "chose the Lord Jesus Christ and, through him, us."[17] To put it another way, "Jesus Christ, the Chosen One *par excellence*, concentrates in himself every divine choice; consequently, Christians are men and women in Christ."[18] We can also say—disregarding the context of "christological concentration" of the following quotation from Karl Barth—that "the chosen one is neither man in

[9] Cf. L. Scheffczyk, "La santidad de Dios, fin y forma de la vida cristiana," *Scripta Theologica* 2 (1979) 1021–36; J. L. Illanes, *Mundo y santidad* (Madrid, 1984), pp. 21–36.

[10] Col 1:16.

[11] See, for instance, F. Ocáriz, "La personne du Verbe, source de Vérité," *Annales Theologici* 4 (1990) 249–62.

[12] See Eph 1:1ff.

[13] Paul VI, *Populorum Progressia*, March 26, 1967, no. 15. Cf. A. Favale, "La vita come vocazione," in A. Favale (ed.), *Vocazione commune e vocazioni specifiche* (Rome, 1981), pp. 23–30; J. L. Illanes, *Mundo y santidad*, pp. 106–112; A. Bandera, *La vocación cristiana en la Iglesia* (Madrid, 1988), pp. 45–48.

[14] A. Pigna, *La vocación. Teología discernimiento*, 2nd ed. (Madrid, 1988), p. 15.

[15] Eph 1:4.

[16] John Paul II, *Address*, May 28, 1986, no. 4. In *Insegnamenti di Giovanni Paolo II*, 9.1 (1986) 1699.

[17] St. Clement of Rome, *Letter to the Corinthians*, ch. 64; Funck 1, 182. Cf. St. Augustine, *Sermo* 304, 1–4: PL 38:1395–1397.

[18] J. Morales, "La vocación en el Antiguo Testamento," *Scripta Theologica* 19 (1987) 61.

general, nor an individual man, but Jesus Christ, through whom the choice extends from Israel to the Church, and thence to man."[19]

All this shows the depth of Vatican II's thinking when it said that it is only in Christ that man is fully revealed to himself: only in the mystery of the Word Incarnate can one find, *ab aeterno* (from all eternity), the source, meaning, and purpose of the existence of every human being, that is, the majesty of his vocation.[20] Therefore, fidelity to the divine call is the only way man can be true to himself, to his entire being: "the gravest commitment to myself, and the fullest honor and consistency in my own being are found in my commitment to God who calls."[21]

2. The Church, the "place" of the Christian vocation

When considering the universal scope of the Christian vocation, what comes immediately to mind is the huge number of men and women who do not know anything about it or have even heard of it. Furthermore, is it not a contradiction to say that God calls a person to be a saint and yet the person knows nothing about that call? Aside from the fact that it is impossible to know the different ways the word of God works in the depths of consciences, the previous statement and this question lead us to two key aspects of the way the word of God becomes present in history:

(a) In the first place, they remind us of the *human mediation in God's word*: when the word of God is addressed to man, it necessarily requires some type of human mediation for it to be heard. Human mediation is indeed a constant datum in the history of Revelation—from the Word of the Covenant and the Prophetic Word up to the fullness of Revelation when the eternal Word became Man in Jesus Christ.

(b) Secondly, they also point to the *individual and at the same time, collective* (personal and communitarian) *nature* of God's call to man,[22] a characteristic that describes also the divinization (sanctity) to which that call is aimed:[23] thus, God used Israel and, later on, the Church to reveal his plans to mankind.

[19] B. Gherardini, "Riflettendo sulla dottrina dell'elezione in Karl Barth," in *Barth Contemporaneo* (Turin, 1990), p. 114. For a valid analysis of this topic in Barth, see especially pp. 105–17.

[20] Vatican Council II, *Gaudium et spes*, no. 22.

[21] P. Rodriguez, *Vocación, trabajo, contemplación* , 2nd ed. (Pamplona, 1987), p. 19.

[22] On this aspect see, for instance, J. Morales, "La vocación en el Antiguo Testamento," especially pp. 33–35.

[23] Cf. International Theological Commission, in *Theology, Christology, Anthropology*, no. I.E.5, "Documenta-Documenti (1969–1985)" (Vatican City, 1988), p. 333.

These two dimensions (human mediation and the individual and communitarian aspects of vocation) merge towards an obvious fact—the *ecclesial nature of the Christian vocation*: God not only calls man to the Church, he calls him through the Church and in the Church. While it is true that the call to holiness is universal, we must not forget that every divine plan is such that (regardless of the way God's word is communicated to each human being—a process that is beyond our understanding) we can only see that that word really is a divine call through the mediation (human and communitarian) of the Church, the general sacrament of salvation and of the communion of men with God and among themselves.[24] "St. Peter," we read in a homily of St. Josemaría Escrivá, "applies to Christians the title *gens sancta* (1 Pet 2:9), a holy nation. And being members of a holy nation, all the faithful have received this vocation to holiness, and must strive to respond to grace and be personally holy."[25] The Church not only is the object of a choice/vocation, prefigured by Israel; she also receives, as something inseparably linked to that vocation, the mission to bring that same vocation to all men by means of the intrinsic efficacy of God's Word, which both calls people to holiness and makes them holy.

The Church is the *Ekklésia*, the assembly of the saints (*hagioi*),[26] who are none other than those who have been chosen (*eklektoi*)[27] and called (*klétoi*).[28] Baptism itself is an effective call to holiness; Christians are "called by means of water" (*aqua vocatos*);[29] they are called to communion with the Father, the Son, and the Holy Spirit, and they are truly involved in that communion, the essence of sanctity: "in the baptism of faith they are truly made children of God and sharers of the divine life, and thus, they are really saints."[30]

And so it is that the Christian vocation is also usually described as "baptismal vocation"; and, by being found within the vocation of the Church,[31] that vocation is a vocation not only to holiness but

[24] Cf. Vatican Council II, *Lumen gentium*, no. 1; see also above, chapter 1, section II, 1; E. Ancilli, "Santitá cristiana," in *Dizionario enciclopedico di spiritualitá* (Rome, 1990), 3:2246–49.
[25] *Love for the Church*, p. 6.
[26] Cf. Acts 9:13–32; 26:10; Rom 12:13; 2 Cor 13:12; Rev 5:8; etc.
[27] Cf. 8:33; Col 3:12; 2 Tim 2:10.
[28] Cf. Rom 1:6ff; 1 Cor 1:24; Rev 17:14.
[29] Tertullian, *De Baptismo*, 16. Cf. J. Morales, "La vocación cristiana en la primera patrística," *Scripta Theologica* 23 (1991) 837–89.
[30] *Lumen gentium*, no. 40.
[31] Cf. J. L. Illanes, "Vocación," in *Gran Enciclopedia Rialp* (Madrid), 23:661; S. Bisignano, "Vocazione," in *Dizionario enciclopedico di spiritualitá*, 3:2672.

to apostolate as well:[32] it entails announcing, fulfilling, and spreading the mystery of communion constituted by the Church, reuniting all mankind and all things in Christ.[33] As St. Josemaría said: "It is up to those millions of Christian men and women who fill the earth, to bring Christ into all human activities and to announce through their lives the fact that God loves and wants to save everyone. The best way for them to play their part in the life of the Church, the most important way and indeed the way which all other ways presuppose, is by being truly Christian precisely where they are, in the place to which their human vocation has called them."[34]

So, the fact that very many people have never heard of the call to holiness does not limit the true universal scope of that call; rather, it reminds us (*pace* the inscrutable ways God speaks to the conscience of each person) that the economy of the redemptive Incarnation continues to operate in the mystery of the Church: the divine Word speaks to all men through the Church's word, through the word of our Lord's disciples.

3. *Unity and diversity in the Christian vocation*

The universal scope of the Christian vocation, in the sense explained above, does not imply that it assumes the same form in everyone; in fact, it is "individualized" in each person. True, it is a *common vocation*, insofar as the call embraces all, and its terminus is the same for all; in this sense the Christian vocation is one and the same for everyone. Nevertheless, this vocation always comes about as a *personal vocation*: it is a calling to each person to attain full communion with God in Christ by following the unique path towards which Providence guides him in ways that are often mysterious. "Every human situation is unique; it is the result of a unique vocation which should be lived intensely, giving expression to the Spirit of Christ."[35] A personal vocation is simply a "manner of living out the Christian dignity shared by all and the universal call to holiness in the perfection of love."[36]

In other words, through a personal vocation God calls every

[32] Cf. Vatican Council II, *Apostolicam actuositatem*, no. 2.

[33] Cf. Sacred Congregation for the Doctrine of the Faith, *Communionis notis*, May 28, 1992, no. 4.

[34] *Conversations*, no. 112.

[35] *Christ Is Passing By*, no. 112.

[36] John Paul II, Apostolic Exhortation *Christifideles laici*, Dec. 30, 1988, no. 55. Cf. A. Pigna, *La vocación. Teología y discernimiento*, p. 106.

105

man and woman to practice the Christian faith in a specific way. Since being Christian affects all facets of one's life, we can say therefore that *one's entire life is a vocation*; in short, the Christian vocation, in each of its individualized forms, is *all-embracing* as far as the life of a person is concerned: "Christian faith and calling affect our whole existence, not just a part of it. Our relations with God necessarily demand giving ourselves, giving ourselves completely. The man of faith sees life, in all its dimensions, from a new perspective—that given us by God."[37] To say that the Christian vocation is all-embracing involves recognizing, through faith, that divine Providence is not only something general; it affects every single dimension of the world and of man. When a person realizes this, he comes face to face with the mysterious ways of God's actions in a history that also depends on created freedom.[38]

Nevertheless, although we say the Christian vocation as found in an individual affects his whole existence, that does not mean that his every decision and action is predetermined to only one choice, thereby reducing Christian freedom to merely accepting a divine plan that is clearly and unmistakably knowable. On the contrary, within the gradual shaping of personal vocation (where, so to speak, God's eternity meets with man's temporality) one's free decisions intervene.[39] What the all-embracing nature of a personal vocation does imply is that in all circumstances and in all decisions and actions (even those not determined specifically as to their *matter*, which are the usual kind) the Christian vocation requires that the person give them the *form* of the love of God and others. Therefore, the Christian vocation is not only all-embracing but is also something that unifies one's whole life. This is what St. Josemaría Escrivá de Balaguer called "unity of life," something that he preached about with such depth and originality.[40]

Since the common or general Christian vocation is never found in its indeterminate form but rather is always received by an individual, theology admits the existence of special vocations that imply not so much the action of the ordinary Providence of God guiding a person's freedom, as a *divine initiative* preceding any

---

[37] *Christ Is Passing By*, no. 46.

[38] Cf. St. Thomas Aquinas, *Summa Theologiae*, I, q. 22, a. 2 and 3.

[39] For example: see M. Bellet, *Vocation et liberté* (Paris, 1963); E. Blanpain, "Contribution à l'évolution d'une théologie pastorale de la vocation," *Nouvelle Revue Théologique* 96 (1964) 511–22; M. Delabroye, "Le Dynamisme de la vocation," *Vie Spirituelle*, suppl. 8 (1967), 41–52.

[40] Cf. I. de Celaya, "Unidad de vida y plenitud cristiana," in *Mons. Josemaría Escrivá de Balaguer y el Opus Dei*, pp. 321–40.

reflection and judgment on the individual's part.[41] Obviously, God can call someone *to do something* (a special mission, even within a limited time-frame) in such a way that the calling does not completely affect his life, or does so only temporarily. Likewise, God can also call someone through a special vocation, in the sense referred to above, to take on a *new way of being* that affects his whole life. A case in point that has explicit biblical basis is the priestly vocation.[42] A person who receives the vocation to priesthood does not strictly speaking have three vocations (the common Christian call, the priestly, and the personal), but only *one personal vocation* that specifies the priestly vocation, which in turn, is a specific mode of the Christian vocation, for the priesthood is not a mere office that affects a person only partially; it influences his entire life. As John Paul II wrote to priests: "you are always and everywhere bearers of your specific vocation."[43]

Let us now focus on special vocations in the last-mentioned sense. Precisely because the call comes from an initiative of God prior to the decision of the person called, and since that call affects the person's whole life, every special divine vocation is *permanent*, because its scope is permanent as are the gifts and the call of God.[44] Consequently, although the person may prove unfaithful to his own vocation, "strictly speaking, no one ever loses his vocation"[45]—neither his Christian vocation nor its special form. The efficacy of the divine Word that calls (we shall discuss this later) does not nullify the responsibility of the person called: in that mysterious fusion of grace and freedom he too has his part to place in making that call fully effective. St. Peter had this in mind when he exhorted the faithful: "Therefore, brethren, strive even more by good works to make your calling and election sure."[46]

On the other hand, by reason of the link between Christian vocation and mission, between personal sanctification and apostolate, it follows that the manner of being Christian called for by a special vocation involves a specific Christian lifestyle (spirituality)

---

[41] For example, see M. Adinolfi, *L'apostolato dei Dodici nella vita di Gesù* (Milan-Turin, 1985), p. 55.

[42] Cf. Heb 5:4; 7:24; 9:11–28.

[43] John Paul II, *Letter* to all priests of the Church, Holy Thursday 1979, no. 6. These special vocations often also called "specific" vocations (see the words of John Paul II we have just quoted). It is a valid analogous term, but must not be taken in its literal meaning, as though they were the "species" of a "genus" (i.e., the general Christian vocation).

[44] Cf. Rom 11:29.

[45] R. Berzosa, *El camino de la vocación cristiana* (Estella, 1991), p. 105.

[46] 2 Pet 1:10.

and a special way of participating in the one mission of the Church. "Vocation, mission and spirituality are intimately connected."[47] *Special vocations* usually involve an institutional dimension—although not necessarily so, in principle. They are vocations in which God calls people to follow a path or a special channel within the Church and pursue that specific spirituality and mission. Since the Church is the place where every authentic Christian vocation is found, it is the Church that has the authority to decide on the ecclesial and Christian authenticity of special vocations.

It is important to underline again the universal scope of the Christian vocation in order to avoid the mistake of thinking that someone whose personal and unique vocation is a personal expression of a special vocation has a "greater call" to communion with God and to the building up of the Church than someone whose personal vocation is directly derived, so to speak, from the general Christian vocation. In this context, and also in view of what we shall go on to say about the connection between vocation and grace, it is customary to consider a special vocation (for example, priesthood) as a special grace of God, or a sign of divine predilection. That is very true; however, the concept of vocation as such (which, in reality, always exists as a personal call) makes it imperative to maintain that these words of God are addressed to every man and woman: "I have redeemed you, and have called you by your name: you are mine."[48] In fact, in one way or another, God has a special love for everyone; his love is universal and reaches the whole person in his uniqueness: "It is not surprising that our Lord, who is a Father, should show special fondness to each one of his children: he may do so in various forms but he does love each person in a special way; to each one he gives what is appropriate, for himself and for the benefit of the family and the apostolate."[49] In other words, "God does not abandon any soul to a blind destiny. He has a plan for all and he calls each to a very personal and non-transferable vocation."[50]

4. *Vocation, grace, and freedom*

In some cases, particularly but not exclusively special vocations, divine Providence (through various channels, but always with the help of some form of human mediation) lets the person have a

[47] J. L. Illanes, "Espiritualidades," in *Gran Enciclopedia Rialp*, 9:207.
[48] Is 43:1. Cf. *Friends of God*, no. 312.
[49] Letter, May 31, 1943, no. 60.
[50] *Conversations*, no. 106.

"psychological experience" of his own vocation. He becomes conscious of the plan for himself and conscious too of the appeal it makes for his free answer.[51]

The founder of Opus Dei described the psychological experience of a calling in this way: "If you ask me how the divine call is perceived, how one becomes aware of it, I would say that it is a new outlook on life. It is as though a new light is lit within us; it is a mysterious impelling force that pushes a person to dedicate his or her noblest energies to an activity which, through practice, becomes second nature. That vital force, somewhat like an avalanche sweeping all before it, is what others call vocation.

"*Vocation* leads us, without realizing it, to take a stance in life which we will maintain eagerly and joyfully, filled with hope until the moment of death itself. It is something that gives a sense of mission to work, that dignifies and gives value to our existence. Jesus authoritatively comes into the soul, into yours and mine; that is what vocation means."[52] These words, written in connection with the vocation to Opus Dei, apply to any consciousness of the radical nature of the Christian vocation.[53]

The divine call manifests itself in a person's conscience as a *light and an impulse*; that is, if it is authentic, it is always the effect of a special divine grace. "Vocation is a grace. It is such that it presupposes and requires the perception of a voice. It is the voice of the Father, through Christ, in the Spirit, giving an ineffable invitation: Come. This is a grace that has the power of attraction, of conviction, and of certainty."[54] But the concept of divine vocation would be unduly restricted if one thought that a real vocation exists only if one has a psychological experience, or thought that only some vocations involved a grace (light and impulse) of God.

The personal and communitarian (ecclesial) "usefulness" of each particular vocation allows us to link the idea of vocation to the concept of charism, charisms being "specific vocations the Holy Spirit directly nurtures in the community of the faithful in order to increase the holiness and apostolate of the Church."[55] What St.

---

[51] The many different biblical accounts of individual vocations are a benchmark. For example, see Favale, *Vocazione comune e vocazione specifiche*, pp. 84–205; J. Morales, "La vocación en el Antiguo Testamento"; R. Berzosa, *El camino de la vocación cristiana*, pp. 18–43; G. Greganti, *La vocazione individuale nel Nuovo Testamento* (Rome, 1969); A. Bandera, *La vocación cristiana en la Iglesia*, pp. 106–28.

[52] Letter, Jan. 9, 1932, no. 9.

[53] For example, see *Christ Is Passing By*, nos. 32 and 45.

[54] Paul VI, "Message for the Day of Vocations," Feb. 15, 1974, in *Insegnamenti di Paolo VI*, vol. 12 (1974) 377.

[55] P. Rodríguez, "Carisma e institución en la Iglesia," *Studium* 6 (1966) 490.

Paul wrote, in the context of the choice between matrimony and celibacy, can have a broader application: "each of us has his own gift [*carisma* in the Greek original] from God, one to live in this way, another in that."[56] Just as some personal vocations are particular modes of special vocations (which, in turn, are forms of the Christian vocation), so some charisms are also *special*, the discernment of which belongs to Church authority.[57]

The divine call's light and impulse is due to the fact that the word of God, in all its manifestations, has not only an intellectual but also a dynamic force. It does not merely transmit a message, an invitation, a teaching; it has an efficacy of its own.[58] Consequently, a vocation, inasmuch as it is the divine word calling, is not a mere external invitation (not necessarily experienced psychologically); it is also an internal grace[59]—a light thrown on the path one's life should take, and an impulse to walk along that path.

Every vocation, as light in the intellect, makes a person "see" concretely—and not only as a general doctrine—the fundamental nature of the demands of holiness and apostolate that are part and parcel of being a Christian. It is a maturing in the faith[60] "that surrenders to the discretion of God one's entire life in all its dimensions, as shown by turning one's Christian life into an offering of oneself and a commitment."[61] And because it is a maturing in the faith, the light of a vocation does not exclude all traces of darkness; rather, it refers to an unconditional openness of the person to an unpredictable future that wholly depends on God. When a vocation is psychologically experienced with its exact special features, it always involves setting out on a journey, with the obedience of faith and trusting in God's word, as Abraham did at the dawn of the Old Covenant[62] and the Virgin Mary at the start of the New and definitive Covenant.[63]

Insofar as it is an impulse in the will, the grace of vocation is love responding to divine love: it is a blossoming of charity,[64] and

[56] 1 Cor 7:7.

[57] *Lumen gentium*, no. 13.

[58] Cf. G. Ziener, "Palabra," in *Diccionario de Teología Bíblica*, col. 744–48.

[59] Cf. St. Thomas Aquinas, *In I Sent.*, d. 41, q. 1, a. 2 ad 3.

[60] Cf. G. Moreschini, "Vocazione e realtà ecclesiale," in *Vocazione e società* (Padua, 1970), p. 63.

[61] P. Rodriguez, *Vocación, trabajo, contemplación*, p. 17.

[62] Cf. Gen 12:1–4. On Abraham's vocation, see, for example, J. Morales, "La vocación en el Antiguo Testamento," pp. 21–24.

[63] Cf. Lk 1:38. On the Virgin Mary's vocation and her answer, marked by faith and abandonment in God, cf. John Paul II, *Redemptoris Mater*, March 25, 1987, especially nos. 13–16.

[64] Cf. *Christ Is Passing By*, no. 33.

therefore, of freedom.[65] The response of love to a vocation is not a denial of one's personal freedom but an exercise of freedom that strengthens freedom itself. As St. Thomas Aquinas put it, "the more charity there is, the greater the freedom."[66] Looking at love as an act of freedom allows us to understand obedience to God not only as a free action, but also as an action that liberates: "The love of God shows the way to truth, justice, and goodness. When we make up our minds to tell our Lord, 'I put my freedom in your hands,' we find ourselves loosed from the many chains that were binding us to insignificant things, ridiculous cares, or petty ambitions. Then our freedom, which is a treasure beyond price, a wonderful pearl that it would be a tragedy to cast it before swine (Mt 7:6), is used entirely to learn how to do good (Is 1:17). This is the glorious freedom of the children of God."[67]

The Christian vocation is simply an initial call which a person refers to as a thing of the past, even though it affects present and future; it is, as mentioned above, *a permanent* call. And it constantly shows itself in numerous calls and appeals of God to a person's conscience; it is a light and a singular impulse or grace for the here-and-now of one's life: "God does not call only once. Bear in mind that our Lord is seeking us all the time."[68] This is why the response—of faith and love—to one's vocation is not just a single action that determines his whole future life; it requires an on-going exercise of freedom—which the founder of Opus Dei called "actual willingness."[69]

In the psychological experience of special vocations, God's call is not ordinarily perceived so clearly that it dispels all doubt; consequently, a person has to make an effort to discern his own vocation. Except in extraordinary cases, that psychological experience does not impose God's call on a person's conscience by tangible evidence; rather, vocation is perceived through moral certainty based on signs that are naturally known, yet illuminated by a maturing faith that acts as the "light" of vocation. This growth in faith, shedding light on the signs of a vocation and leading to moral

---

[65] There is no need for us to dwell further on the ontological aspects of vocation as grace (light or voice, attraction or impulse). On vocation as grace, see, for instance, R. M. Gay, *Vocazione e discernimento degli spiriti* (Rome, 1963), pp. 55–88.

[66] "Quanto aliquis plus habet de caritate, plus habet de libertate" (St. Thomas Aquinas, *In III Sent.*, d. 29, q. 1, a. 8 ad 3). Cf. C. Cardona, "Libertad humana y fundamento," *Scripta Theologica* 11 (1979) 1037–1055.

[67] *Friends of God*, no. 38. Cf. C. Fabro, "El primado existencial de la libertad," in *Mons. Escrivá de Balaguer y el Opus Dei*, pp. 341–56.

[68] *Friends of God*, no. 196.

[69] Cf. *The Way*, no. 293; *The Forge*, no. 396.

certainty, is above all the conviction that God really calls every person to holiness and exercises a loving Providence over our lives. In short, while faith tells an individual that there is a general vocation to sanctity (communion with God in Jesus Christ), the existence of a special vocation for oneself is not the direct object of theological faith; it comes from natural knowledge of signs which, when seen in the light of the grace of that special vocation, lead the mind to a moral certainty that one is being called.

The fact that God (normally) does not impose a special vocation as an evident truth allows us to think that he wants the person's freedom to come into play not only in the moment of answering the call but in its shaping as well. In every theological reflection on personal vocation, the mystery of God's eternal action is projected onto the world's temporal condition and it is within this dim brightness that we can understand in some way that God calls "since before the world was created," but also through the free choice of the person called. This choice is the product of human freedom and of divine grace (vocation acting as an impulse, as described above). Clearly, this does not destroy or lessen the *priority* of call over personal decision, which we have referred to as a feature of special vocations, but it puts this priority in the context of the whole mystery of the presence of divine eternity in man's life on earth.

The ascetical and pastoral implications of the above are noteworthy, but since they are not what concern us in this present study, suffice it to say that when a person is uncertain about the existence of a special call of God for him, he must ask the Holy Spirit for "light to see" his vocation. But if the person concerned and those whose role it is to help in the discerning of vocations (for example, through spiritual direction) see no objective impediment, and if Providence (ordinarily through human channels) has actually guided him towards that experience, then in addition to continuing to ask for "light to see," it is important (a first priority, I would say) to ask the Holy Spirit for "strength to want to," so that by that strength which lifts up freedom in time, the divine vocation itself may take shape.

(II)

ASPECTS OF THE UNIVERSAL SCOPE
OF THE CHRISTIAN VOCATION

The universal scope of the vocation to communion with God in Christ, which means that *all are called*, contains various aspects which need to be explained at this point. This more direct meaning of the universal call to holiness could be designated as the "subjective" dimension, in the sense that all men and women are personally called. Closely linked to it is what we might call the "objective" dimension of the universality of the Christian vocation—the fact that everything that shapes the life of a person, situating him or her in the Church and in the world, constitutes *the place* and the *medium* of his or her Christian sanctification and apostolate. In turn, this implies another dimension that we can describe as *cosmic*, in the sense that one is called to sanctify all created things. Lastly, the universality of vocation has an *ecclesial* dimension, for it is a call that never isolates a person; on the contrary, by its very nature it leads to the universal communion of the Church.

1. *Subjective and objective dimensions*

From the very start of his mission as a founder, St. Josemaría Escrivá de Balaguer constantly preached the universal call to holiness.[70] Then, and for many years to come, that teaching was not common in Christian thought. The subjective aspect of the universal scope of the call to holiness, even when found in the preaching and writings of many saints and spiritual writers of various times (just to mention a few—St. Augustine, St. Thomas Aquinas, St. Francis de Sales, St. Thérèse of Lisieux),[71] was usually not stated emphatically: holiness was considered as possible for any Christian, but at the same time it was seen as probably exceptional for the majority, namely, those involved in the affairs of the world.

It was even less common for people to perceive what we have referred to as the "objective" dimension of the universal call to holiness, namely, that all the situations and circumstances of ordinary life can and should be the place and medium of communion with God, of sanctification. For the majority of Christians,

---

[70] Cf. A. del Portillo, *Una vida para Dios. Reflexiones en torno a la figura de Josemaría Escrivá de Balaguer* (Madrid, 1992), pp. 69–73.

[71] For a partial but useful summary, see J. Daujat, *La vita soprannaturale* (Rome, 1958), pp. 561–73.

immersed as they are in temporal activities and situations in the midst of the world, holiness is possible not "in spite of"—not even "outside of"—ordinary life: it is to be found precisely *in and through* the incidents of that ordinary life. "For those who knew how to read the Gospel, how clear was that general call to holiness in ordinary life, in one's profession, without leaving one's own environment! But for many centuries most Christians did not understand this: there was no evidence of the ascetical phenomenon of many people seeking sanctity in this way, staying where they were, sanctifying their work and sanctifying themselves in their work. And soon, by dint of not practicing it, the doctrine was forgotten." [72]

Nowadays, especially as a result of Vatican II, [73] this teaching is fairly well known, although the idea that sanctity is objectively extraordinary and existentially attainable by only a few is still rooted in the minds of many people. As a result, it has been remarked that "the word 'saint' has undergone a dangerous restriction in meaning with the passage of time, which is still very much around. When we think of the saints on the altars, and of miracles and heroic virtues, we regard all that as something reserved for a chosen few among whom we have no place. Let us then leave holiness for these few unknown people and settle for being what we are. Josemaría Escrivá has shaken people out of this spiritual apathy: no, holiness is not an unusual thing; it is something common and normal for all the baptized. It does not involve epic achievements of a vague and unattainable heroism; it assumes countless forms, and can be achieved in any state and condition in life." [74]

Holiness (communion with God in Christ) is the "fullness of divine filiation." [75] It is total identification with Jesus Christ, the only Son of the Father. [76]

Total identification with Christ is inseparably united with the perfection of charity, because charity is a "a kind of participation in

---

[72] Letter, Jan. 9, 1932, no. 95. Regarding the "forgetting of this doctrine," see the concise historical summary of J. L. Illanes, "Dos de octubre de 1928: alcance y significado de una fecha," in *Mons. Josemaría Escrivá de Balaguer y el Opus Dei*, especially pp. 96–101, and his *Mundo y santidad*, pp. 65–79.

[73] Cf. Second Vatican Council, *Lumen gentium*, nos. 51, and also 39–41.

[74] J. Ratzinger, Homily, May 19, 1992, in *17 Maggio 1992. La beatificaziene di Josemaría Escrivá, fondatore dell'Opus Dei* (Milan, 1992), p. 113.

[75] Letter, Feb. 2, 1945, no. 8.

[76] Cf. Rom 8: 29–30. Cf F. Ocáriz, "La filiación divina, realidad central en la vida y en la enseñanza de Mons. Escrivá de Balaguer," in *Mons. Josemaría Escrivá de Balaguer y el Opus Dei*, pp. 173–214.

infinite Love, who is the Holy Spirit." [77] And it is through the Holy Spirit that we are "regenerated as children in the Son." [78] That being so, charity is the "fullness of the law" [79] within the operative order of the virtues: "By practicing charity—Love—you practice all the human and supernatural virtues required of a Christian. These virtues form a unity and cannot be reduced to a mere list. You cannot have charity without justice, solidarity, family and social responsibility, poverty, joy, chastity, friendship. . . ." [80]

Holiness, the perfection of charity, is not necessarily nor generally linked to certain actions that are more or less extraordinary or have little bearing on ordinary life; charity can and should influence all that a person does, including seemingly unimportant actions; in and through those actions a person can live in communion with God. St. Paul wrote: "Everyone should remain in the state [*vocation*, in the Greek original] in which he was called." [81] What this means is that the Christian vocation as such (except for some of its specific forms), does not require changing one's position in the world. Moreover, that vocation, inasmuch as it asks each person to stay where he is, reveals the validity of ordinary life in the midst of the world as the place and medium for attaining the goal of the vocation—holiness. [82]

Every noble human reality can therefore be a channel for the Christian spirit, and for the love which is the source of the fullness of the law. St. Josemaría emphasized this point on several occasions, for it is part of the very core of his message. For instance, with reference to a very basic human reality, work, he said: "Man ought not to limit himself to producing things. Work is born of love; it is an expression of love and is directed toward love. We see the hand of God, not only in the wonders of nature, but also in our

---

[77] St. Thomas Aquinas, *Summa Theologiae*, II–II, q. 24, a. 7, c. On holiness as the perfection of charity, see q. 184, a. 3.

[78] John Paul II, Apostolic Exhortation *Christifideles laici*, Dec. 30, 1988, no. 12. Cf. no. 11. Thus, the dynamics of Christian life can be summarized as: "*to the Father, in the Son, through the Holy Spirit*": encyclical *Dominum et Vivificantem*, May 18, 1986, no. 32. For a further study on these points, see, for example, F. Ocáriz, *Hijos de Dios en Cristo. Introducción a una teología de la participación sobrenatural* (Pamplona, 1972).

[79] Rom 13: 10. Cf. 1 Cor. 13: 1–3.

[80] *Conversations*, no. 62.

[81] 1 Cor 7: 20.

[82] On the exegesis of 1 Cor 7: 20, see A. Garcia Suárez, "El misterio de la Parusía y el apostolado de San Pablo," *Misiones Extranjeras* 11 (1964) 144–46; P. Rodríguez, *Vocación, trabajo, contemplación*, pp. 37–42; M. A. Tabet, "La santificazione nella propria condizione di vita (Commento esegetico di 1 Cor 7: 17–24)," *Romana* 4 (1988) 169–76.

experience of work and effort. Work thus becomes prayer and thanksgiving, because we know we have been put on earth by God, that we are loved by him and made heirs to his promises. We have been rightly told: 'So, whether you eat or drink, or whatever you do, do all to the glory of God' (1 Cor 10: 31)." [83]

To recognize this "objective" aspect of the universal scope of the call to holiness one needs a deep understanding of the mystery of the Incarnation—that reality summarized in John Paul II's words as the time when "the *first-born of all creation* (Col 1: 15), becoming incarnate in the individual humanity of Christ, unites himself to the whole reality of man, who is himself flesh—and thereby unites himself to all *flesh*, to the whole of creation." [84] The world, which is *good* and has a *logic*, for it was created by God through the *Logos*,[85] has been given a *new goodness* and a *new logic* through the redeeming Incarnation. This is why "we must love the world and work and all human things. For the world is good. Adam's sin destroyed the divine balance of creation; but God the Father sent his only Son to reestablish peace, so that we, his children by adoption, might free creation from disorder and reconcile all things to God." [86]

2. The call to reconcile all creation to God

The divine call to holiness, considered in the "objective" aspect of its universality (all the noble things of the world can and must be the medium for communion with God) is therefore not just a vocation to sanctify oneself and cooperate in the sanctification of others. It is also a vocation to liberate creation from disorder, to reconcile all things to God; in a word, to sanctify the world. Hence the cosmic dimension of the Christian vocation: "Everything on earth, both material things and the temporal activities of men, need to be directed to God (and now, after man's sin, to be re-deemed and reconciled), in accordance with the nature of each thing, and the immediate end given it by God, but without losing sight of its supernatural final end in Jesus Christ: 'for in him all the fullness of God was pleased to dwell, and through him to reconcile to himself all things, whether on earth or in heaven, making peace by the blood of his cross' (Col 1: 19–20). We must put Christ at the

---

[83] *Christ Is Passing By*, no. 48.

[84] John Paul II, encyclical *Dominum et Vivificantem*, May 18, 1986, no. 50.

[85] Cf. Jn 1: 3; Col 1: 16; Heb 1: 2. Cf. J. Ratzinger, *Creazione epeccato* (Rome, 1986), pp. 1–20.

[86] *Christ Is Passing By*, no. 112. The topic of *Christian love of the world* will be discussed thoroughly in chapter three, section II, below.

summit of all human activities."[87] The sanctification of the world and all temporal activities and structures therefore entails respecting above all their own nature and purpose, that is, their created value that points to their divine origin. This is a prerequisite for discovering "their supernatural final end in Jesus Christ."

The vocation and mission to sanctify the world applies to the whole Church, and thus all the faithful, according to the personal vocation of each one. As Vatican II has stated, the laity have the role of sanctifying the world *from within* temporal structures and endeavors.[88] However, it would be narrow-minded to think, for instance, that a contemplative religious in a cloister does not directly cooperate in the mission of reconciling all things to God. That attitude would mean denying or forgetting the ecclesial nature of every vocation and the unity of the Church as the general sacrament of salvation.[89]

The universality of the call to holiness, taken in its different aspects, is a clear and emphatically positive appraisal of the world and of all secular concerns (particularly human work), and places them in their theological context. Consequently, it is not only far removed from naturalism, but it further demands the theoretical and practical acknowledgment of the primacy of divine grace in the plan of the redeeming Incarnation. "Humility, and recognition of man's dignity (especially the overwhelming fact that grace has made us children of God) are one and the same thing for a Christian. It is not our own strength that saves us and gives us life; it is the grace of God."[90]

So it is not really our own ability that allows us to sanctify the world but the strength that Christ grants us in the Holy Spirit. To illustrate this point, let us recall St. Mark's short account of the calling of the apostles: our Lord "appointed twelve, *to be with him*

---

[87] Letter, March 19, 1954, no. 7. Regarding the expression "putting Christ at the summit of all human activities," frequently found in the preaching and writings of the founder of Opus Dei, see P. Rodriguez, "Omnia traham ad meipsum. El sentido de Juan 12: 32, en la experiencia espiritual de Mons. Escrivá de Balaguer," *Annales Theologici* 6 (1992) 5–34.

[88] Cf. Second Vatican Council, *Lumen gentium*, nos. 31, 33, 36. Decree *Apostolicam actuositatem*, nos. 2, 5; John Paul II, Apostolic Exhortation *Christifideles laici*, Dec. 30, 1988, no. 15. Also see A. del Portillo, *Fieles y laicos en la Iglesia*, 3rd ed. (Pamplona, 1981), pp. 191–97; a translation of the 1969 Spanish edition of this book appeared in English as *Faithful and Laity in the Church* (Shannon, Ireland, 1972).

[89] It follows that every Christian condition has a secular dimension, but that the *secular* nature be specific to the laity. This topic is dealt with in chapter III, below.

[90] *Christ Is Passing By*, no. 133.

and to be sent out to preach and have the authority to cure diseases and to cast out demons." [91] *Being with Christ* is the premise and condition for the effectiveness of the apostles and of all Christians, called as they are to participate actively in the apostolic mission of spreading the Gospel which is "an instrument of God's power, that brings salvation to all who believe in it," [92] able to alleviate every human pain and free man from the power of evil.

This eagerness *to be with Christ* is fully expressed in the eucharist, in which our Lord gives us his Body and transforms us into one Body.[93] The eucharist has therefore a central and fundamental place in Christian life; the eucharistic sacrifice is truly "the center and the root of the spiritual life of a Christian." [94] It is from the eucharist, where the mystery of the Church in its most essential form[95] is fulfilled and expressed, that the entire life of a Christian becomes *the life of the Church*, and therefore, a sign and instrument of salvation of the world.[96]

3. *The ecclesial dimension of the universal character of vocation*

Turning once again to the *divine gift*, the love poured into our hearts by the Holy Spirit[97] (on the perfection of which depends holiness), we can clearly see the *ecclesial dimension of the universal scope of the Christian vocation*. This vocation is a call to holiness; and, being a communion with God, is also necessarily *a communion with all the saints*, with the universal Church. It is a life of communion in charity which is *the bond of perfection;*[98] charity, together with the eucharist, the source of its nourishment, is the root of Church unity.[99]

Consequently, discovery of the Christian vocation in any of its personal modes never isolates a person or makes him self-centered. It rather entails openness to the universal communion of the

---

[91] Mk 3: 14–15.

[92] Rom 1: 16.

[93] Cf. J. Ratzinger, "Kirche," in *Lexicon für Theologie und Kirche*, vol. 6, col. 176. A broad study by the same author of the eucharistic character of the Church as Body of Christ is found in his *El Nuevo Pueblo de Dios* (Barcelona, 1972), pp. 87–102

[94] *Christ Is Passing By*, no. 87.

[95] Cf. Congregation for the Doctrine of the Faith, letter *Communionis notio*, no. 5.

[96] Cf. Second Vatican Council, *Lumen gentium*, no. 1.

[97] Cf. Rom 5: 5.

[98] Col 3: 14.

[99] "Ecclesia est una . . . ex unitate caritatis, quia omnes connectuntur in amore Dei, et ad invicem in amore mutuo" (St. Thomas Aquinas, *Expositio in Symbol. Apost.*, 9).

Church and, in the Church, to all men and women, "always acknowledging whatever is good in others, never falling into the narrowness of a closed, cliquish outlook, but being men and women with an open and universal heart." [100]

Since ecclesial communion does not mean uniformity but rather unity in diversity, [101] the ecclesial aspect of the universality of the Christian vocation does not prevent internal diversification in the People of God. "In heaven as in the holy Church, which is the house of God on earth, there is room for everyone, and all forms of apostolic works, each with its own characteristics: *unusquisque proprium donum habet ex Deo: alius quidem sic, alius vero sic* (1 Cor 7: 7); everyone receives from God his own special gift, one of one kind and one of another. [102] However, this always goes hand in hand with everyone remaining in the "unity that only the Pope gives to the whole Church, and that the bishop, in communion with the Holy See, gives to his diocese." [103]

(III)

CHRISTIAN VOCATION AND VOCATION TO OPUS DEI

1. *The existence of a special vocation to Opus Dei*

In the light of the preceding general considerations concerning vocation, we can now tackle the main subject of this chapter. Incorporation into Opus Dei is the result of a vocation, of a divine call. In other words, it is not the outcome of a mere personal decision to undertake what one has seen to be something good— "signing up" for a job, as they say; it is a decision a person makes upon realizing that he is being called by God. The fact that this vocation is a special one does not make the person who receives it any different from an ordinary member of the faithful and, in the case of a priest, it does not distinguish him from other secular priests.

Theological reflection on this subject needs to focus both on the

---

[100] Letter, Oct. 24, 1965, no. 58.
[101] Cf. Congregation for the Doctrine of the Faith, letter *Communianis notio*, nos. 15–16. A commentary on this text is found in F. Ocáriz, "Unita e diversita nella communione ecclesiale," *L'Osservatore Romano*, June 21, 1992, p. 11.
[102] Letter, August 15, 1953, no. 15. Cf. John Paul II, apostolic exhortation *Christifideles laici*, Dec. 30, 1988, nos. 55–56.
[103] Letter, May 31, 1943, no. 31.

existence of that vocation and on its special nature; it needs to examine the features of special vocations already studied above, in particular their all-embracing nature and (perhaps their key feature) their *priority* in time over any personal decision; without this feature, all the others may be present but, strictly speaking, they will not point to a special vocation, in the sense we have given this term. All of these factors will refer us to a foundational light coming from God and recognized by the Church. Therefore, our study will revolve around the testimony of St. Josemaría regarding the foundational light, the divine inspiration, that gave birth to Opus Dei in the bosom of the Church.[104]

The founder of Opus Dei continually affirmed in direct and clear terms that there is a "special vocation to Opus Dei," as we have read from a letter of his to the members of the Work, quoted at the beginning of this chapter: "You and I are in Opus Dei not because we decided to carry out some good, or even a very noble, work. We are here because God called us, with a special and personal vocation."[105] These words do not simply refer to the vocational nature of a particular dedication to a good work, in the sense that all of human life is a vocation; they refer to a vocation which is personal (as is any form of the Christian vocation) but at the same time special, being rooted in a divine initiative prior to one's own personal freedom.[106] Helped by a foundational light St. Josemaría saw that vocation to Opus Dei had this primary attribute of every authentic vocation, and (this is the clinching factor) this was later confirmed to be so by the judgment of the Church.

The divine initiative of choosing and calling is not, in Opus Dei, a summons to do some particular things, or to give a particular confirmed direction to some aspects of one's own life; it is an invitation to give a new meaning to one's whole existence, in all its dimensions. St. Josemaría explained this, by saying, for instance, that vocation to Opus Dei is a "full vocational encounter" that affects one's whole life. "It is a full vocational encounter, I say, because—whatever civil status a person may have—his is a full dedication to his work and to the faithful fulfillment of the duties of his state, in accordance with the spirit of Opus Dei. Therefore, to dedicate oneself to God in Opus Dei does not mean choosing to

[104] As mentioned in chapter I, the Founder declared from the very beginning that Opus Dei was the fruit of a divine inspiration, a fact that is expressly noted in John Paul II, apostolic constitution *Ut sit*, Nov. 28, 1982, introduction.

[105] Letter, Feb. 14, 1944, no. 1.

[106] Recall what was previously said about this "prior" nature within the mystery of eternity–time relationship.

do certain things, nor does it mean devoting some of our time to do good works, instead of doing other things. Opus Dei affects our whole life." [107] It is, then, a call not only "to do something," but "to be something": "each of us, by means of his or her self-giving in the service of the Church, must be Opus Dei—that is, *operatio Dei*—work of God, in order to do Opus Dei on earth." [108] The comprehensive nature of vocation implies that "to be Opus Dei" is simply one way of "being Church"—one of the many present and future ways of "being Church"—because the Church is the *place* where God calls and where the purpose of every vocation—communion with God—is achieved.

For lay people, that is, Christians whose personal vocation does not require them to withdraw from the ordinary situations of secular life, the comprehensive nature of the Christian vocation involves, includes, what is usually known as "human vocation" or, more specifically, "professional vocation." By "human vocation" is commonly understood the inclination of a person, resulting from his natural talents, education, and circumstances in life, that lead him to have a particular lifestyle. Faith enables a Christian to see in all that the ways of divine Providence that "calls each person to carry out a task in the world." [109]

St. Josemaría explained in a homily how human vocation "belongs" to divine vocation: "Your human vocation is a part—and an important part—of your divine vocation. That is why you must strive for holiness, contributing at the same time to the sanctification of others, your fellow men, precisely by sanctifying your work and your environment—that profession or job that fills your day, putting its stamp on your human personality (your way of being in the world), your home and family, and your country where you were born and which you love." [110] Naturally, he gave the same teaching to members of Opus Dei: "Your professional vocation, my children, forms part of your divine vocation because God our Lord wants that you sanctify your profession, sanctifying yourselves in your profession, and sanctifying others through your profession. This has been my teaching since 1928." [111] At times, he put this

[107] Letter, Jan. 25, 1961, no. 11.

[108] Letter, Feb. 14, 1950, no. 4.

[109] A. Pigna, *La vocación. Teología y discernimiento*, p. 12. This gives rise to the Christian view of that inclination as vocation—human vocation. Nevertheless, it is obvious that Providence counts on the free choices of a person in the shaping of his human vocation; therefore, it is neither restricted to only one possibility nor immutable.

[110] *Christ Is Passing By*, no. 46. Cf. *Friends of God*, no. 60.

[111] Letter, May 6, 1945, no. 16.

idea even more strongly, saying that "your professional vocation is not only a part, but a principal part, of your supernatural vocation." [112]

Given that vocation to Opus Dei is as we have described above (a calling coming from a divine initiative prior to human freedom, and one that affects one's whole life), then it must also be permanent. That is how St. Josemaría saw it from the very beginning. Because it does not originate in the person called, but rather in God's initiative, this vocation "is not a 'state of mind'"; [113] it leads to a definitive and permanent self-surrender to God. "Our self-surrender to God," the founder wrote members of Opus Dei in 1934, "is not a 'state of mind,' a temporary affair." [114] Due to the close link between the comprehensive nature and the permanent character of the vocation, the founder used to say that the latter is the result of the former. Using a graphic illustration, he told the members of the Work: "Our commitment of love to God and of service to his Church is not like an article of clothing you put on and then take off: it affects our whole life, and our desire (counting on our Lord's grace) is that that always be so." [115]

As regards the other feature of special vocations we referred to above—the fact that they involve a particular *manner of Christian living* (a particular *spirituality* and way of sharing in the one *mission* of the Church), which is also a consequence of their affecting a person's entire life—this was something the founder also taught from the very start. The Statutes of Opus Dei explain it thus: "The prelature, in accordance with the norms of its particular law, aims at the sanctification of its members through the practice of the Christian virtues, each in his own civil state, profession, and social position according to its specific spirituality which is totally secular.

"Moreover, the prelature tries to do all it can to help people of every walk of life and civil state, particularly intellectuals, sincerely to follow the precepts of Christ the Lord and put them into practice in the midst of the world, also through the sanctification of the professional work of each one, in order to orientate all things to the will of the Creator; it also trains men and women to do apostolate in civil society." [116]

---

[112] Letter, May 31, 1954, no. 18. Of course, professional vocation—for the faithful of Opus Dei, as well as for other people—does not entail a need to keep forever the same professional work, nor does it leave a person without any choice, since it is the most general human vocation.

[113] Instruction, Dec. 8, 1941, no. 74.

[114] Instruction, April 1, 1934, no. 20.

[115] Letter, March 11, 1940, no. 10.

[116] *Statuta*, no. 2.

With the light of the foundational event, St. Josemaría Escrivá de Balaguer clearly saw that, for someone to form part of what he would soon call Opus Dei, a divine vocation was required. This vocation, preceding the person's response, embraces his whole life, and is definitive or permanent, entailing a specific manner of Christian living. When he spoke of a vocation he did so in this strict sense of a "special vocation," which has, besides, the "institutional dimension" usually, although not necessarily, present in what we have called "special vocations." This dimension is found in Opus Dei not as a mere matter of fact, but as part of its essence; in other words, it forms part of the foundational charism itself.[117]

Like any other special vocation in the Church, the vocation to Opus Dei involves "becoming aware" of a divine calling, that is to say, the person has a "psychological experience" of the call, in the sense explained above (as a light and an impulse of the grace of vocation). It is a light that makes one see the way for him to live to the fullest the demands of being a Christian in his ordinary life in the world (his work, family, social relations, etc.). Thus, the founder used to say that the vocation to Opus Dei "is the same as that which those fishermen, peasants, merchants, or soldiers received in their heart as they sat at Jesus' feet in Galilee and heard him say, 'You must be perfect as your heavenly Father is perfect' (Mt 5: 48)";[118] also pointing out the particular institutional channel (Opus Dei) to which God calls, and encouraging the person to take that path.

2. *Special vocation and ecclesial mission of Opus Dei*

We have so far considered the existence of a special vocation to Opus Dei as attested to by the founder's own explanation of the various features of such a vocation. Let us now move on to consider the *content of its special nature*. The key element in this regard (on which the other elements studied thus far depend) is the *mission* to which the vocation summons.

From the beginnings of Opus Dei, St. Josemaría underscored its special mission as being closely connected to the universal call to holiness. He wrote the members of the Work: "My daughters and sons, as part of divine Providence's care for the Holy Church and for the conservation of the spirit of the Gospel, our Lord has entrusted to Opus Dei since October 2, 1928, the task of showing,

---

[117] Cf. John Paul II, *Ut sit*, introduction. Regarding this aspect, see chapter I, section 1.

[118] *Conversations*, no. 62.

of reminding, all souls by the example of your life and your word, that there is a universal call to Christian perfection, and that it is possible to follow that call." [119]

It is always possible to follow the divine call to holiness because, as explained above, the universal scope of the Christian vocation is not only "subjective" (everyone is called) but also "objective": ordinary life can and should be the place and the medium of sanctification, leading to communion with God the Father, in Christ, and through the Holy Spirit. St. Josemaría thus expressed this point in a letter already quoted above: "We have come to say, with the humility of one who knows himself to be a sinner and not worth talking about—*"homo peccator sum"* (Lk 5:8), we say with St. Peter—but with the faith of someone who lets himself be led by God's hand, that holiness is not something for the privileged few. Our Lord calls us all; he expects Love from all of us—from everyone, wherever he may be; from everyone, whatever his state in life, profession, or job. That common, ordinary, apparently unimportant life can become a means of sanctity: it is not necessary to leave one's own place in the world to seek God, if the Lord has not given one a religious vocation; all the ways of the earth can be occasions of finding Christ." [120]

The founder of Opus Dei would usually explain (also when referring to the mission of Opus Dei) that the sanctification of ordinary life is ultimately a matter of sanctifying everyday work: "Our Lord desires that through us all Christians at last discover the sanctifying value and power of ordinary life—of professional work—and the efficacy of the apostolate of giving doctrine through one's example, friendship, and confidence." [121] It is certainly not a matter of reducing all that can be sanctified in ordinary human life to ordinary work, but rather of referring to something quite complex by one of its characteristic elements. Besides, it is a particularly good way of stressing, among other things, the social and apostolic dimensions of personal sanctification. [122]

At the core of St. Josemaría Escrivá's spiritual message is the very clear teaching that the vocation/mission to sanctify oneself

---

[119] Letter, March 11, 1940, no. 25.

[120] Letter, March 24, 1930, no. 2. See also *Christ Is Passing By*, no. 20.

[121] Letter, Jan. 9, 1932, no. 91.

[122] On professional work as means of sanctification and apostolate, in the teachings of the founder of Opus Dei, see, for example, J. L. Illanes, *La santificación del trabajo*, 8th ed. (Madrid, 1981) [see also below, chapter III, note 5]; P. Rodríguez, *Vocación, trabajo, contemplación*, pp. 59–84; F. Ocáriz, "El concepto de santificación del trabajo," in *La misión del laico en la Iglesia y en el mundo*, pp. 881–91.

and to spread that call, and help others to practice it, is something all Christians have; furthermore, it is proper to the laity to carry it out *in the midst of the world*, that is, *ab intra* secular activities. The founder defines the mission of the members of Opus Dei in this manner: "What our Lord wants is that each of you strive for holiness in the specific circumstances of your condition in the world: *haec est enim voluntas Dei, sanctificatio vestra* (1 Thess 4: 3), this is the will of God, your sanctification. It is frequently a hidden sanctity—without any outward glitter—ordinary, heroic: in order to co-redeem with Christ and save all with him, directing all human affairs to him." [123] And in one of his Letters we read: "(God) has called us to seek our holiness in our ordinary, daily life; and to teach others the way of sanctification in one's own state, in the midst of the world—*providentes, non coacte; sed spontanee secundum Deum* (1 Pet 5: 2)—prudently, without any coercion; spontaneously, according to God's will." [124]

The special features of vocation to Opus Dei parallel the special ecclesial mission for which God brought it into being. It is apparent from the quotations above that it is a mission that involves reminding all souls, by word and example, about the call to holiness in the midst of the world—helping them see that ordinary life, in particular one's work, can and must be a means of Christian sanctification and apostolate; it also involves teaching the individual how to go about sanctifying himself in practice according to his personal circumstances.

After describing the call to Christian holiness and apostolate in the world, through one's work and the ordinary vicissitudes of human life, St. Josemaría goes on: "What I have just said is applicable to Catholics in general. But you, my daughters and sons— who, like all other Christians, have been consecrated to God by baptism, and by the sacrament of confirmation have later renewed that consecration and been made *milites Christi*, soldiers of Christ —have freely and willingly renewed *your dedication to God* once more by answering the specific calling we have received, in order to try to seek sanctity and do apostolate in the Work." [125] It is, then, a call to a self-giving or dedication to God required by the baptismal vocation, but at the same time it is a special call, because (as we read in the text just quoted) God calls a person to live that general Christian condition "in the Work," that is, by being a member of a particular Church institution (Opus Dei) which, according to the

[123] Letter, March 11, 1940, no. 25.
[124] Letter, March 24, 1930, no. 1.
[125] Letter, Aug. 15, 1953, no. 35.

judgment of the Church, requires its members to have a special divine vocation.[126]

To underline even more the mission to which the vocation calls, the founder wrote: "we have been sent to be salt and supernatural leaven in all human activities. Also, as Christian faithful we have heard Christ's command: *euntes ergo docete omnes gentes*! It is not a function delegated by the ecclesiastical hierarchy, an extension of its own mission to suit particular circumstances; it is the specific mission of the lay faithful insofar as they are living members of the Church of God.

"It is a specific mission which in our case (by the will of God) has for us the support and assistance of a special vocation. We have been called to the Work to impart doctrine to all men, in a lay and secular apostolate, *in and through the practice of professional work*, in the personal and social circumstances of each one, precisely in the sphere of those secular activities which have been left to the free initiative of men and the personal responsibility of Christians." [127] In other words, the mission to which vocation to Opus Dei summons is nothing other than the specific mission of the laity in the Church (and, analogously, of secular priests).[128] But, as the words of the founder quoted above attest, vocation to Opus Dei gives special "strength and aid" to enable a person to meet the full demands of the baptismal vocation.

He also said: "Opus Dei welcomes and channels the beautiful fact that any state and any professional work, as long as it is upright, can lead one to God. Our Work takes up that possibility in a well-defined vocation—a *personal dedication* to God in the midst of the world, so as to turn our ordinary life and our professional and social work into means of sanctification and apostolate, whatever one's age and circumstances." [129]

The concepts used here by St. Josemaría are very enlightening: vocation to Opus Dei "takes up, welcomes, channels" the self-surrender or dedication to God and to others as required by the Christian vocation; the only special element "added" is, precisely, the "channel"—that the same dedication be carried out by forming

[126] The Statutes of the Prelature expressly say so (see *Statuta*, nos. 1 § 2, 6, 11, 58).

[127] Letter, Oct. 2, 1939, no. 3.

[128] In fact, as John Paul II said, Opus Dei, "from its beginnings, has been the forerunner of the theology of the laity that later on marked the Church of the Council and of the post-council period": address, Aug. 19, 1979, in *Insegnamenti di Giovanni Paolo II*, 2.2 (1979) 142. On Opus Dei and the modern process of evolution of the laity, see *Conversations*, no. 58.

[129] Letter, Aug. 15, 1953, no. 12.

part of a particular institution of the Church (Opus Dei) which has a specific spirituality and also specific means of formation and apostolate in keeping with the condition of its members as ordinary lay people or secular priests. Those means are the channels through which the "support and assistance and aid" needed to fulfill the vocation's mission are received.

Although the present study is not about spirituality (besides, spirituality as such is much broader than vocation), it is nevertheless not superfluous to point out that—as mentioned earlier regarding the objective universality of the call to holiness—"a deep grasp of the richness contained in the mystery of the Incarnate Word was the solid basis of the founder's spirituality." [130]

In the same way that a vocation affects not just a part of one's life but encompasses it entirely, so too is the mission *special* but (as stated in chapter I) not sectional since it is aimed at heightening all aspects of *Christian life*. For this same reason, one can see why the best institutional channel for this pastoral reality should be within the framework of the ordinary hierarchical structure of the Church—and such is a personal prelature; moreover, it should be a channel that neither takes the place of nor constitutes an alternative to a particular Church. [131]

3. *A special vocation for ordinary Christians*

On several occasions, particularly in the last years of his life, St. Josemaría Escrivá used a comparison to illustrate graphically the connection between Christian vocation and vocation to Opus Dei. He was often asked this sort of question: "What makes members of Opus Dei different from other ordinary members of the faithful?" The founder would answer: "Have you ever seen a lamp that is lit, and another that is not? The two are the same, but one is lit, and the other is not. Well then, the lamp that is burning is what a member of Opus Dei is; understood? So one Christian is very much the same as another, but if one is set ablaze within . . . and responds, and the flame keeps burning—that one belongs to Opus Dei. There lies the difference: he gives light, warmth, and draws others." [132]

The comparison is important and deserves further comment:

(a) Its starting point is, first of all, the common Christian condition, specifically the rebirth worked by baptism that causes a

---

[130] A. del Portillo, in C. Cavalleri, *Entrevista sobre el Fundador del Opus Dei* (Madrid, 1992), p. 70.

[131] This point was dealt with in detail in chapter I, section III, 2.

[132] Quoted from a gathering he had in Brazil, May 26, 1974

Christian to have, ontologically, a new life within (every Christian is "a lamp," capable of giving light); secondly, there is the fact that this life does not always show forth its full strength.

(b) What the lamp needs is, therefore, an impulse (an operation of grace) that "lights up the lamp." Obviously, the action of grace can take various forms. It can take place when a person meets Opus Dei, but that is not the only way: Opus Dei is *one* channel—not the channel—to attain that light and spread it. The special ecclesial mission of Opus Dei is to do what it can, through its own spirituality and particular modes of apostolate, to see that all lamps end up lit, each in its own way and with its own flame—keeping in mind that the only and true light of all men is Christ.[133] In fact, "Opus Dei never has tried to put itself forward as the last word or the most perfect thing in the history of spirituality. When a person lives by faith he understands that the fullness of time is already found in Christ, and that all forms of spirituality that stay true to the Magisterium of the Church and to their own foundational charism are current and valid. [. . .] Opus Dei loves and reveres all institutions—the old as well as the new ones—that work for Christ in filial unity with the Magisterium of the Church." [134]

(c) The metaphor goes further, because it underlines the fact that the light shining in Opus Dei makes someone give light but without ceasing to be an "ordinary lamp," so to speak. Through the metaphor of the lamps, St. Josemaría was trying to show that vocation to Opus Dei does not involve, for the person who receives it, any difference with respect to his condition as an ordinary Christian. What it does is to help him fully assume that condition of being an *ordinary Christian*, called to be holy—to have within himself the light of God—and to give an apostolic meaning to his whole life, which means continuously to spread that light to others.

From the preceding discussion one can see that it is an essential feature of vocation to Opus Dei that *no one be moved from his place*.[135] It is a calling that does not require any change in one's civil status or type of life: "We all do what we would have done if we were not in Opus Dei, but with one difference: we carry ablaze in our soul the light of a divine vocation, of a special grace of God that does not take us from our place but gives a new and divine

[133] Cf. St. Cyprian, *De unitate catholicae Ecclesiae*, 3: PL 4:512.

[134] A. del Portillo, "El camino del Opus Dei," in *Mons. Josemaría Escrivá de Balaguer y el Opus Dei*, p. 40.

[135] Instruction, April 5, 1934, no. 23; *Letter*, May 31, 1954, no. 18. This point will be discussed further in chapter three, below.

flavor, a supernatural efficacy, to our ordinary life and work." [136] To describe that supernatural efficacy, the founder applies the evangelical image of *leaven*, inasmuch as it implies a transforming strength *from within*: "I like using parables, and, following the example of our Lord, I have often compared our mission to that of leaven which, from within the dough (Mt 13:33), ferments it until it transforms it to delicious bread." [137]

Not taking anyone away from his place has not merely a civil-sociological significance but also a theological-ecclesial one; in fact it implies appreciating the capacity of grace to vivify human situations and conditions. As we have said, vocation to Opus Dei is not a vocation involving a special "consecration" to God over and above baptismal consecration. The founder was particularly insistent on these points as he ran into difficulties about finding a juridical form fully suited to the theological and pastoral nature of Opus Dei (its actual and definitive juridical status as personal prelature).[138] In this context, let us read once again the words of St. Josemaría quoted earlier: "You, my daughters and sons—who, like all other Christians have been consecrated to God by baptism, and who by the sacrament of confirmation later renewed that consecration, being made into *milites Christi*, soldiers of Christ— have freely and willingly renewed once again *your dedication to God* upon answering the specific vocation with which we have been called, in order to try to seek sanctity and do apostolate in the Work." [139]

In the members of Opus Dei, therefore, there is no consecration other than the sacramental one (baptism, confirmation and, in the case of priests, their ordination); so as regards their state in life "each one has, in the Church and in civil society, the same position as he had before being a member of the Work, because joining Opus Dei *does not create a state in life*. The layman stays a layman, celibate or married, and the secular priest stays a secular and diocesan priest. [140] This is not simply a juridico-canonical fact but an integral part of the theological and pastoral nature of Opus Dei: "It is the will of our Lord—part of the imperative command, of the vocation given us—that you, my daughters and sons, be ordinary Christians and citizens." [141]

---

[136] Letter, July 29, 1965, no. 7.
[137] Letter, March 24, 1930, no. 5; cf. *Letter*, Feb. 14, 1950.
[138] Cf. A. de Fuenmayor, V. Gómez Iglesias, J. L. Illanes, *El itinerario jurídico*.
[139] Letter, Aug. 15, 1953, no. 35.
[140] Letter, Jan. 25, 1961, no. 12; *Conversations*, no. 70.
[141] Letter, Feb. 14, 1944, no. 2.

Although the idea of ordinary Christian will be the subject of the next chapter, it is useful to point out here that "the concept of vocation goes beyond the limits of the canonical concept of *status*; but we must not forget that there are different missions, gifts and charisms in the Church—a diversity that must ordinarily have a juridical expression, even though frequently it does not entail a change of *status*—giving rise to the numerous vocations that make the Mystical Body of Christ what it is—an organized body, not an amorphous mass." [142] Only someone with a very narrow concept of vocation (a not uncommon phenomenon in the old days) could argue that every vocation that gives a special channel to the universal vocation to holiness and apostolate is also a vocation to a change of state in the Church and in the world.

Opus Dei's being a personal prelature also perfectly suits the condition of its faithful as ordinary Christians: it is an institution of the ordinary structure of the Church wherein the linking of the faithful with the institution belongs to the same theological category as, although not identical with, their link with particular Churches. For example, the jurisdiction of the prelate and the other authorities of the prelature does not come from a vow of obedience (none exists in Opus Dei) nor from a legal right to demand the fulfillment of the rules of an association; it is rather a particular expression (that is, special in regard to the matter it covers) of the *ordinary jurisdiction of the Church*.[143]

One important consequence of the above is that not only is each member of Opus Dei an ordinary Christian, but all of them together—that is, Opus Dei itself—do not constitute an apostolic "group." In a phrase used by the founder, mentioned at the beginning of this book, Opus Dei is "a little bit of the Church," that does not cut any of its faithful off from the *pars Ecclesiae* (the particular Church where each belongs). Every member of Opus Dei tries to to do his own, deep Christian apostolate in his surroundings, in the particular Church to which he belongs. This is the main apostolate of Opus Dei—the apostolate each member of the prelature personally does in his work, family, and social setting, thereby rendering a special service to the Church and the world: "we have received *God's call* to carry out a special service to his Church and to all souls. The sole ambition, the only desire of

---

[142] Letter, Aug. 15, 1953, no. 4.

[143] This point has been discussed in detail in chapter I, above, and it will be brought up again in chapter III. Cf. P. Rodríguez, *Iglesias particulares y Prelaturas personales*, pp. 128–29; F. Ocáriz, "La consacrazione episcopale del Prelato dell' Opus Dei," in *Studi Cattolici* 359 (1991) 22–29.

Opus Dei and each of its children is to serve the Church the way the Church wants to be served, within the specific vocation our Lord has given us.

"*Nos sumus servi Dei caeli et terrae* (1 Ezra 5:11), we are servants of the God of heaven and earth. That is what our entire life is, my daughters and sons—a service with exclusively spiritual aims, because Opus Dei is not, and will never be—nor could it be—a tool for temporal ends. But at the same time, it is also a service to mankind, because all you are doing is trying in an upright way to achieve Christian perfection, acting most freely and responsibly in all the areas of civil life. It is a self-sacrificing service that is not degrading, but uplifting; it expands the heart (making it more *Roman*, in the most noble meaning of the word) and leads one to pursue the honor and the good of people of every nation—to try to see that every day there are fewer people who are poor and uneducated, fewer souls without faith, without hope; fewer wars, less uncertainty, and more charity and peace." [144]

Opus Dei as such has no role other than the doctrinal, spiritual, and apostolic formation of its members and all those who want to avail themselves of that formation, and the pastoral service provided by its prelate, priests, and deacons. The founder put it very neatly: "The Work itself has as its *only* task the formation of its members." [145] This formation, insofar as it is an invitation to build up a deep and sincere piety, pass on Church teaching, and encourage people to live according to a refined apostolic spirit, will then lead the individual members of the prelature to strive to sanctify their everyday work and engage in a variety of apostolic initiatives developed with personal spontaneity, freedom, and responsibility. [146]

Obviously, this does not prevent some members of Opus Dei, together with many other people, carrying out some apostolic undertakings (for example, in education, and social work) through their professional work, undertakings whose Christian orientation and spiritual direction the prelature takes responsibility for; these are known as "corporate undertakings" of Opus Dei. [147]

[144] Letter, May 31, 1943, no. 1.
[145] Instruction, Jan 9, 1935, no. 11.
[146] Cf. *Conversations*, nos. 19 and 27.
[147] Cf. *Conversations*, nos. 18 and 27. Of course, the prelature as such takes responsibility for the Christian integrity of an apostolic undertaking of this kind only if it can in fact guarantee it by making use of the means that are suitable and necessary for every particular case. The prelature can assume that responsibility only if the promoters and owners of these activities agree to it.

(IV)

UNITY OF VOCATION AND
VARIETY OF MEMBERS IN OPUS DEI

Opus Dei is made up of a whole range of Christian faithful—lay faithful and priests, men and women, celibates and married couples, coming from all walks of life and occupations. This variety, a reflection of what is to be found in the People of God as a whole, implies different modes of being a member of Opus Dei; but these modes are not degrees of a greater or lesser belonging to Opus Dei, nor do they denote different vocations. The founder clearly explained it: "And so, in the Work, there are no degrees or categories of membership. The vocation to Opus Dei is one and the same. It is a call to commit oneself personally, freely, and responsibly to carry out the will of God, that is, what God wants each individual to do. What there is, is a multitude of personal situations, the situation of each member in the world, to which the same specific vocation is adapted." [148]

Of course, the fact that this special vocation is common to all does not mean that every member of Opus Dei, like any human being, has not got a personal vocation that is unique and is his alone, for God's plan for each man and woman is unique and embraces his whole life. Just as in the Church no two vocations are identical, yet all of them are specific forms of the same Christian vocation, so too the various personal vocations of the members of Opus Dei are, in turn, specific modes of one and the same special mode of the Christian vocation, the vocation to Opus Dei.

1. *People from different professions and walks of life*

The subjective aspect of the universal call to holiness (that is, the fact that every person is called to be holy) implies its objective aspect—acknowledgment of the fact that holiness can be achieved in all the situations and conditions of human life. This theological reality has been present in Opus Dei from its beginnings, as one might expect, because its *raison d'être*, its original charism, is precisely the spreading of the universal call to holiness. "Since the foundation of the Work in 1928, my teaching has been that holiness is not reserved for a privileged few. All the ways of the earth, every state in life, every profession, every honest task can be divine." [149]

[148] *Conversations*, no. 62.
[149] *Conversations*, no. 26.

The above statement, aside from its doctrinal significance, also has pastoral and juridical implications: people in all kinds of professions and walks of life can be, and in fact are, members of Opus Dei. Because of its relevance to the present topic, let us quote again what the Statutes say: "The prelature tries to work with all its resources so that people from all walks of life and civil status in society, above all, intellectuals, would sincerely follow the precepts of Christ the Lord and put them into practice in the midst of the world, through the sanctification of the professional work of each one";[150] the subsequent points of the Statutes say that people in all situations and conditions in life can be admitted as faithful of the prelature.[151]

In an interview he gave in 1966, Monsignor Escrivá said: "People of all social conditions belong to Opus Dei: men and women, young and old, workers, businessmen, clerks, farmers, members of the professions, etc. It is God who gives the vocation, and with God there is no distinction of persons."[152] To express the openness of Opus Dei to all, that is, the non-sectional nature of the specific mission of the prelature (using the term we used before), the founder at times compared it to "a sea without shores,"[153] and other times he spoke of the un-specialized character of its apostolic work, describing it as "an unorganized organization."

The same idea is found in one of his Letters. He wrote that in Opus Dei "all contemporary society is present, and it will be always that way: intellectuals and businessmen; members of the professions and craftsmen; merchants and manual workers; people in the diplomatic corps, commerce, farming, finance, and the humanities; journalists, theatre and movie actors and actresses, circus entertainers, athletes. The young and the old, the healthy and sickly. An unorganized organization, marvellous like life itself." He added: "You know very well, my children, that our apostolic work has no specialized purpose: it has all kinds of specializations, because it is rooted in life's diverse forms of specialization; it exalts and raises to the supernatural order all the forms of service people render one another in their social relations, and turns them into a genuine apostolate."[154]

It is in this context of the universal reach of the apostolate of Opus Dei that the phrase "above all, intellectuals"[155] in number 2

---

[150] *Statuta*, no. 2 § 2.
[151] Ibid., nos. 6ff.
[152] *Conversations*, no. 40.
[153] Letter, Dec. 8, 1949, no. 6.
[154] Letter, Jan. 9, 1959, nos. 11 and 14.
[155] Regarding this idea, see *El itinerario jurídico*, especially pp. 44–45, 459–61.

of the Statutes should be understood. As Monsignor Escrivá de Balaguer explained on several occasions, that phrase refers not to a sphere of apostolate, but to a pastoral method, so to speak. When in 1928 he saw himself being called to promote the universal call to holiness, he realized at once that in order to reach all sectors of society he would have to start with those who, with their intellectual professions, would have the mobility and qualities that would facilitate this outreach. He worked in line with this criterion, and included it in his foundational and juridical writings, while underlining at the same time the universal reach of his apostolate. He used to say that "out of a hundred souls we are interested in a hundred": "That is precisely why I have always taught that we are interested in each and every person. Out of a hundred souls we are interested in a hundred. We discriminate against no one, for we know for certain that Jesus has redeemed us all, and that he wishes to make use of a few of us, regardless of our personal nothingness, to make his salvation known to all." [156]

It should be noted that the fact that Opus Dei is for everyone (that is, any ordinary Christian, any person called to sanctify himself in the midst of the world, regardless of his profession, race, social condition, or job) and the real diversity of its members do not imply any juridical or theological difference between one member and the next, because as we have said before the vocation is one and the same for all. They have different professions or jobs and conditions in life, but all of them are called to sanctify their particular circumstances of their life, whatever they may be, and to do apostolate in their own surroundings. The pastoral and theological phenomenon is therefore one and the same for all.

So, all the members have the same spirit, and even receive the same formation (which obviously needs to be adapted to the capacity and needs of each); the aim is always basically the same—to transmit the Christian faith and the spirit of Opus Dei undiluted, showing their capacity to vivify all human realities. St. Josemaría explained this unity of spirit by making a graphic comparison, taken from ordinary experience: the fact that in families where members are united and healthy, everybody eats from *the same cooking pot*. "We are *a healthy family*—he wrote in one of his Letters—so we have only one cooking pot. [. . .] We have only one kind of food, only one cooking pot: we have to say the same things to everyone, because the Work is for souls, and everyone has the same chance to sanctify himself as anyone else [. . .]. Nevertheless,

---

[156] *Friends of God*, no. 9

it is true that my children are involved in a wide variety of activities: you can find among them people of different cultures, ages, and states in life—some are single, others are married, widows, or widowers, others are priests; it is likewise true that they have different temperaments. So those children of mine who train the others imitate mothers, who are very practical people: they adapt the common cooking pot to the specific needs of each [. . .]. But it is always the same cooking pot." [157]

2. Single and married people: Numeraries, Associates, Supernumeraries

The words of St. Josemaría we have just quoted, describing the different situations in life of the faithful of the prelature—the fact that single or married people form part of it—deserves comment. Besides, this fact reflects the objective universal reach of the spirit and apostolate of Opus Dei.

From the very start of his work as founder Monsignor Escrivá de Balaguer knew that the spirit of Opus Dei can be put into practice in all kinds of human situations—and therefore in married life or in celibacy; and he also saw that Opus Dei needed to have people who commit themselves to celibacy (with the availability for apostolic work it brings) in order to fulfill the mission that God wanted him to carry out. Thus he orientated his initial work towards those people whom he perceived as having the vocation to live "apostolic celibacy," as he liked to call it; at the same time, he vigorously and in clear terms preached the Christian value of marriage. [158] Opus Dei developed as a result of that apostolic work, and it was stated from the very beginning that married people as

---

[157] Letter, Sept. 29, 1957, no. 57.

[158] To show the content and the tone of preaching of the founder of Opus Dei since the early years we have chosen some points of *The Way*: "Do you laugh because I tell you that you have a 'vocation to marriage'? Well, you have just that—a vocation. Commend yourself to St. Raphael that he may keep you pure, as he did Tobias, until the end of the way" (no. 27); "How frankly you laughed when I advised you to put your youthful years under the protection of St. Raphael, 'so that he'll lead you, as he did young Tobias, to a holy marriage, with a girl who is good and pretty—and rich,' I added jokingly. And then how thoughtful you became, when I went on to advise you to put yourself also under the patronage of that youthful apostle John, in case God were to ask more of you" (no. 360); "It's good to give glory to God, without seeking a foretaste (wife, children, honors . . .) of that glory which we will enjoy fully with him in the eternal life. . . . Besides, he is generous. He returns a hundredfold; and this is true even of children. Many deprive themselves of children for the sake of his glory, and they have thousands of children of their spirit—children, as we are children of our Father in heaven" (no. 779).

well as celibates could form part of it, although the manner of belonging to Opus Dei of the former would have a juridical form different from that of the latter, in line with what canon law then allowed, until eventually full recognition came of the fact that both married and celibate persons could be members of Opus Dei with full rights.[159]

The presence in the prelature of people who are committed to celibacy and of others who are married (or, more broadly, those who are open to marriage)—together with factors related to availability, is reflected in the existence of different forms or conditions of incorporation into Opus Dei; thus there are *Numerary, Associate, and Supernumerary members*—men and women. The Statutes refer to these forms of belonging to the prelature in this way: "Depending on each person's normal availability to devote himself or herself to the tasks of formation and to particular apostolic undertakings of Opus Dei, the faithful of the prelature, men as well as women, are called Numeraries, Associates, and Supernumeraries, without thereby forming different classes. Their availability depends on the varied and permanent circumstances—personal, family, professional, etc.—of each one." [160]

In the subsequent points of the Statutes this general provision is made specific by giving the details of the different forms of bond with the prelature:

(a) The Numeraries are the faithful of this prelature who, living apostolic celibacy, have the greatest degree of personal availability for its special apostolic undertakings. They can live in the centers of the prelature in order to take charge of those apostolic undertakings and of the formation of the other members of Opus Dei.[161]

(b) The Associates are the faithful of the prelature who, living apostolic celibacy, ordinarily live with their own families since they have to attend to particular and permanent personal, family, or professional responsibilities, which affect their availability for certain apostolic tasks or formative activities of Opus Dei.[162]

(c) The Supernumeraries are the faithful of the prelature—married or single, but in either case, without any commitment to celibacy—who, having the same vocation as the others, fully par-

[159] This is one of the areas where Monsignor Escrivá de Balaguer had to open up new paths, until it was fully recognized that married people have received a Christian vocation and can seek Christian perfection (which allows for their full membership of Opus Dei). More information about that process could be found in *El itinerario jurídico*, chaps. 3, 4, 7.

[160] *Statuta*, no. 7 § 1.

[161] Cf. *Statuta*, nos. 8, 9, and 10.

[162] Cf. *Statuta*, no. 10.

ticipate in the apostolate of Opus Dei and have such availability for the apostolic activities as may be compatible with the fulfillment of their family, professional, and social obligations.[163]

From these descriptions, it is clear that they are personal specific forms of the vocation to Opus Dei through which the faithful of the Prelature devote themselves to the activities needed for its institutional life, in ways determined by the objective and permanent circumstances of each; in no way do they imply *degrees* of bonding with Opus Dei or of the pursuit of Christian perfection. It must be emphasized that these diverse ways of being available for apostolic tasks presuppose that all the faithful of Opus Dei have one and the same special vocation, for "whatever civil status a person may have, his dedication to his work and the faithful fulfillment of the duties of his state is complete, in accordance with the spirit of Opus Dei."[164] The first point in the Statutes where the faithful of the prelature are referred to repeatedly and forcefully underlines the fact that all those who form part of the Prelature do so *"moved by the same divine vocation,"* such that *"*all of them *have the same apostolic goal,* they *practice the same spirit and ascetical means."*[165]

This matter is of prime importance, as the founder never tired emphasizing. He never used expressions that might even remotely erode the idea of the unity of the vocation to Opus Dei—expressions such as "classes of members" or "categories of members." It is precisely in and *through* their own situation in the world that each member of Opus Dei carries out the Christian mission of spreading the universal call to holiness and helps others live according to that call. One and the same spirituality, the same mission, the same permanent and all-embracing effect on one's life—all these features reveal a vocation that is completely identical in all aspects, from the call to holiness and apostolate up to the implementation of that call in a secular milieu.[166]

It should also be pointed out, in connection with vocation being exactly the same for all, that for the Numeraries and Associates of Opus Dei the charism of celibacy—as for any person who receives that charism—is an integral aspect of their *personal* vocation, and

---

[163] Cf. *Statuta,* no. 11.

[164] Letter, Jan. 25, 1961, no. 11.

[165] *Statuta,* no. 6 (my italics). See also no. 11 § 1, where the unity of the vocation is stressed.

[166] The basic fact of unity of vocation not only discourages the attitude of considering the availability of some members of the Opus Dei to tasks of formation and government in Opus Dei as a higher calling, but it also prevents that same availability from lessening their condition as ordinary Christian faithful. (This idea will be discussed below, in chapter three, section III, 4, within the topic of secularity.)

not a *special* aspect of the vocation to Opus Dei. Of course, this does not mean that God "initially" calls someone to celibacy and "later on" to Opus Dei (a person has only one vocation); what it does mean is that God calls people to Opus Dei in celibacy and in marriage; in both cases it is a matter of "dimensions" of vocation, as is true for other Christians.[167]

As to marriage, St. Josemaría Escrivá clearly preached that "for a Christian, marriage is not just a social institution, much less a mere remedy for human weakness. It is a genuine supernatural calling, a great sacrament, in Christ and in the Church, says St. Paul (Eph 5:32). At the same time, it is a permanent contract between a man and a woman, for whether we like it or not, the sacrament of matrimony, instituted by Christ, cannot be dissolved. It is a sacrament that sanctifies, being an action of Jesus, who fills the souls of the couple and invites them to follow him. He transforms their whole married life into an occasion for God's presence on earth." [168]

Christian marriage as a vocation was constantly present in the preaching of Opus Dei's founder since its beginnings. Aside from all what we have quoted above, he also wrote: "We must deeply respect and revere the married state; it is noble and holy—*sacramentum hoc magnum est* (Eph 5:32), matrimony is a great sacrament—and we regard it as another vocation to be followed, as a marvellous sharing in the creative power of God." [169]

In the same Letter, immediately after the point just mentioned, he states—in agreement with Tradition—that "it is certain doc-

---

[167] At any event, let it be noted that celibacy is not a charism that is necessarily linked to the consecrated life (see Vatican II, *Apostolicam Actuositatem*, no. 4; John Paul II, *Christifideles laici*, no. 56; A. del Portillo, *Escritos sobre el sacerdocia*, 6th ed. (Madrid, 1991), p. 94; J. L. Gutiérrez, "El laico y el celibato," in *La misión del laico en la Iglesia y en el mundo*, pp. 995–1006. In particular, in Opus Dei the formal reason for the celibacy of Numeraries and Associates is not the renouncing of the world, but the service to the mission; for this reason, after taking into account the obvious differences, it is a celibacy that is more akin to the formal reason of priestly celibacy than that of religious celibacy. (As with other matters related to secularity, this point will be studied further in chapter III, section III, 4.) We can cite, from the considerable bibliography on priestly celibacy: E. de la Lama, "El celibato, compromiso de amor pastoral," in *La formación de los sacerdotes en las circunstancias actuales* (Pamplona, 1990), pp. 137–56.

[168] *Christ Is Passing By*, no. 23. For Monsignor Escrivá's teaching on marriage and the family, see an interview given in 1968 to *Telva*, a Spanish magazine (*Conversations*, nos. 87–112); a homily he gave on Christmas Day 1970 (*Christ Is Passing By*, nos. 22–30); J. M. Martínez Doral, "La santidad de la vida conyugal," *Scripta Theologica* 21 (1989) 867–85.

[169] Letter, March 24, 1931, no. 45.

trine of the faith that, in itself, the vocation to virginity is more noble." We cannot examine here the justification for and the meaning of that statement (the whole question is much more complex than people think). Be that as it may, it does not mean that married people are called to a "second-class" holiness (which is, anyway, a theologically absurd idea). The reason is not only the one given by St. Clement of Alexandria, who wrote: "That man is truly superior who—in the midst of the temptations and care he gets from his wife, children, servants, and riches—manages to control his sensuality and sorrow, and keeps his union with God through love";[170] it is also because, for those who have a vocation to marriage, the family and marriage itself are a medium for holiness. In other words, marriage is not a place wherein "despite everything" one can stay united with God; it is in fact a means and a path to achieve that union.[171] Really, "for each individual, the most perfect thing is, always and only, to do God's will." [172]

It is, then, very much part of the theological substance of Opus Dei as a pastoral phenomenon that the Numeraries and Associates (the celibates who have a special availability for apostolic tasks) *are not the paradigm* of a member of Opus Dei. The Supernumeraries, who are the majority, do not merely try to "approach" to that paradigm. We say once more that all have the same special vocation to holiness and apostolate.

3. *Men and women*

Given the specific characteristics of vocation to Opus Dei as discussed above, the fact that it is for women as well as for men is evident.[173] Furthermore, the three general modes in which the special vocation is personalized also apply to women: there are also women in Opus Dei who are Numeraries, Associates, and Supernumeraries.[174] Consequently, the scope of their apostolic action is the same as the men's. So, in theory and in fact, women—married or single—can become members. And they come from all walks of life and diverse professions—university professors, farmers,

[170] Clement of Alexandria, *Stromata* 7, 12; PG 9:509. On the Christian vocation to holiness according to Clement of Alexandria, see J. Morales, *La vocación cristiana en la primera patrística*, pp. 862–70.

[171] Cf. Second Vatican Council, *Lumen gentium*, nos. 11 and 35; *Gaudium et spes*, no. 52.

[172] *Conversations*, no. 92.

[173] Also see *Statuta*, no. 4 § 3.

[174] Cf. ibid., no. 7 § 1. Obviously, what concerns the priesthood of some male Numeraries and Associates does not apply to female Numeraries and Associates.

workers, pharmacists, doctors, engineers, etc.—each called to sanctify her own state in life and work.

This section of the chapter could well end here; however, it is worthwhile continuing our reflection and dwelling more on the aspect of Opus Dei as a family, already referred to in chapter I.[175] The reason is that the presence of women in Opus Dei not only implies the obvious fact that the spirituality and mission of the prelature is not only for men but—in the same degree and extension—also women; their presence is also necessary for a family spirit—that of a family linked by supernatural bond—to actually exist in Opus Dei. As stated earlier, this family spirit is nothing but a specific manner of fulfilling an aspect of the nature of the Church, that is, the Church as *familia Dei*.

This is the ecclesiological context into which the work of the *catering staff* of Opus Dei apostolic undertakings fits. This work is supportive of the apostolic undertakings of the men and women of the prelature. The women of the Prelature, particularly some Numeraries, are in charge of it; they regard it as one of their special tasks, though not their only duty, because they are also engaged in all kinds of professional work as the male Numeraries are. Some Numeraries, called Assistant Numeraries, dedicate themselves to this domestic work as their own professional work.[176] They are like the other Numeraries in all other aspects of their vocation (celibacy, and the corresponding special availability for the apostolic works), except for their professional specialization in household management of the centers of Opus Dei; it should be noted that aside from the Assistant Numeraries, other Numeraries are also involved in these activities. The Assistant Numeraries take part in all the prelature's activities,[177] but their dedication to domestic work is an expression of the availability specific to all women Numeraries; it is their principal (but not their only) work, and also their usual (not necessarily permanent) duty. One thing certain is that their work is very much needed if the apostolic undertakings are to have the air of a Christian family, so much in keeping with the spirit of Opus Dei.

We need not dwell here on the importance and dignity of this kind of work; suffice it to say that the founder underlined its objective importance by calling it the "apostolate of apostolates."[178] He wrote to his daughters explaining why: "By your

[175] Cf. above, chapter one, section IV, 3.
[176] Cf. *Statuta*, no. 9.
[177] Cf. Letter, July 29, 1965, no. 24.
[178] Letter, Aug. 8, 1956, no. 43.

work in the domestic staff you participate in all our apostolic undertakings, and play a part in all that the Work does. The smooth functioning of the household affairs is a necessary precondition, and the best push for the whole Work, if you do everything for the love of God. Without the apostolate you are doing, we could not pursue other apostolic undertakings according to our spirit." [179]

It must also be noted that when Assistant Numeraries and other women Numeraries look after the domestic management of the centers of Opus Dei, they do so not as employees in someone else's home. They are more like mothers or sisters in their own home, although because they do their work so professionally they may have job descriptions like housekeeper or manager.

4. *Laymen and priests*

As discussed at length in chapter I the relationship between the common priesthood and the ministerial priesthood that constitutes the hierarchical structure of the Church is essential to the Opus Dei prelature. It was also emphasized that the clergy of the prelature come from the ranks of the lay faithful of Opus Dei (the Numeraries and Associates).[180] Although there is no need to consider these points further, it would be helpful to bear them in mind for their relevance to the present chapter.

The faithful of the prelature who are ordained to the priesthood—the founder explained—"do not change their vocation." [181] While it is true that the priesthood implies a genuine divine call that radically shapes the *personal* vocation of the one receiving it, it does not, however, change the special nature of the vocation to Opus Dei; by analogy, the ministerial priesthood does not constitute the Christian vocation as such but only the personal vocation of some Christians. However, it is quite evident that this does not make the ministerial priesthood any less necessary in Opus Dei than it is in the entire Church. As St. Josemaría said: "Ordination therefore can in no way be regarded as a crowning of a vocation to Opus Dei: it is simply a calling given to a few people so that they can serve others in a new way." [182] It follows that priests and laymen, insofar as they are members of Opus Dei, "are, and feel

---

[179] Letter, July 29, 1965, no. 11.
[180] Cf. *Statuta*, no. 1 § 2; no. 37 § 1.
[181] *Conversations*, no. 69.
[182] Ibid.

themselves to be, on a par; and all live the same spirit—sanctification in one's own state in life." [183]

The founder used to say, in stressing the equality between priests and laymen in Opus Dei, that they do not form distinct classes: "the members of Opus Dei who are called to the priesthood continue to form with the lay members, within the Work, only one class. This is a very remarkable providence of God, whom we have to thank from the bottom of our hearts." [184] As these words reveal, St. Josemaría gave a lot of importance to this phenomenon, as it very much facilitates the practice of the priesthood for what it really is—*a service*. Consequently, "priests do not let their brothers who are laymen render them unnecessary service. Each of us has in his heart the same sentiments of Jesus Christ who said: *Filius hominis non venit ministrari, sed ministrare* (Mt 20:28). Like our Lord, we have not come to be served, but to serve." [185] In sum, "although the vocation is the same for all, the priest—I say again—has a duty to be a servant of his brothers, an instrument of unity and of effectiveness, one who awakens in others desires for holiness, particularly by his example; at the same time, he is aware of the fact that in the Work he is just one of many." [186] This way of acting "makes it easy for priests not to clash with laymen, or laymen with priests; it ensures that no priest interferes in the affairs of laymen, and no layman interferes in what is proper to priests." [187] The fact of having the same special vocation—and the corresponding equality among priests and laymen insofar as they are members of Opus Dei—"is the reason why there can never be any clericalism in the Work." [188]

The Priestly Society of the Holy Cross was already referred to in chapter I from the ecclesiological-institutional viewpoint. Let us now consider it in the context of the diversity of members in Opus Dei having the same special vocation. We should remember that the Society is "an association of clerics intrinsically linked to the prelature," [189] and therefore together with the prelature it constitutes one single thing; [190] furthermore, the members of this associa-

[183] Ibid.
[184] Letter, Feb. 2, 1945, no. 20.
[185] Letter, March 28, 1955, no. 10.
[186] Letter, Aug. 8, 1956, no. 6.
[187] Letter, March 19, 1954, no. 21.
[188] Ibid.
[189] John Paul II, *Ut sit*, no. 1.
[190] We read in the Statutes of the Prelature that the Priestly Society of the Holy Cross "est Associatio clericalis Praelaturae propria ac intrinseca, unde cum ea aliquid unum constituit et ab ea seiungi non potest" (*Statuta*, no. 36 § 2).

tion of priests are the priests and deacons incardinated in the prelature[191] as well as other priests and deacons incardinated in different dioceses.[192] The latter, who are not incardinated in the prelature of Opus Dei and, consequently, do not form part of its clergy, are called Associates and Supernumeraries of the Priestly Society of the Holy Cross; they form part of the clergy of the diocese to which each belongs. Obviously, in everything to do with their incardination they exclusively depend on their respective diocesan bishops, and not on the prelate of Opus Dei.[193] With the president general of the Priestly Society of the Holy Cross—the prelate of Opus Dei—they have a relationship that is purely associative in nature, which means that they do not come under his power of jurisdiction. That associative bond exclusively refers to their spiritual life, that is, to aspects which each priest or deacon is free to arrange as he wishes.[194]

Referring to the Priestly Society of the Holy Cross and associations of priests in general, recommended by Vatican II, St. Josemaría Escrivá de Balaguer said: "Within the general limits of morality and of the duties proper to his state, a secular priest is free to arrange as he wishes, individually or together with others in an association, all the spiritual, cultural, and financial aspects of his personal life. He is free to look after his own development in accordance with his personal preferences or abilities. He is free to lead the social life he wishes, and to organize his life as he thinks best, provided he fulfills the obligations of his ministry. He is free to dispose of his personal property according to the dictates of his conscience. And above all, he is free to follow in his spiritual and ascetic life and in his acts of piety what the Holy Spirit's inspirations may suggest, and to choose, from among the many means which the Church counsels or permits, those which best suit his own particular circumstances." [195]

---

[191] Cf. ibid.

[192] Cf. ibid., no. 42.

[193] Cf. ibid.

[194] For these clerics of the Priestly Society of the Holy Cross, "nulla enim viget oboedientia interna [Praelaturae], sed solummodo normalis illa disciplina in qualibet Societate existens, quae provenit ex obligatione colendi ac servandi proprias ordinationes; quae ordinationes, hoc in casu, ad vitam spiritualem exclusive referuntur" (*Statuta*, no. 58 § 2).

[195] *Conversations*, no. 8. Regarding associations of priests, see A. del Portillo, "Le associazioni sacerdotali," in *Liber amicorum Mons. Onclin* (Gembloux, 1976) pp. 133–49; J. Polo Carrasco, "Las asociaciones sacerdotales en el Decreto Presbyterorum Ordinis," *Teología del sacerdocio* 7 (1975) 545–67; R. Rodriguez Ocaña, *Las asociaciones de clérigos en la Iglesia* (Pamplona, 1989). Concerning priestly formation

Membership in the Priestly Society of the Holy Cross of priests and deacons incardinated in different dioceses does not lessen, in law or in fact, their union and dependence on their own bishops. On the contrary, their belonging to the Priestly Society of the Holy Cross necessarily helps them to keep that union and dependence with utmost fidelity since it is an essential element of the spirituality of Opus Dei that each person seek his own sanctification in and through the duties of his state in life. St. Josemaría explained it this way: "An essential characteristic of Opus Dei is that it does not take anyone out of his place—*unusquisque; in qua vocatione vocatus est; in ea permaneat* (1 Cor 7:20). Rather it leads each person to fulfill the tasks and duties of his own state, of his mission in the Church and in society, with the greatest perfection possible. Therefore, when a priest joins the Work, he neither modifies nor sets aside any part of his diocesan vocation. His dedication to the service of the local Church in which he is incardinated, his full dependence on his Ordinary, his secular spirituality, his solidarity with other priests, etc., are not changed. On the contrary, he undertakes to live his vocation to the full, because he knows that he must seek perfection precisely by fulfilling his obligations as a diocesan priest." [196]

All this shows that priests and deacons who join the Priestly Society of the Holy Cross as Associates or Supernumeraries do so inspired by the same special vocation as other members of Opus Dei have[197]—the call to practice all the demands common to their Christian vocation (which for them is specified in their being diocesan priests) in a particular "channel," that is, Opus Dei. It is a channel which is perfectly compatible with their position in the Church and in the world for it does not take them away from their place; it provides them with a specific spirituality which they feel called by God to follow, as well as formative activities and spiritual direction geared towards their sanctification in their ministry as diocesan priests. St. Josemaría once wrote that these priests "by their vocation to the Work, confirm and strengthen their love for

and the contribution which associations of priests can make in this matter, the most important document of the recent ecclesiastical Magisterium is certainly the Apostolic Exhortation *Pastores dabo vobis*, promulgated by John Paul II as a result of the Synod of Bishops held in 1990 and devoted to the formation of priests. Among the writings on the formation and spirituality of priests produced during the preparatory phase of the Synod, we can refer again to the collection *La formación de los sacerdotes en las circunstancias actuales*.

[196] *Conversations*, no. 16.
[197] Cf. *Statuta*, no. 58 § 1.

their own diocese, and their veneration, affection, and obedience to their own bishop: in the souls of these sons of mine, from the spiritual and psychological point of view this can only have the effect of strengthening their cheerful ministry and their self-denial in the service of the diocese to which they belong, and all souls, and of course their filial submission to the diocesan Ordinary." [198]

The fact that the members of the Priestly Society of the Holy Cross have the same special calling as the other members of Opus Dei makes it logical that they, too, can be considered members. However, they do not form part of the *presbyterium* or clergy of the prelature; they are linked to it only insofar as the Priestly Society of the Holy Cross—as stated above—constitutes *aliquid unum* with the prelature.

To conclude this chapter, let us summarize its main points. Like any other special vocation in the Church, vocation to Opus Dei is a specific mode of living the Christian vocation; as such, it radically depends on a divine initiative that precedes the person's exercise of his freedom; it is something permanent, and affects the person's whole existence. The special character of this vocation is manifested in a spirituality and a mission that lead him to fulfill the all-embracing demands of the baptismal vocation, in his own state or condition in the midst of the world, and to be a ferment of Christian life in all secular activities, with the help of an institutional channel of the Church—the prelature of Opus Dei. This mission, although special, is never sectional; as to its institutional channel, it is not an alternative to, nor is it disconnected from, the particular Churches, since it belongs by ecclesiastical law to the hierarchical structure of the Church: one of its essential features is to serve the mission of particular Churches. In short, it is a vocation that does not make the person who receives it different from an ordinary member of the faithful and, as far as priests are concerned, they do not become different from other secular priests.

The diversity found in members of Opus Dei, that is, the various ways in which the members dedicate themselves to the institutional activities of Opus Dei, is not the result of their having different special vocations; participating in one way or another in these activities is not the most important, nor the most essential, part of belonging to Opus Dei, of "being Opus Dei." What matters most in Opus Dei, so to speak, is not the institutional aspect, but that which all that is institutional is designed to serve—the free,

[198] Letter, March 28, 1955, no. 45.

responsible Christian life, of each of its members. That is simply an instance of a general point: what is important in the Church is not the ecclesial structure but what the structure tries to promote—the Christian life of all the faithful and the spreading of the Gospel to all mankind, the salvation of mankind for the glory of God.

CHAPTER III.

THE CHURCH IN THE WORLD: THE SECULARITY OF MEMBERS OF OPUS DEI

JOSÉ LUIS ILLANES

In January 1933, Josemaría Escrivá de Balaguer, then a young priest, sensing that his apostolic work to establish Opus Dei had reached a certain stage of development, decided to extend the range of formational activities he provided for a growing number of university students; to informal conversations and meetings he now added study circles. He fixed the first of these for January 21, to be held at a venue made available to him in the Portacoeli Home, a charitable institution in Garcia de Paredes Street, Madrid, run by nuns to whom he devoted some of his time.

Although he invited a number of students, only three in fact turned up. Despite this poor turn-out, Fr. Josemaría did not lose heart; on the contrary, he decided not only to go ahead with the planned meeting, but to do it particularly well. When the talks were over, they all went to the chapel; he exposed the Blessed Sacrament and gave Benediction. At that very moment he had an experience to which he often referred and which he recorded in his "Apuntes intimos" (private notes), a notebook he kept at the time: "Only three came," he commented some forty years later. "What a flop, you're thinking? Well, it wasn't at all. I was very happy, and when it was over I went to the nuns' oratory, placed our Lord in the monstrance, and gave Benediction to those three fellows. To me it seemed that the Lord was blessing not three, nor three thousand, nor three hundred thousand, nor three million: he was blessing a whole multitude of people, of every color under the sun." As he put it on another occasion, when speaking to a large multi-racial gathering in Guatemala: "I could see three hundred, three hundred thousand, thirty million, three thousand million . . . , whites, blacks, yellows, people of every color, of all the color combinations human love can produce." "And still I fell short," he added, with emotion in his voice, "because it has all come true, less than fifty years later. I fell short, because the Lord has been much more generous." [1]

This experience, this look, full of faith, at those three students in the little chapel of the Portacoeli, seeing in them a limitless future reality, was a kind of extension, in Josemaría Escrivá's prayer, of an earlier key event—when, on October 2, 1928, he saw that God wanted him to launch out and spread all over the world the universal call to holiness—when he realized that he had to dedicate his life to spreading to all and sundry an awareness of the fact that God loves every human being and invites us all to be on intimate terms with him all the time, even in and through the ordinary circumstances of human life and work.

Those two events, that of October 1928 and that of January 1933, are the backdrop to what I now propose to describe and study—the lifestyle, the secularity, of members of Opus Dei. This study consists of three sections: in the first I give an overview of the subject, and then I go into it in more detail—in the second section examining the various features of secularity with special reference, naturally, to the spirit and practice of Opus Dei; and, in the third, examining the link or bond members of Opus Dei have with the prelature as something which presupposes their secular condition and inspires their lifestyle.

(1)

THE SECULARITY OF AN ORDINARY CHRISTIAN

1. *Doing Opus Dei by being Opus Dei oneself*

Some years ago, when co-authoring a study of the "legal itinerary" of Opus Dei up to the point when it was made a prelature, I found

---

[1] On this episode in Monsignor Escrivá's life and in general on historical events in his life, the following published biographies are a useful source: A. Vázques de Prada, *El Fundador del Opus Dei* (Madrid 1983); F. Gondrand, *At God's Pace* (London and New York, 1989); P. Berglar, *Opus Dei: Life and Work of Its Founder, Josemaría Escrivá* (Princeton, 1994); Ana Sastre, *Tiempo de caminar. Semblanza de Mons. Josemaría Escrivá* (Madrid, 1989), pp. 145–47.

it necessary to describe the very earliest stages of its founder's work; the entire juridical journey of Opus Dei made sense only if viewed from the perspective of the moment of its foundation: everything flowed from that point and referred back to it.

"What Don Josemaría," I wrote at that time, "discovered on October 2, 1928, was, first of all, an apostolic panorama—that of Christians scattered all over the world, involved in the most varied kinds of jobs and occupations: sometimes aware of their faith and its demands; sometimes superficial, forgetful of the life born in them at baptism and accepting, at least in practice, a divorce between their faith and their everyday life, a fabric made up of secular involvements and interests. At the same time, and inseparably from this panorama, he discovered a calling, a mission: God wanted him to devote all his energies to developing an institution—a Work, to use a term he employed from the start—whose purpose it would be to spread among Christians living in the world a deep awareness of the calling God has been addressing to them from baptism onward. A Work, furthermore, which is identical with the pastoral phenomenon it promotes, and which is made up of Christians who, on discovering what the Christian vocation really means, commit themselves to this vocation and strive from then on to communicate this discovery to others, thereby spreading throughout the world an awareness that faith can and should inspire, from within, human life and all that it involves." [2]

We have here a message about the universal call to holiness; a pastoral phenomenon of a genuine search for holiness in the midst of the world which that message provokes; and an institution at the service of the message and of its spiritual and apostolic impact—all combined in one. What the paragraph I have quoted says, and the summary of it I have just given, has been commented on at length in chapter I of this book;[3] but I do think it necessary to recall it, however briefly, at the start of this chapter, because it governs everything I shall go on to say about secularity. In fact, it should be stressed that these three elements (message, pastoral phenomenon, and institution) are so intimately involved with each other in the life of Opus Dei—as they were in Josemaría Escrivá's own life—as to constitute one, single thing.

(a) First and foremost the message and the pastoral phenomenon are very closely linked, because what Josemaría Escrivá

---

[2] *El itinerario jurídico del Opus Dei. Historia y defensa de un carisma*, written in collaboration with A. de Fuenmayor and V. Gómez Iglesias, 4th ed. (Pamplona, 1990), p. 27.

[3] See above, chapter one, sections I and II.

sensed himself called to on October 2, 1928, was not merely to proclaim the universal call to holiness and apostolate in general terms, but to do so in a personal, lived way, embodying it in actual commitments and decisions. This explains why his life was one of constantly addressing individual men and women, to open up horizons of Christian life for them. His writings also (there are many, some going back to the first years of the foundation) always grew out of his life, and kept very close to it; they are not treatises: in fact almost all of them are letters and homilies, that is, texts written in a direct style—texts in which the doctrine of the universal call to holiness and apostolate, and teachings connected with that doctrine, were formulated there and then, as he invited people to accept that call and live their lives in accordance with it.

(b) There are also (and perhaps this is the point which most concerns us here) profound links between the pastoral phenomenon and the institution. What Monsignor Escrivá realized he was called to on October 2, 1928, was not just to awaken Christians around him to an awareness of their divine vocation, but to found and develop an institution which, by bringing about a growth of holiness in the midst of the world, would contribute by its own dynamic to the spread of that holiness: that is, his mission was to look for men and women, engaged in all kinds of jobs and occupations, who, on appreciating the divine call that baptism implies, would commit themselves to answering that call in their own lives and spreading it to others until, if possible, it reached all mankind.

For the founder of Opus Dei there was never any problem of discontinuity between the pastoral phenomenon of Christian life in the world which he felt impelled to promote, and Opus Dei as a concrete ecclesial institution. From October 2, 1928, onward he did everything he could to open up horizons of Christian life to everyone he had any contact with, either personally or through his priestly ministry. Some of these people gave signs of not only taking to heart what he said and sharing the ideal of a deeply Christian life in the midst of the world, but of being totally in tune with his spirit, indeed of sharing his ideals and being ready to commit themselves to the task of spreading (by an example and word growing out of their personal lives) the practice of Christian faith in a secular context. That was how Opus Dei began to take shape, and how it continued to grow: the pastoral phenomenon and the institution becoming one and the same thing, because the member of Opus Dei, the lay person in the prelature of Opus Dei, is just a lay person, an ordinary Christian who, taking to heart the implications of baptism, commits himself or herself to spread that ideal by actually putting it into practice, that is, striving to express it in everyday actions. It was a matter then, and is a matter now, basically, in Monsignor Escrivá's own words, of "doing Opus Dei by being Opus Dei oneself."

Obviously, all this involves the contribution of the priestly ministry, without which there is not and cannot be any Christian life, and it also implies a grasp of the meaning of Christian life which impacts on one's understanding of what priestly ministry is. The founder of Opus Dei was very aware of that, not only because his priestly and theological training made him so, but also because these things were part and parcel of his foundational charism: from the very beginning, he depicted Opus Dei as an institution made up of priests and laity; in intimate, organic cooperation. This is not at odds with the fact that, to understand the physiognomy and life of Opus Dei, one needs to begin with the lay person, the ordinary Christian who strives to live in a manner consistent with his or her faith in every sort of ambience and occupation, conscious of the fact that there, in those secular realities, one can find Christ and, by becoming one with Him, draw the entire world toward God the Father. This is the viewpoint which allows one to appreciate what Opus Dei is, and the secularity which is such a feature of it.[4]

From a historical point of view, all that I have said (as I have already pointed out) harks back to October 2, 1928, and to later events which filled out that experience; from a theological point of view, we can see it as a growing appreciation of the Gospel that comes about thanks to the light Monsignor Escrivá received at foundational moments. That is why, referring to the Work he founded, he said that it was "old as the Gospel, and like the Gospel new"—in other words that it goes right back to the heart of the Gospel, finding there its strength and vigor.

To sum up, one can say that this growing appreciation turns on two basic nuclei: the regenerating efficacy of baptism and the unity between creation and redemption. For it is baptism that confers new life and gives historic consistency to the universal call to holiness and apostolate, extending and reflecting the incorporation into Christ and the Church that baptism effects. And it is the union between creation and redemption that evidences and highlights the Christian value of all human conditions and situations: they become not just the setting in which a redemption alien to them

---

[4] Again we refer the reader to chapter one, above, where the connection between the common priesthood and the ministerial priesthood, and also the form it takes in Opus Dei, is discussed.

occurs; they are actually something taken up by the action of redemption and totally imbued with its dynamism.[5]

2. Sanctification in one's own state in life

The last decades of the nineteenth century and the first third of the twentieth century saw a flourishing of lay associations. A very large proportion of these aspired to social and civic action; in a historical and cultural context in which, on the one hand, people were conscious of significant sociocultural changes and in which, on the other, laicist and secularizing policies tended to reduce the impact of the faith, it was natural for initiatives and groups to develop which sought to encourage Catholics, and therefore the Christian spirit, to influence social customs and institutions.

During those same years Fr. Josemaría Escrivá was given the light that brought Opus Dei into being, and it was then too that he began to work to consolidate and develop that institution. Those who witnessed this process, by hearing his preaching and his vigorous assertion of the divine vocation of the ordinary Christian, might have thought (and in fact in some cases did think) that Opus Dei was simply one more example of all those Christian social-action bodies to which I have just referred. But that was not in fact so, because the inspiration which gave rise to Opus Dei had accents of its own, which marked it out as different, as Josemaría Escrivá himself stressed, from the very beginning.[6]

It is true that even at the start of his pastoral activity, the founder's apostolic horizon did include the idea of spreading the Christian message in the world at large, and restoring harmony between Christian faith and social life, and therefore putting into practice the ideal of charity and justice and social harmony through

---

[5] The first of these two nuclei has been discussed at length in chapters one and two, above, from the perspective of an analysis of the configuration of the Church and also in connection with the concept of vocation. Some reference is also made there to the second nucleus, which we shall examine in more detail later. On both subjects, see also A. del Portillo, *Una vida para Dios: reflexiones en torno a la figura de Josemaría Escrivá de Balaguer* (Madrid, 1992); J. L. Illanes, *La santificación del trabajo* (Madrid, 1990); P. Rodriguez, *Vocación, trabajo, contemplación* (Pamplona, 1986); C. Fabro, S. Garofalo, and M. A. Raschini, *Santos en el mundo. Estudios sobre los escritos del Beato Josemaría Escrivá* (Madrid, 1992); and *Mons. Josemaría Escrivá de Balaguer y el Opus Dei* (Pamplona, 1985). [Earlier editions of Professor Illanes' *La Santificación del trabajo* were translated into English, the most recent as *On the Theology of Work* (Dublin and New Rochelle, 1982), a translation of the sixth edition (Madrid, 1980)—trans. note.]

[6] This point is dealt with fully in *El itinerario jurídico*, pp. 51ff.

Christian living. The fact that a new historical scenario was emerging, often bringing with it a cultural crisis, was something quite easy to see at that time, as was also the need to foster among Christians, especially those involved in secular or temporal activities, an attitude of faith which was both open and active, and which would encourage them to imbue their activities and thereby human institutions with the spirit of Christ. Many people at the time, including the founder of Opus Dei, must have seen all this; and he obviously realized that the Work he was called to develop could and should make a substantial contribution to this great apostolic objective.

However, as I have already said, Opus Dei did not become part of this movement of ideas and institutions, the reason being that by its very nature it was located and is located on a different level. In fact, even if, as is the case, one finds references even in early writings of Monsignor Escrivá's to cultural events, these references never form the core of his preaching: that preaching always harks back not to those events and their possible echo in the Christian conscience, but to October 2, 1928, and its message of sanctification. In other words, the Christian transformation of the world is not, from the perspective of Opus Dei or its founder, an end, but an effect, foreseen, desired and even expected, but only as a result of what the prelature directly promotes, namely, holiness sought and found in the heart of the world.

An oft-quoted point from *The Way* puts this particularly clearly: "A secret, an open secret: these world crises are crises of saints. God wants a handful of men 'of his own' in every human activity. And then . . . '*pax Christi in regno Christi*—the peace of Christ in the kingdom of Christ.'"[7] Josemaría Escrivá's main objective, that mission he knew was his from October 2, 1928, onward, was to foster, among people of every walk of life, in all professions and trades, a deep conversion of soul and heart which leads them to orient their entire lives toward God. Obviously, this conversion, this really making the faith one's own, transforming faith into life, cannot but have repercussions on the world and on history; but, as I have said, these repercussions were not the specific purpose of Josemaría Escrivá's pastoral ministry; and, in keeping with its foundational charism, neither are they what defines Opus Dei, whose reason for being is on a more radical level—the call to each person to communion with the will of God, indeed with God himself.

For this reason, even though (as we noted earlier) Monsignor

---

[7] *The Way*, no. 301.

Escrivá was conscious of the need to point out the differences between Opus Dei and associations and institutions seeking the Christian renewal of society (and he did so unambiguously), this was not what absorbed most of his attention. He was much more emphatic in pointing to differences in another direction—where the call to holiness, that is, to complete and radical surrender of oneself to God, was and is presumed to be present, that is, the religious state and consecrated life in general.

In the early decades of this century (as also in later ones, though with a different accent), in theology, canon law, and in pastoral practice, there was a strong tendency to identify the fullness of Christian life with the religious state. Life in the world, with all that it involved in terms of everyday work, social relationships, and family life, was viewed very much as an obstacle to holiness. Obviously no Catholic thinker was unaware of the infinite power of grace and therefore the possibility of holiness, even outstanding holiness, in the context of secular occupations (the teachings of a St. Francis de Sales, centuries earlier, had not gone with the wind); but the general view was that holiness in the world was in practice something very exceptional. Normally (the thinking went) the search for and actual achievement of holiness meant that one needed to turn one's back on the world and temporal occupations; only by abandoning the world would one remove the obstacle these occupations implied and be able to have a lifestyle which made it quite possible to have the kind of close relationship with God that sanctity involves.[8] To put it in technical language, holiness or Christian perfection tended to be viewed (not always in theory, but very often in practice) as the preserve of those in one particular way of life: the religious state, defined as "the state of perfection." [9]

The message Monsignor Escrivá was spreading was obviously not on a collision course with the religious state as such (the importance of that state has always been recognized and promoted by the Church), but it was at odds with the theological line of thought just described, that is, with the tendency *in practice* to think that the call to holiness and the call to the religious life were one and the same.

[8] The situation I describe, in outline but accurately, is well known; so there is no need to document it here. The following texts are particularly useful: Y. M. Congar, *Jalons pour une théologie du laïcat* (Paris, 1953), chap. 1; J. B. Torelló, "La espiritualidad de los laicos," in *La vocación cristiana. Reflexiones sobre la catequesis de Mons. Escrivá de Balaguer* (Madrid, 1975), pp. 47–75.

[9] The concept of state of perfection, whose roots go back to Roman law and the structure of medieval society, was spelled out by St. Thomas Aquinas and reworked later by Suarez and Passerini; for more on the concept and on the modern debate on the subject, see J. Fornés, *La noción de 'status' en derecho canónico* (Pamplona, 1975).

"Your duty is to sanctify yourself. Yes, even you. Who thinks that this task is only for priests and religious? To everyone, without exception, our Lord said: 'Be ye perfect, as my heavenly Father is perfect,'" he says in *The Way*,[10] in words which simply echoed his constant teaching from the very start of Opus Dei. The light he was given on October 2, 1928, the vision of a vast multitude of Christians, of all kinds and conditions, practicing and spreading the call to holiness in the world, led him to assert, vigorously, that holiness is not something reserved to a particular group or lifestyle: it is something open to every human being, no matter what his or her position or state in life.[11]

Furthermore, he held (and this is the key point, because without it the proclamation of the universal call to holiness runs the risk of being just a nice idea, which never comes down to earth, never touches real life)[12] that it is in fact by availing of the realities, circumstances, and interests that each state-in-life implies that one can and should seek and attain holiness. In order to find God and become one with him a person does not need to leave the world and his or her own particular state in life, because it is quite possible to find God and love him in the world and through the world: the light of faith and the strength of grace in fact enable us to recognize the world as something God-given and to direct it toward him. The whole purpose of Opus Dei is to proclaim this truth and encourage its practice by people living in the world, or, more precisely, people who belong to the world because they have been born into it and are being called to give themselves to all the various earthly realities.

"We don't take anyone out of his place," rather, we teach him to seek God there, where he lives, Fr. Escrivá said from the very beginning.[13] Our thing, he would also say, summing it up more technically, "is not the state of perfection; [we encourage] everyone to seek perfection in his own state in life."[14] Vocation to Opus

[10] *The Way*, no. 291.
[11] On this point and the following one, see above, chapter two, section II.
[12] See the previous note and my essay "La llamada universal a la santidad" in *Mundo y santidad* (Madrid, 1984), pp. 65–96.
[13] On the importance of the idea of "place" in *The Way* and other texts from the early years of Monsignor Escrivá's work, see P. Rodriguez, "Camino y la espiritualidad del Opus Dei" in *Teología espiritual* 9 (1965) 213–45 (later published in *Vocación, trabajo, contemplación*, pp. 97ff.) and especially his "Sobre la espiritualidad del trabajo" in *Nuestro Tiempo* 35 (1971) 359–88.
[14] This is an idea he often spoke about, and it frequently appears in the course of canonical approvals of Opus Dei; some particularly important texts appear in *El itinerario jurídico*, pp. 321–23, 327–31, 354–56.

Dei does not create a new state in life, does not lead a person to look for a new set of circumstances (different from the ordinary circumstances in which he already lives); rather, it encourages him to focus on his own situation in life, to evaluate it properly and commit himself to it in full fidelity to the spirit of Christ.

Sanctification in and through one's own state in life: this is the ideal which the ordinary Christian, involved in shaping the world, can and should propose to himself; the goal to which he should aspire. Christians, men and women who have received the gift of faith, must not, as Monsignor Escrivá put it in a homily in 1967, "lead a kind of double life. On one side, an interior life, a life of relation with God; and on the other, a separate and distinct professional, social and family life full of small earthly realities. No! We cannot lead a double life!" he goes on, very emphatically. "We cannot be like schizophrenics, if we want to be Christians. There is just one life, made of flesh and spirit. And it is this life which has to become, in both soul and body, holy and filled with God. We discover the invisible God in the most visible and material things." [15]

This message, this vigorous assertion of the calling to find God in one's own state in life, using the events, great and small, of everyday life, is developed in his preaching and writings by, on the one hand, reference to the dogmatic presuppositions which justify it and underpin it (the intimate connection between creation and redemption we referred to earlier) and, on the other (and this is the aspect which most directly affects us here), through making its consequences explicit, that is, by spelling out what the sanctification of ordinary life actually means. Without attempting to be exhaustive, I shall mention some of his basic teachings in this regard:

—viewing everyday work in the midst of the world as the axis or hinge of spiritual and apostolic life, in such a way that the individual realizes that he is called "to sanctify work, to sanctify himself in work and to sanctify others by his work";[16]

—proclaiming the value of "little things," that is, of the details and incidents which go to make up not just one's life, but one's

[15] *Conversations*, no. 114.
[16] See, for example, the homilies "In Joseph's Workshop" (*Christ Is Passing By*, nos. 39ff.) and "Working for God" (*Friends of God*, nos. 55ff.); an attempt to study this teaching at some length is in J. L. Illanes, *La santificación del trabajo* (Madrid, 1990; a first, shorter edition appeared in 1966); P. Rodríguez, *Vocación, trabajo, contemplación*, pp. 59–84; J. M. Aubert, "Santificación del trabajo," in *Mons. Josemaría Escrivá de Balaguer y el Opus Dei*, pp. 215–24; F. Ocáriz, "El concepto de santificación del trabajo," in *La misión del laico en la Iglesia y en el mundo*, pp. 881–91.

156

every day, and which, by "turning them into big things through Love," enable one's entire life to be filled with God;[17]

—inviting people to a life of prayer which, based on a sense of divine filiation and on awareness of the fact that God is always near us, leads a person to have such continuous contact with Him that one becomes a "contemplative in the midst of the world";[18]

—proposing the ideal of "unity of life," whereby the theological, ascetical and apostolic aspects of one's life integrate with one's secular involvements, so that one's entire existence in the world is raised to the level of communion with God and helps to effect the plan of salvation manifested in Christ.[19]

As I have already said, this list is not exhaustive (many further examples could be given), but it does, I think, show the basic idea—how the calling to holiness in the world is spelt out in a series of teachings which indicate how, in ordinary secular life and all that it involves, the full range of dimensions implied by Christian life can and should express themselves.

It shows what is implied by the call to sanctification in one's own state in life, and it also shows that the invitation to unite life in the world and Christian life is not just a vague proposal, or something to be accepted as just a theory or a nice idea: it is an ideal which really can be attained, because one is also being shown the route which, with the help of grace, leads to that goal.

3. *Christians and ordinary citizens*

"I dream—and the dream has come true—of multitudes of God's children, sanctifying themselves as ordinary citizens, sharing the ambitions and endeavors of their colleagues and friends. I want to shout to them about this divine truth: if you are there in the midst of ordinary life, it doesn't mean Christ has forgotten about you or hasn't called you. He has invited you to stay among the activities and concerns of the world. He wants you to know that your human vocation, your profession, your talents, are not omitted from his

---

[17] The basic source in this regard is, undoubtedly, the long chapter devoted to it in *The Way* (nos. 813–30); see also the homily "The Richness of Ordinary Life" in *Friends of God*, nos. 1ff.

[18] In the second section of this chapter we shall return again to this expression, and the life of prayer that it implies; on divine filiation, the basis of the spiritual life according to the teaching of the founder of Opus Dei, see F. Ocáriz, "La filiación divina, realidad central en la vida y en la enseñanza de Mons. Escrivá de Balaguer," in *Mons. Josemaría Escrivá de Balaguer y el Opus Dei*, pp. 173–214.

[19] I shall also deal with this point later in the chapter.

divine plans. He has sanctified them and made them a most acceptable offering to his Father." [20]

The passage I have just quoted, taken from a homily Monsignor
Escrivá gave in 1963 commenting on the ordinary life of Jesus in
Bethlehem and Nazareth, allows us to take a step further, because
it brings in the expression "ordinary Christians." This has appeared in earlier chapters, but I should like to go into it in some
detail now because, for one thing, it focuses our attention on that
homogeneity between message, pastoral phenomenon, and institution which, as I said earlier, is basic to our understanding of Opus
Dei and of its members' secularity. For, if Monsignor Escrivá
devoted his life to proclaiming, to "shouting," that "divine truth"
to which the homily refers, that is, the Christian value of ordinary
life, he did so not only in his preaching, in his spiritual guidance of
souls and in his writings, but also and especially by founding Opus
Dei, developing an institution made up of men and women who,
taking to heart the ideal of sanctification in the midst of the world,
commit themselves to making this a reality and thereby spreading
it among those around them.

Monsignor Escrivá was acutely aware that the essence of his
mission and destiny lay in proclaiming and defending the fully
secular status of the members of Opus Dei. From October 2, 1928,
he saw absolutely clearly that the mission he had been given involved asserting, unequivocally, the universal call to holiness and,
as a consequence, the possibility of sanctification in the midst of
the world, in and through temporal realities and involvements. But
he also realized, equally clearly, that that was not enough: he also
needed to proclaim and stand up for the ordinary Christian condition of members of Opus Dei, not just (though it would have been
enough) out of fidelity to his foundational charism, but also, and
inseparably, for the sake of the universal call to holiness itself.

In other words, those who, when they hear mention of radical-
ness in Christian life (which Opus Dei undoubtedly involves) tend
to think of the religious state, showing that, as they see it, the
fullness of Christian life and the religious or consecrated state are
one and the same thing; they act, in effect, as if they do not accept
or do not fully accept the universality of the call to holiness. To put
it the other way: asserting the universal call to holiness implies
recognizing that the fullness of Christian life and the religious state
are not synonymous, and therefore recognizing that it is possible
for there to be an institution whose members commit themselves

[20] *Christ Is Passing By*, no. 20.

to a fullness of Christian life without themselves being religious or like religious, and without imitating religious spirituality. And that is precisely what identifies Opus Dei. Asserting the universal call to holiness and recognizing the secular condition of members of Opus Dei are one and the same thing.[21]

That is why its founder emphasizes secularity so much, even to the point of sounding boring: the members of Opus Dei, he stressed time and time again, are not religious; they are Christian men and women who want to work at their jobs, live in the world, engage in their family and social affairs in a manner fully consistent with their faith; by encountering Opus Dei their Christian lives have deepened, their apostolic endeavors increased, their awareness of the need to follow Christ has become sharper—but their situation in the world has not changed, for it is precisely there, in the world, in their own state in life, where they have to really follow Christ. To sum up, they were, they are, and they will continue to be ordinary Christians—which brings us back to that expression I said we needed to explore.

It is an expression whose origin goes back to the earliest days of the founder's preaching. In his "Apuntes intimos" we find, for example, the following note: "Ordinary Christians. Dough being leavened. Ours is to be ordinary, natural. The means: everyday work. All saints! Silent self-surrender." [22] The expressions "ordinary Christians" or "ordinary faithful" continue to appear in later texts. Very soon he uses "ordinary Christians" so often that we could almost say it acquires a technical meaning. It carries all sorts of resonances, particularly (as often happened in his writings) if he combined it with another expression with a somewhat different and yet very close meaning, "ordinary citizens."

---

[21] From a general theological point of view, all this obviously ties in with the whole question or debate on the subject of states or conditions of life in the Church. Without going into that subject, which would take us beyond the scope of this essay, I might say that contemporary theological thinking (and the Magisterium, as can be seen in the *Lumen gentium* and other more recent documents, particularly *Christifideles laici*) has moved from an ontological-moral approach to an ecclesiological-symbolic one: in other words, it has ceased to focus on the idea of the distinction between conditions of life determining states of perfection, which leads nowhere, and instead is concentrating on the real life of a Church in which there exists a range of vocations, states, and charisms, which differ from one another and yet are complementary—that is, all are necessary for the perfecting of the whole. On this point, see the brief summary given in my article "Llamada a la santidad y radicalismo cristiano" in *La misión de los laicos en la Iglesia y en el mundo*, pp. 803–24.

[22] "Apuntes intimos," no. 25.

Let me quote some texts, which I shall then comment on:

—"It is the Lord's will—part of the imperative command, part of the vocation you have received—that you, my daughters and sons, be ordinary Christians and citizens: not in any way differentiating yourselves from others, sharing with them noble earthly interests, doing your everyday work in a responsible way, having an active, genuine presence in social and civic life, in keeping with your own personal position." [23]

—"Ordinary work, in the midst of the world, puts you in touch with all the problems and concerns of mankind, for they are your own concerns, your own problems: you are ordinary citizens, citizens the same as others." [24]

—"Opus Dei aims to encourage people of every sector of society to desire holiness in the midst of the world. In other words, Opus Dei proposes to help ordinary citizens like yourself to lead a fully Christian life, without modifying their normal way of life, their daily work, their aspirations and ambitions." [25]

—"The Work was born to help those Christians who, through their family, their friendships, their ordinary work, their aspirations, form part of the very texture of civil society, to understand that their life, just as it is, can be an opportunity for meeting Christ: that it is a way of holiness and apostolate. Christ is present in any honest human activity. The life of an ordinary Christian, which to some people may seem banal and petty, can and should be a holy and sanctifying life." [26]

—"What members of Opus Dei, who are ordinary Christians, have to do is to sanctify the world from within, taking part in the whole range of human activities." [27]

—"The men and women who want to serve Jesus Christ in the Work of God are simply *citizens the same as everyone else*, who strive to live their Christian vocation to its ultimate consequences with a strong sense of responsibility." [28]

I could quote from other writings of Monsignor Escrivá's, but I think the above passages give a good idea of the way he used to speak and will allow us to see the meaning and scope of the expression "ordinary Christians":

(a) The ordinary Christian is, simply, as the words indicate, the

---

[23] Letter, Feb. 14, 1944, no. 2.
[24] Letter, Oct. 15, 1948, no. 28.
[25] *Conversations*, no. 24.
[26] Ibid., no. 60.
[27] Ibid., no. 61.
[28] *Conversations*, no. 118.

typical plain member of the faithful, a person who, incorporated into Christ by baptism and thereby made a participant in the Church's mission, lives in the ordinary circumstances of life in the world, sharing the social conditions, interests and problems of other citizens; in this reference to the state or situation common to everyone lies the full force of the words "ordinary Christians," because it contains both the canonical-theological element (the "lay status") and the "ordinary way of life" element, thereby accentuating that community of life with others which the lay condition connotes, and, consequently, that mission to sanctify earthly realities from within those very realities, which is the mission of the lay member of the faithful.

(b) The expression "ordinary Christian" has therefore a sociological content, because it indicates normality, sameness of circumstances and lifestyle as other citizens (and this explains how it is reinforced and spontaneously filled out by its analogue, "ordinary citizens"); but it transcends sociology, because its substance is theological: it is an expression designed with the very purpose of indicating that the world and all that goes to make it up are not something alien to God and his plan: divine vocation lifts up human vocation, endowing it with a new and basic meaning, but without doing it violence: on the contrary, respecting human vocation's own dynamic (which is why one can in fact speak of "ordinary citizens").

Obviously, the expressions "ordinary Christian" and "ordinary citizen" cover a huge variety of situations: there is no single type of ordinary Christian or ordinary citizen, but rather a whole range of extremely varied possibilities (as befitting lives which are not devised to comply with a preconceived model or an *a priori* rule); yet these lives coincide in the fact that they are all ordinary, that is, all of them are located in a setting of ordinariness and are in no way disconnected from that setting. The fact that there is no disconnection or, to put it positively, the fact there is continuity, both theological and sociological, is the basic datum.

It is also obvious that the fact that one is an ordinary Christian does not exclude (in fact it presupposes) either practice of the faith and vital connection with the Church, without which you cannot have genuine Christian life, or, therefore, involvement in ecclesial things or institutions; provided, of course, that those institutions, and one's connection with them, do not take from but, on the contrary, respect and even reinforce one's position as a Christian called to sanctify himself within the coordinates of the ordinary life of men. The only thing that is excluded, very definitely, is any kind of approach or attitude which involves a distancing, even if only psychological, from the common condition and from the relationship with the world which that implies.

Monsignor Escrivá was very uncompromising on this point: he always underlined, as I have said, the fact that the spirit of Opus Dei does not "take anyone out of his place," but, rather, leads him to discover the meaning of that "place" in God's mind, and therefore to recognize that it is not just a "place" but an integral part of one's own divine mission and vocation. So, not only did he insist that the ordinary Christian has to love his condition and the world in which he lives and which by divine vocation he is called to sanctify,[29] but he must scrupulously avoid any tendency to speak in a way which might even remotely give the impression of being separate or distanced from the world.

Perhaps the best example of this attitude (reflecting a profound conviction concerning the nature of the foundational charism entrusted to him) was his decision to avoid using the comparative adverb "like" which, even though it means identity, sameness, also implies distinction: instead he speaks directly and consistently of "equality": "Your task, my beloved daughters and sons," he said in one of his Letters, and this is just one example, which I could multiply, "is a secular, lay work, a task of ordinary Christians—the *equals* of other citizens, and *not* 'like' other citizens—who seek their holiness and do apostolate *in* and *from* those occupational involvements you have in the midst of the world." [30]

[29] "Passionately loving the world" is in fact the title Monsignor Escrivá gave to one of his homilies (*Conversations*, nos. 113ff.), to which we shall return in section II of this chapter. It is also worth mentioning here, in addition to other texts to which I have referred, the occasions when he criticized what he graphically called "mystical wishful thinking": day-dreaming about being in another situation instead of grasping the present moment and facing up to it (see, e.g., *Conversations*, no. 116).

[30] Letter, May 31, 1943, no. 18. And elsewhere: "The supernatural mission we have received does not lead us to differentiate ourselves or cut ourselves off from others; it leads us to join up with everyone, because we are the *equals* of other citizens of our country. We are, I repeat, equal to others (not, 'like' others) and we share with them the concerns of a citizen, of a profession or job which is ours, other involvements, the world around us, the way we dress, the way we work. We are ordinary men or women who in no way differentiate ourselves from our companions and colleagues, from those who live with us in our milieu and our walk of life": letter, March 24, 1930, no. 5.

The same concern to avoid any use of language that implies separation or external difference is to be found in those texts in which he shows his distaste for expressions such as "making oneself present in the world": a Christian does not go into the world or move into the world: he is there to begin with; in fact he belongs to the world, because that is where he was born and that is where he lives. "I hope the time will come when the phrase 'the Catholics are moving into all sectors of society' will

4. Secularity

Up to this point I have been going through teachings (and texts) of Monsignor Escrivá's to do with the secular condition of members of Opus Dei, ordinary Christians called to sanctify themselves in the day-to-day circumstances of human life. Before going on, I think it would be useful to refer to the recent theological debate on the subject of secularity. That will involve a change of method and intellectual focus, but I think it will provide a useful reference point for evaluating the scope of some of the statements already made or soon to be made.

The term *secularity*, like many other abstract nouns, has come into common use only in recent times, even though its antecedent, the adjective *secular*, is to be found in Christian writing from very early on; in fact its Greek precedents (the adjectives *cosmikos* and *biotikos*) go back to pre-Christian language. In recent theological literature the noun *secularity* refers to things to do with the world, that is, secular, earthly, temporal realities and more specifically their positive Christian value; and so it is applied to the Christian or to the Church to indicate that they, in one way or another, to some degree or other, have reference to the world, whose Christian value they manifest and bring out.[31]

In fact, not only is the noun *secularity* fairly new: the positive meaning it contains is also something new. In Christian writings of the patristic and medieval periods the adjective *secular* was used to refer to occupations and activities proper to Christians living in the world (the *negotia saecularia*, in a well-known Latin expression) and to the attitudes which those occupations involved; and sometimes it was used as a noun (*saeculares* or *laici*, as opposed to clerics and

---

go out of circulation because everyone will have realized that it is a clerical expression. In any event, it is quite inapplicable to the apostolate of Opus Dei. The members of the Work have no need to 'move in on' the temporal sector for the simple reason that they are ordinary citizens, the same as their fellow citizens, and so they are *there already*": *Conversations*, no. 66.

[31] The literature on secularity is very extensive, because the debate on this subject ranges very widely, from historico-cultural to theological-spiritual studies. I shall therefore mention only a few studies that are more directly connected with what we are discussing here. J. L. Illanes, "La secularidad como elemento especificador de la condición laical," in *Vocación y misión del laico en la Iglesia y en el mundo* (Burgos, 1987), pp. 276–300; "Secolarità," in *Dizionario enciclopedico di spiritualità*. vol. 3 (Rome, 1990) 2278–82; "La discusión teológica sobre la noción de laico," in *Scripta Theologica* 22 (1990) 771–89; P. Rodriguez, "La identidad telógica del laico," in *La misión del laico en la Iglesia y en el mundo*, pp. 265–302; S. Piei Ninot, "Aportaciones del Sínodo de 1987 a la teología del laicado," in *Revista española de Teología*, 48 (1988) 321–70.

monks or, later on, religious in general). All these uses of the adjective *secular* were affected by the negative attitude to earthly realities which, as we have said, characterized the time, an attitude originating in a tendency to extend to human society the severe judgment that biblical texts reserve for "this world," regarded as the kingdom of the devil.

At the very least that theological tendency is very one-sided. The world has indeed been affected by sin, but it does not cease to be something created by God and ordained to redemption—in fact, something already redeemed by Christ Jesus. The world as seen by Christian eyes is not only a world controlled by sin which should be fought and avoided, at least spiritually; it is also (or, better, above all) a world called to redemption, something which should feel the impact of that life of Christ given to the Christian in the form of grace.

This whole theological horizon, much richer and more balanced, came onto center stage due to the broad movement of ideas and ecclesial developments which has led, in our own century, to an assertion of the value of the lay situation, a recognition that the lay person, the ordinary Christian living in the midst of the world, is called to holiness and apostolate—and called to that not in spite of or without regard to his presence in the world but, in fact, in and through the secular activities which shape his life. Secularity now comes across as something positive, as a specifying characteristic of a particular Christian status—that of the lay person. The Constitution *Lumen gentium* of the Second Vatican Council (specifically its fifth chapter, dealing with the laity) was the high point of this process. "Their secular character," the Council says, "is proper and peculiar to the laity"; it belongs to them "by reason of their special vocation to seek the kingdom of God by engaging in temporal affairs and directing them according to God's will. They live in the world, that is, they are engaged in each and every work and business of the earth and in the ordinary circumstances of social and family life which, as it were, constitute their very existence. There they are called by God that, being led by the spirit to the Gospel, they may contribute to the sanctification of the world as from within, like leaven, by fulfilling their own particular duties." [32]

This theological and spiritual clarification brought about by Christian life and reflection in the earlier part of this century, and confirmed by the Council, establishes a fixed point of reference, from which there is no going back. However, in the 1970s there

---

[32] Second Vatican Council, *Lumen gentium*, no. 31.

were instances not so much of querying the basic idea (the assertion of the Christian value of the world and everything that derives from it) as of questioning other aspects of the conciliar teaching or at least its possible interpretations. The Council had not only underlined the Christian meaning of earthly realities but had described one of the possible Christian vocations in reference to that meaning: the vocation of those Christians we call "lay people." It was apropos of this last point that the queries arose: Is it only the lay person who has this reference to the world; is that not a feature of all Christians? By depicting one possible Christian vocation as being actually defined by a connection with the world, do you not risk proposing too rigid a division of functions, which is at odds with the way things in fact are—the world for the laity, the Church for the priests and religious?

We do not need here to go into the various stages of this debate in the seventies and eighties up to the time of the 1987 Synod of Bishops and the Apostolic Exhortation *Christifideles laici* which it produced. I shall simply refer to that document and the synthesis it achieved.

Christifideles laici locates its teaching in the context of the ecclesiology of communion; it presupposes, then, a view of the Church as a living, pluralist communion, in which there is plurality of offices, vocations, and ministries, where these are distinct from but not opposed to one another, and complementary, in such a way that the mission common to all is carried out thanks to the action of each and every member. This leads to a first conclusion: there is no Christian condition or vocation that constitutes a world apart or that can be considered in isolation, for it acquires its full meaning only when set within the Church, in communion with the rest of the ecclesial body, to whose life it contributes.

This first idea then goes on to impact on the document's view of the Church–world relationship, which brings us into the area that interests us here. The Church has been sent by God to men, to proclaim to the world that union with God is the reason-of-being and ultimate destiny of everything. The notion of proclamation clearly contains the idea of words announcing a message, and this also applies to the Christian message, except that in this case it must also be proclaimed by one's life: one needs to testify by deeds to the truth of the love of God which one proclaims in words. To sum up, the Church must not wash its hands of temporal realities, of the concrete events of history, because it is right there, in concrete daily life, in the things that go to make up ordinary human existence, that it should express the truth of that divine love which has been given to it to proclaim. The entire Church therefore, *Christifideles laici* concludes, "has an authentic secular dimension, inherent in her inner nature and mission, which is deeply rooted in the mystery of the Word Incarnate."[33]

And so, just as the Word, the only-begotten Son of the Father, took on our human condition, sharing everything that goes to make it up and define it—family, work, friendships, sorrow, joy, suffering—even incorporating them into the mystery of his intimate relationship with the Father, so too the Church realizes that it has solidarity with all mankind, sharing man's interests and destiny, sharing the concrete events of human history, while at the same time showing men and women the infinite horizon of the love of God.

Understood in this sense, the "secular dimension," that is, reference to the world and to history, is something that belongs to the whole Church and therefore to each and every member; independently of his vocation or state: no Christian should feel detached from the situation of those around him and from what is happening in the world; indeed he should feel it as something that belongs to him, not just as a man living in human society but as a Christian, because he could not fulfill his role as a Christian if he turned his back on human problems and needs. However, the text of *Christifideles laici* goes on, while it is true that "all the members of the Church are sharers in this secular dimension," they are so "in different forms." "In particular," it adds, "the sharing by the lay faithful has its own manner of realization and function which, according to the Council, is properly and particularly theirs. Such a manner is designated by the expression *secular character*."[34]

The distinction between the words *dimension* and *character* enables *Christifideles laici* to harmonize all the various data. The Church as a whole and every Christian calling considered separately have a secular dimension, have a relationship with the world, sanctify the world. This relationship with the world is part of the make-up of the Church, though it is not the source of its life (that source is none other than Christ himself), nor does it define everything about it; we can see this from the language used, specifically the word *dimensions*, which means aspects or features which may be important and even decisive in constituting an entity or an action, but which are added to other aspects or facets; this is not the sum total of its essential nucleus which, in the case we are discussing,

---

[33] John Paul II, *Christifideles laici*, Dec. 30, 1988, no. 15, quoting an address given by Paul VI on Feb. 2, 1972.

[34] *Christifideles laici*, no. 15, referring to *Lumen gentium*, no. 31.

refers to Christ and to his mystery. It is in Christ and from Christ and in line with each person's particular share in the Church's mission, that the secular dimension, the relationship with the world, needs to be accented and developed.

All this is valid, naturally, for the lay member of the faithful too: his vocation is founded on Christ, in whose life he shares through baptism; but (*Christifideles laici* goes on) in his case the secular dimension is so relevant that one can speak of a secular *character*, that is, a specific condition, a defining feature, some thing which identifies and determines the vocation one has received and the task one is called on to do—in a word, one's whole life. Other ecclesial vocations and conditions do have a secular dimension; however, they are defined not by it but rather in relation to other things (priestly ministry, consecration, and bearing witness to things eschatological, etc.), whereas the lay state is defined and specified in relation to nothing other than secularity. The lay member of the faithful not only contributes to the transformation and sanctification of the world (as every Christian can and should do) but he lives in the world, in the society of men; his entire life is intertwined with secular institutions, settings, and activities; he inserts therein, through his own life and action, the spirit of Christ, that is, sanctifies them from within.

Secular condition and Christian vocation interconnect in the life of the lay person; they combine to make one thing; they imbue each other completely: Christian life and dynamism unfold in and through secular realities and occupations; and secular experience and all it implies about living in harmony with others and a spirit of service reveals its full meaning when it takes place in the light of and under the influence of Christian life. "The ecclesial condition of lay members of the faithful," *Christifideles laici* concludes, "comes to be fundamentally defined by their newness in Christian life and distinguished by their secular character." [35] Newness in Christian life (the life of grace derived from baptism) and secular experience form an intimate unity, expressing the harmony of creation and redemption. The lay vocation thereby testifies to the Gospel's ability not only to reveal the ultimate goal toward which history is making its way, but also to give life here and now to temporal things, causing the spirit of Christ to throb in them.

If, having reached this point, we now look back and compare these ideas with those we looked at earlier, we will easily notice how much they are in line with each other. In fact, what *Lumen*

---

[35] Ibid., no. 15; see also nos. 16 and 17, where this teaching is extended with reference to the call to holiness.

gentium and *Christifideles laici* have to say about the secular character being proper to lay people and what Monsignor Escrivá taught about naturalness and the condition of the ordinary Christian illuminate each other—which fits in with what I said earlier about any attempt to understand Opus Dei needing to begin with the notion of lay person, given the fact that what Opus Dei aspires to do (in keeping with its foundational charism, as defined on October 2, 1928) is precisely to foster among lay people or ordinary Christians of the most varied different social conditions and occupations an awareness of their Christian vocation, of the calling God is addressing to them—to sanctify their life and sanctify others in and through the circumstances and events of their life in the world.

It is, at the same time, worth noting that secularity asserted in that way embraces the entirety of the pastoral and institutional phenomenon of Opus Dei. For example, in the first instance, it affects the priests who form part of Opus Dei (both those who make up its presbyterium and those who are incardinated in their own dioceses and become members of the Priestly Society of the Holy Cross),[36] who are not only canonically and theologically secular priests, but also, in keeping with the spirituality and mission of the prelature, are expected to have a deep appreciation of secular things and to be fully available, and indeed zealous, to spread among lay people an awareness of their Christian vocation.[37] Secularity affects all the apostolate, too—including those apostolic works (in the field of education and social welfare) the members of Opus Dei may promote—which will always have "eminently secular characteristics," as befits activities for personal, cultural, and social advancement carried out by citizens, who naturally try to make them "reflect the light of the Gospel and to enkindle them with Christ's love," and who always act in a lay and secular manner, conscious that they are "engaged in professional work (undertaken) by lay people, citizens the equals of colleagues who engage in the same task or work."[38]

In both cases secularity is not just an external dressing or some-

---

[36] Both are discussed above, in chapters one and two.

[37] Various teachings of the founder of Opus Dei might be cited here, but space does not allow. See particularly *Conversations*, nos. 3–8, 16, 20–21, 47, 58–59, 69; and the homily of April 13, 1973, in *In Love with the Church*, pp. 37ff.

[38] *Conversations*, nos. 119 and 18 (also nos. 27, 31, 51); the same ideas appear in many of his letters; in one, for example, he says that corporate apostolates "are activities which (always with an apostolic aim) are undertaken within the terms of civil law, not as an ecclesiastical initiative but as what they are: professional initiatives of citizens," April 15, 1953, no. 22. On corporate works of apostolate, see D. de Tourneau, *What Is Opus Dei?* (Cork, n.d.), pp. 86ff.

thing which is bonded onto the Christian condition from outside, as it were; it is an intrinsic component of Christian existence: the Christian grasps this when he takes his faith seriously and realizes that God is calling him to sanctify himself while staying in the world and, therefore, realizes that divine vocation and human vocation blend to form the one thing, each illuminating and complementing the other.[39]

Monsignor Alvaro del Portillo has put this very well in words which I shall use to end this section: "Secularity is not for us a camouflage we put on to obtain a particular result; it is not a matter of pastoral or apostolic tactics; it is actually the place where the Lord puts us in his Heart, in order that we may do his Work and sanctify this world, where we share the joys and sorrows, work and leisure, daily hopes and activities of other Christians, our equals. . . . So, secularity is not a route [designed] to make *Christianity easy*, it is not a sham worldliness [but] a connatural participation in the realities of life—in work well done, in shouldering of family and social obligations, in sharing in the sorrows of others and striving to build the earthly city peaceably and in the light of God."[40]

(II)

ASPECTS OF SECULARITY

1. *Unity of life*

Ordinary Christians, sanctification of one's state in life, secularity—all these different expressions refer to one and the same thing: the Christian value of the ordinary, the fact that God is seeking out man in the context of his everyday life and inviting him to respond to him in and through what that life involves.

The theological nucleus I have just described is something complete in itself (it has a clear, well-defined meaning), but to demonstrate its scale and scope we need to examine its basic implications: only then will we see what an "acted out" secularity means. That is

[39] On the connection between divine vocation and human vocation in Opus Dei spirituality, see above, chapter two, section III; also J. L. Illanes, *La santificación del trabajo*, pp. 84–93.

[40] A. del Portillo, letter, Nov. 28, 1982, no. 22. This is a letter Monsignor del Portillo sent to all the members of Opus Dei on the occasion of its establishment as a personal prelature and in which he comments on the main features of its spiritual make-up that this juridical development underlined and guaranteed; very much to the fore among these features is secularity. On this letter and its historical context, see *El itinerario jurídico*, pp. 444–46.

what I propose to do in this second section, and I shall do so, naturally, with special reference to the life and apostolate of Opus Dei.

Among the facets of secularity there is one which according to the spirituality of Opus Dei (and very probably in all cases) has pride of place: I refer to "unity of life."

Anyone who goes to the writings of St. Josemaría Escrivá to see what words and phrases he uses to describe that encounter with God in which vocation to Opus Dei consists will notice that two words have special importance: light and commitment.[41] Light, or, as the first chapter of *The Forge* puts it,[42] "dazzle," a strong bright light illuminating one's life, referring partly to God, from whom this light comes, and partly to the person concerned and to the world, to his ambience, which is given its fullest meaning by being lit up by God. In other words, knowledge; not an abstract or disincarnated knowledge but a living, real knowledge. A calling or invitation, which leads to a commitment, if the person really answers it.

Every Christian vocation is structured in that way. In the case of members of Opus Dei, both elements—light and commitment—have to do with one's personal life in the world, in and through which the relationship with God and consciousness of mission (self-surrender, and service of others) which derive from that relationship must be expressed and articulated.

"What do members of Opus Dei do? some may ask, used to seeing apostolate as a special, extra, activity," Monsignor Escrivá wrote in one of his Letters, going on to give a short, incisive reply: "What do they do? *They do their duty*, no more, no less."[43] The Statutes say the same thing, in the tight, precise language typical of legal documents: the prelature, we are told, "seeks the sanctification of its members through the practice of the Christian virtues, each in his or her own state, occupation and circumstances, following its specific spirituality, which is a thoroughly secular one."[44]

In line with this initial statement, the Statutes go on to point out that, as a consequence, all the members of the prelature "undertake not to cease to engage in professional or equivalent work, because

---

[41] Vocation as a light that gives a deep understanding of the meaning and scope of the Christian vocation and what it means in one's personal life has already been dealt with in chapter two, above; what is said there should be borne in mind when reading the following.

[42] *The Forge*, nos. 1ff.

[43] Letter, May 6, 1945, no. 10.

[44] *Statuta*, no. 2 § 1; see also no. 27 § 3.

it is through that that they seek holiness and carry out their own specific apostolate"; in fact, "they strive to carry out with maximum fidelity their duties of state and the activity or social role each has."[45]

To show the spiritual and theological scope of these expressions (although their meaning is quite clear), it might be useful to link them with the founder's previously cited phrase: "sanctifying work, sanctifying one-self in work, sanctifying others through work"; or also, going from everyday work to the entire area of secular life, of which that work is such a key component, "sanctifying ordinary life, sanctifying oneself in ordinary life, sanctifying others through ordinary life.[46] This "dazzle," the projection of the light of faith on to ordinary life, the realization that one is called by God to practice and foster holiness in the world: all this implies an awareness of meaning and therefore of mission and role, which unfolds in three complementary and closely connected dimensions:

(a) A call to personal sanctification to meet God and to attain union with him in everyday life, recognizing in the obligations of one's own state in life and job and in the circumstances which go to make up one's day, an echo and sign of God's will and an invitation therefore to respond to his love in and through those very obligations and circumstances;

(b) A call to serve others in line with the commandment of charity which sums up the law of Christ; and therefore a sense of mission, an awareness of the need to contribute through one's work and through family and social relationships to the good of those around us, and to open up for them horizons of Christian life involving an apostolate of "friendship and trust," that is, an apostolate which, availing of the little events of daily life, expresses itself in actions both authentic and simple, in conversations between friends, between colleagues.

(c) Finally, and presupposing what has just been said, a calling to sanctify work and daily life as such—that is, doing everything well in a technically and humanly perfect way and imbuing it with the light of the Gospel, by evaluating it from the viewpoint of Christian faith and doing it in a way which truly reflects the spirit of Christ.

We do not need to comment in any greater detail here about

---

[45] *Statuta*, no. 3 § 2.

[46] The expressions cited ("sanctifying work," "sanctifying oneself in work," "sanctifying others by means of work") and equivalent expressions were used by Monsignor Escrivá repeatedly; see, e.g., *Christ Is Passing By*, no. 46; *Friends of God*, no. 9; *Conversations*, no. 70.

this ideal or program of secular life;[47] but it is useful to point out that this program needs to be seen not in a static framework but rather as something dynamic; in fact, in terms of a rhythm which develops from the center and influences one's whole life. As is true of every Christian experience, the Opus Dei ideal has its starting point in faith or, better, in faith-put-into-practice, in that consciousness of communion with God which faith provides; it then proceeds to affect one's entire life; one sees and lives everything in the light of faith; life becomes a manifestation of the love that emanates from faith.

St. Josemaría Escrivá described this by using an expression which always carries a very definite meaning—unity of life.[48] By "unity of life" he meant not just an ascetical ideal (an upright intention, inner calm, making an effort to avoid distractions and to focus one's thoughts and affections on a governing value . . .); he was referring to something deeper, something which was of course reflected in daily existence and involved ascetical effort, but whose roots go down to the depths of one's being, to that real communion with God made possible by grace. Indeed, although his writings do contain references to asceticism, the strongest note they strike is that of inviting the person to let faith influence his mind and therefore his heart, so that it ends up affecting all dimensions of his life, including (this is a key part of his message) profane and secular aspects.

In one of his homilies, given on the feast of the Ascension, he reminded his listeners that Christ is in heaven, at the right hand of the Father, and therefore they needed to raise their minds toward higher things, eschatological things; and then he came back immediately to everyday life: transcendence should not cut us off from that life but, rather, refer us to it, by focusing light on it and revealing its full meaning. "In this life, the contemplation of supernatural things, the action of grace in our souls, our love for our neighbor as a result of our love for God—all these are already a foretaste of heaven, a beginning that is destined to grow from day

---

[47] This would entail giving a detailed account of the spirit of Opus Dei, which would obviously be beyond the scope of this essay. I shall simply refer the reader to short accounts in R. Gómez Pérez, *El Opus Dei. Una explicación* (Madrid, 1992), pp. 63–119; D. le Tourneau, *What Is Opus Dei?*, pp. 25ff.; G. Romano, "L'uomo, Cristo, la Chiesa," in *Il vangelo del lavoro. Josemaría Escrivá* (Milan, 1992), pp. 37–121; and, for more detailed theological studies, the works cited in note 4, above, the opening chapters of *El itinerario jurídico*, and the various contributions in *La vocación cristiana. Reflexiones sobre la catequesis de Mons. Escrivá de Balaguer*.

[48] On the presence of this expression even in the very early days of Monsignor Escrivá's preaching, see *El itinerario jurídico*, pp. 42–43.

to day." This leads on to a clear conclusion: life must not be divided into two separate sections—yearning for heaven, on the one hand; everyday existence, on the other—because awareness of things supernatural pushes one to a God-conscious practice of one's each and every activity; "we Christians must not resign ourselves to leading a double life; our life must be a strong and simple unity into which all our actions converge." [49]

This text, while vigorously asserting the ideal of unity of life which definitely includes the secular element, also targets that dynamism or spiritual rhythm which, as we said earlier, is integral to the notion of unity of life. This is made even clearer in other texts—for example, the following passage, which is particularly relevant because it comes from one of Monsignor Escrivá's earliest "Instrucciones" (Instructions): "Combining everyday work, ascetical struggle and contemplation (something which might seem impossible, yet it is necessary if we are to help reconcile the world to God), turning that ordinary work into a means of personal sanctification and apostolate: is this not a great and noble ideal, worth giving one's life for?" [50] Or this other passage from a Letter where, when speaking about prayer life, he says that cultivation of God, and particularly of Christ in the Eucharist, "will give you a supernatural instinct to purify all your actions, raise them to the order of grace and turn them into a means of apostolate." [51]

The entire phrase describes a movement or dynamic process which begins, as we saw, by deepening one's faith and which then overflows into one's life, into all one's actions, discovering their Christian meaning and turning them into opportunities to meet God and serve others. The expression "supernatural instinct," to which Monsignor Escrivá often resorted in this context, gives the phrase a special weight, because it implies that this reference to God can and should become second nature to a person, so that one's mind and heart tend spontaneously and instinctively, as it were, to evaluate from God's viewpoint the various events which go to make up one's life, thereby paving the way for a genuine Christian life.

Holiness and apostolate, union with God and fulfillment of the mission which God gives one, are thereby depicted as inseparable things, fused together to form one, both designed (in the case of the Christian called to sanctify himself in the world, as the member of Opus Dei is) to merge with the secular situation and all that goes

[49] *Christ Is Passing By*, no. 126; see a very similar text in *Conversations*, no. 113.
[50] Instruction, March 19, 1934, no. 33.
[51] Letter, Feb. 2, 1945, no. 11.

with it, because it is precisely in the world and in social and professional affairs that that Christian should express and develop his vocation. The idea of unity of life is caught very well in this summary by St. Josemaría himself: "The twin aspect of our aim (ascetical and apostolic) is so intrinsically and harmoniously united and merged with the secular character of Opus Dei that it makes for a unity of life which is simple and strong (a unity of ascetical, apostolic, and professional life) and which turns everything we do into prayer, sacrifice and service."[52]

Unity of life understood in that sense is what underpins Christian awareness of things secular. Secularity, the way secular involvements shape one's life, is depicted in this way, in line with what we saw earlier, as something which goes far beyond the merely sociological: it produces a deeply and radically Christian form of life, an extension and an effect of that ability to divinize which the gift of grace implies, that is, the gift God makes of himself by entering into communion with man.

2. Naturalness

If, from a deeper, theological perspective, secularity refers us to unity of life and to the communion with God which makes that unity possible, from the psychological and social point of view the fact that someone is an ordinary Christian connotes a lifestyle or tone which Monsignor Escrivá often referred to as "*naturalness*."

Naturalness means, above all, normality: that quality which leads someone not to differentiate himself from his peers; so although he has his own personality and his personal tastes, he dresses, speaks, and acts in line with the language and customs of the area he comes from and the kind of work he does; this quality is what the *Epistle to Diognetus* is referring to when describing the lifestyle of the early Christians (these are words Josemaría Escrivá liked to quote): "The difference between Christians and the rest of mankind is not a matter of nationality, or language, or customs. Christians do not live apart in separate cities of their own, speak any special dialect, or practice any eccentric way of life. The doctrine they profess is not the invention of busy human minds or brains, nor are they, like some, advocates of this or that school of human thought. They pass their lives in whatever township—Greek or foreign—each man's lot has determined; and con-

---

[52] Letter, Feb. 14, 1950, no. 5. For a fuller study of unity of life, see I. de Celaya, "Unidad de vida y plenitud cristiana," in *Mons. Josemaría Escrivá de Balaguer y el Opus Dei*, pp. 321–40.

form to ordinary local usage in their clothing, diet, and other habits."[53]

The founder of Opus Dei dealt with this subject not only in his preaching but even in legal or juridical contexts. In the "regulations" he drew up in 1941, for example, in preparation for the first written diocesan approval, he goes into details which he considered particularly necessary, given the ambience of the time: "The members of the Work," we read, "in no way differentiate themselves externally from others of their profession or social class. Therefore, it will never be allowed, on any grounds whatever, for them to wear a uniform or anything distinctive in their dress." The same naturalness applies to the "centers" where members of Opus Dei carry out apostolic work: "their tone and ambience" should be as befits a normal "Christian home."[54] The current Statutes, using more formal language, make it clear that the faithful of the prelature, priests as well as lay people, "conduct themselves in everything like other secular clergy and lay people, their equals."[55]

"The very nature of our vocation, our way of seeking holiness and working for the Kingdom of God," he noted, in one of his Letters written for the formation of members of Opus Dei, "leads us to speak about divine things in the very language of men, to have the same wholesome lifestyle as they, to share their noble outlook; to see God, I would say, from the same angle, secular and lay, as they approach or might approach the transcendental problems of life."[56] "The way members of Opus Dei dress, live and behave," he added in another letter, written at a time when one still had to spell out the implications of the universal call to holiness, "would be typical of anyone else of the same social background. . . . One can understand very well why religious wear a habit, have common life, reside in convents or monasteries, etc. And one can see even more easily why members of Opus Dei, who are not

---

[53] *Letter to Diognetus*, V, 1–4. In his teaching, Monsignor Escrivá sets his references to this letter in a wider context: that of the early Christians (not only the apostolic generation but also the generations immediately after it) as the model or archetype of the outlook and apostolate of members of Opus Dei; see, e.g., *Conversations*, no. 24; *Christ Is Passing By*, nos. 96, 134, 151; *Friends of God*, nos. 63, 242, 269, etc.; for an overview, see the pages on the subject in R. Gómez Pérez, *La fe y los días* (Madrid, 1973).

[54] The documents for the 1941 approval comprise a series of regulations and five accompanying texts; the phrases mentioned occur in a document entitled *Espiritu*, nos. 14 and 23. On these documents, see *El itinerario jurídico*, pp. 98ff.

[55] *Statuta*, no. 80 § 2.

[56] Letter, March 11, 1940, no. 31.

religious but ordinary Christians, dress like their professional colleagues or fellow workers, tailor their schedule to the needs of their work, live usually with their families or wherever their work brings them, etc." [57] That is why it is so hard, or even impossible, to describe the life or lifestyle of members of Opus Dei, because Opus Dei does not give a person a lifestyle but rather a disposition of soul designed to imbue whatever lifestyle a person happens to have: "Belonging to Opus Dei does not mean following a particular lifestyle, but of trying to incarnate a spirit into all aspects of one's everyday existence." [58]

This descriptive, sociological side of naturalness has its importance, but it does not manage to express all that naturalness implies. As St. Josemaría Escrivá used the word, it referred not to mere external behavior, statistical normality, or being in tune with one's ambience, but to an attitude welling up within one's heart: a conviction that the Christian (and, more specifically, the ordinary Christian) called by God to sanctify himself or herself in the midst of the world is not an outsider in human society but someone who belongs there by right and can therefore act spontaneously, with the "amazing naturalness of the things of God," [59] expressing simply, in a way second nature to him, a faith which, far from cutting him off from earthly realities, allows him to appreciate their value and bearing on man's supernatural end.

We can readily notice here once again that connection in real life between creation and redemption which I referred to earlier and which is revealed to us in Christ; redemption is that action whereby Christ, in obedience to the Father, takes all reality on his shoulders so that, by liberating it from sin, he can give it back its original harmony and, by sending the Spirit, enable history to reach its God-given goal. Naturalness, creation, and redemption are all-embracing *and* overlapping realities and can be fully understood only in terms of their reference to each other: creation, the act whereby God causes the entire universe to be, is not simply a matter of causing existence; it is initiating a history, it is a calling to a destiny to which God is channelling created things. Christian consciousness of belonging to the world and of its being possible (and a duty) to act in the world in a spontaneous, natural way not only *qua* man but indeed *qua* Christian—this is really an existential reflection of a dogmatic truth; it shows that redemption and cre-

---

[57] Letter, March 19, 1954, no. 3, referring, where I have put ellipses, to the *Letter to Diognetus*.

[58] R. Gómez Pérez, *El Opus Dei*, p. 114.

[59] *Christ Is Passing By*, no. 120.

ation, holiness and world, eternity and time, are not heterogeneous things: they actually compenetrate.

"Being a Christian," we read in one of the homilies in *Christ Is Passing By*, "is not something incidental; it is a divine reality that takes root deep in our life. It gives us a clear vision and strengthens our will to act as God wants." There are those, he adds, who reduce Christianity to "a collection of devout practices, failing to realize the relation between them and the circumstances of ordinary life," and there are others who "tend to imagine that in order to remain human we need to play down some central aspects of Christian dogma. They act as if the life of prayer, an on-going relationship with God, implied fleeing from responsibilities." Both kinds of people fail to understand the meaning of the Incarnation; they show "they do not yet realize what it means that the Son of God has become man, has taken the body and soul and voice of a man, has shared our fate"; they regard Christ "as a stranger in the world of man"; they do not seem to have grasped that "Jesus was the one who showed us the extreme to which we should go in love and service." [60]

When viewed and appreciated from the vantage point of the Incarnation, from the fact that God made the human condition his own, naturalness is seen as something completely theological, implying both normality (membership of a society and a milieu and all that that means) and, at the same time, Christian witness, bearing testimony before that milieu and that society (or, to put it better, from within that society) to the message of the Gospel and all its life-giving power; and sometimes criticizing and changing that world, as a point of *The Way* so eloquently puts it: "And in a paganized or pagan environment when my life clashes with its surroundings, won't my naturalness seem artificial? you ask me. And I reply: Undoubtedly your life will clash with theirs; and that contrast—faith confirmed by works!—is exactly the naturalness I ask of you." [61]

Monsignor Escrivá well knew that Christian witness will meet with resistance and that it sometimes has to touch on thorny subjects, even to the point of confrontation. Without denying that (as he makes clear quite often in his writings), he always stressed that even in situations of that kind and, certainly when we look at

---

[60] Ibid., no. 98.

[61] *The Way*, no. 380; see also no. 376. Along the same line, we could cite his teaching on daring, understood in a sense very similar to the apostolic *parresia*; see, e.g., *The Way*, nos. 11, 479, 482, 841, 857; *Furrow*, nos. 96, 101, 106, 109, 110, 121, 124; *The Forge*, nos. 218, 260, 716.

things long-term, the witness borne by the ordinary Christian is something that should always grow from within society itself; finding its channels in one's everyday work, in the exercise of one's own duties, in conversations between friends and colleagues, in the free exchange of views, in the consistency shown in the way one approaches and solves those problems which social living occasions.

Opus Dei, Monsignor Escrivá said in a 1967 homily to which I have already referred, is made up of "a small percentage of priests who have previously exercised a secular profession or trade; a large number of secular priests of many dioceses throughout the world ...; and the great majority made up of men and women—of different nations, and tongues, and races—who earn their living by their everyday work ...; they work with personal responsibility, shoulder to shoulder with their fellow men and experiencing with them successes and failures ... as they strive to fulfill their duties and exercise their social and civic rights. And all this with naturalness, like any other conscientious Christian, without considering themselves special. Blended into the mass of their companions, they try at the same time to detect the flashes of divine splendor which shine through the commonest everyday realities." [62] "A man of faith who practices a profession, whether intellectual, technical, or manual," he said on another occasion, "feels himself and is in fact at one with others; he is the same as others, with the same rights and obligations, the same desire to improve, the same interest in facing and solving common problems"; he will, "through his daily life, bear witness to his faith, hope, and charity: a simple and normal testimony without need for pomp and circumstance. The inner consistency of his life will show the constant presence of the Church in the world." [63]

That naturalness, that simple, spontaneous, consistent way of doing things, will allow the presence of Christ to emerge (every Christian draws his life from Christ) and will establish the basis for an apostolic dialogue which will help others to discover God, starting right in the midst of the world." "How are we to bring others to know God and Christ?" Monsignor Escrivá asked on one occasion, going on to reply: "Naturally, simply, living as you live in the midst of the world, devoted to your professional work and to the care of your family, sharing the noble interests of men, respecting the rightful freedom of everyone." If we act in this way, he went on, "we will give those around us the example of a simple and normal life which is consistent, even though it has all the limita-

[62] *Conversations*, no. 119.
[63] *Christ Is Passing By*, no. 53.

tions and defects which are part and parcel of the human condition. And when they see that we live the same life as they do, they will ask us: Why are you so happy? How do you manage to overcome selfishness and comfort-seeking? Who has taught you to understand others, to be honorable and to spend yourself in the service of others?" Then, he concluded, "We must tell them the divine secret of Christian life. We must speak to them about God, Christ, the Holy Spirit, Mary. The time has come for us to use our poor words to communicate the depth of God's love which grace has poured into our hearts."[64]

3. *Loving the world*

As we well know, the term *world* has many meanings. Sometimes it refers to the universe, all created things, just in general, or bringing in the notion of the order and harmony that reigns among them. In the Bible, for example, the word often also means the cosmos, but in the sense of being under the control of sin and in need of redemption. At other times it means the world of man, the earth we live on, the societies that make it up, and their checkered history.[65]

In the preaching and writings of Opus Dei's founder, this third meaning is very much to the fore, as one would expect, given the fact that his basic concern was to show the value of the vocation and mission of a Christian who lives and works in the normal conditions of human life, being just another member of society. Bearing in mind that meaning of the word *world*, an analysis of his writings shows that (in keeping with his original inspiration) he values it positively; indeed, we can go further and say that he went out of his way to proclaim and defend that positive valuation, as a point from *The Forge* clearly shows: "The Lord wants his children, those of us who have received the gift of faith, to proclaim the original optimistic view of creation, the 'love for the world' which is at the heart of the Christian message. So you should always be keen on your professional work and your effort to build the earthly city."[66]

One would not be wrong to see in this text, and others like it, a conscious argument, a desire to correct and get beyond the kind of approach (very much to the fore in most of spiritual theology until

[64] Ibid., no. 148.
[65] My *Cristianismo, historia, mundo* (Pamplona, 1973), pp. 37–52, contains a more detailed analysis of these and other meanings of the term.
[66] *The Forge*, no. 703.

after the middle of the twentieth century) which tended to speak of the world largely as the "enemy of the soul," as a whole series of social customs inspired by frivolity, ambition, vanity, greed, etc.— attitudes which had nothing Christian in them or were even hostile to Christianity and therefore obstacles to holiness (which, beside, was something that we could achieve only by adopting a confrontational attitude to the world). That is not, St. Josemaría Escrivá will say, the primary, basic meaning of the word *world*: it should be used, in an unprejudiced way, as meaning human society, which does have its defects and disfigurements, but which also contains values, noble qualities, and virtues, and which the ordinary Christian, at all events, must see as somewhere God wants him to live and something he can and should strive to have reflect the spirit of the Gospel.

To sum up, the world cannot be simply seen as the setting (favorable or hostile) in which Christian existence occurs; no, it is something intrinsic to Christian life and therefore an assignment[67] given the Christian or, in Monsignor Escrivá's words, "something sanctifiable and something that sanctifies,"[68] the material out of which holiness is made. Obviously, this teaching is closely connected with that deep awareness of the connection between creation and redemption we referred to earlier, and which can be detected in a number of particularly profound passages where he offers a very concise synthesis of the history of salvation designed specifically to point up the Christian value of the world.

I shall quote from one of them, a homily given one Easter Sunday: "Nothing can be foreign to Christ's care. If we enter into the theology of it instead of limiting ourselves to functional categories, we cannot say that there are things—good, noble, or neutral—which are exclusively worldly. This cannot be, now that the Word of God has lived among the children of men, felt hunger and thirst, worked with his hands, experienced friendship and obedience and suffering and death." And, he concluded, revealing the spiritual echoes of the dogmatic dimensions to which I have recently referred: "We must love the world and work and all human

---

[67] On the difference between world as setting and world as assignment, and its importance for spiritual theology, see J. L. Illanes "El cristiano en el mundo. Análisis de vocabulario en los sermones de John Henry Newman," in *Scripta Theologica* 19 (1987) 563–93; and P. Rodriguez, *Vocación, trabajo, contemplación*, pp. 37–52.

[68] *Christ Is Passing By*, no. 47, refers us directly to work; obviously the teaching concerning the union between divine vocation and human vocation is closely connected with what we are discussing here; it is referred to earlier in this chapter, and especially in chapter two, section III.

things. For the world is good. Adam's sin destroyed the divine balance of creation; but God the Father sent his only Son to reestablish peace, so that we, his children by adoption, might free creation from disorder and reconcile all things to God."[69]

The ethical and spiritual implications of this approach to history and, specifically, its implications for the meaning of secularity, that is, of living in the world being conscious of its human value, are multiple. Let us look at three such implications: love for the world, respect for creation, and optimism toward history.

(a) Love for the world, because we can and should see it as something positive, endowed with a goodness that reflects the goodness of God; without forgetting, in line with what has been said, that this world, which is lovable, is not, in the writings of St. Josemaría Escrivá, just the material cosmos, endowed with harmony and beauty, but also the world as history, wherein God makes himself known and through which he issues callings and invitations: "We must love the world, because it is in the world that we meet God: God shows himself; he reveals himself to us in the happenings and events of the world."[70] We must therefore love this world of history, in which we live and to which we belong, and love it not just any old way but "passionately,"[71] with all our personality; and this implies, to be specific, being in active sympathy with human ideals and yearnings, taking an active part in temporal affairs, being really interested in one's work, sincere in one's friendships . . . ; in other words, conscious of the positive value of human existence.

(b) Respect for creation, because it is endowed with value, in fact, with a value given it by God its creator. As human beings we appreciate the value and beauty of things; as Christians, who know that they are created by God, we have even more reason to appreciate the world and respect it. This meaning, this beauty, this value connect with man and ultimately with God: the world is ordained to man, who in turn is ordained to God ("All things are yours, you are Christ's and Christ is God's," is how St Paul puts it).[72] But this ordination presupposes the reality, the ontological "density," of the world and everything that goes to make it up. All earthly things, all reality, has to be brought to God, but "each according to its nature,

---

[69] *Christ Is Passing By*, no. 12.

[70] *Conversations*, no. 70.

[71] "Passionately loving the world" was the title he gave one of his homilies: *Conversations*, nos. 113ff.

[72] See 1 Cor 3: 22–23, which Monsignor Escrivá often quoted: see, e.g., *Conversations*, no. 70.

according to the direct purpose God has given it";[73] therefore, the Christian, when he lives in the world, when he acts in society, and when he works, knows well that one "is obliged not to sidestep or play down the values that earthly things have in themselves";[74] he knows he must not manipulate reality in an arbitrary or despotic way, but rather direct it toward its goal (the service of man, recognized as a son of God), respecting it, that is, recognizing and appreciating its internal features and laws.[75]

(c) Optimism, because the world can and should be viewed from the perspective of Christ's Resurrection (that is, in the light of his victory over sin, pain, and death) as something strengthened by love and grace; this implies that the yearnings, interests, and activities which go to make up the fabric of human history can and should be approached with conviction and confidence, with a keen interest which is constantly renewed and not eroded by fatigue and difficulties. "The Christian life has to be shot through with optimism, joy, and the strong conviction that our Lord wishes to make use of us";[76] and these attitudes should also affect our earthly tasks and activities, because, being grounded on "faith in Christ, who has died and risen," the Christian does not pass through history like an "expatriate," but as "a citizen of the city of men," who takes a keen interest in its problems and has a hopeful attitude to life, that is, looks forward to the future and yet well knows that the fulfillment Christ proclaims comes at the end of time: "His soul longs for God. While on earth he has glimpses of God's love and comes to recognize it as the goal to which all men on earth are called."[77]

Assertion of the goodness of the world never led St. Josemaría Escrivá to adopt a naïve or superficial approach: his great realism and deep faith always meant he could avoid making that mistake. He was quite aware of the reality of evil and therefore of the need for both effort and sacrifice, that is, the need for the cross, because only by uniting himself to Christ's redemptive sacrifice and death

---

[73] Letter, March 19, 1954, no. 7.

[74] *Christ Is Passing By*, no. 184.

[75] Connected with this point are two of Monsignor Escrivá's key teachings (to consider them here would be a digression): the importance of human perfection in work, and the importance of human virtues. On the former, see quotations in J. L. Illanes, *La santificación del trabajo*, pp. 94–105; on the latter, the homily "Human Virtues" in *Friends of God*, nos. 73–93, and some particularly graphic points in *The Way* and *Furrow*.

[76] *Christ Is Passing By*, no. 160.

[77] *Christ Is Passing By*, no. 99.

can the Christian defeat evil and sin.[78] "Christ," he says, "rises in us, if we become sharers in his cross and his death. We should love the cross, self-sacrifice, and mortification"; so, he concludes, "Christian optimism is not something sugary, nor is it a human optimism that things will 'work out well.' No, its deep roots are awareness of freedom and faith in grace. It is an optimism which makes us be demanding with ourselves. It gets us to make a real effort to respond to God's call."[79]

From another viewpoint, that of love for the world, this led him to say that, for this love to be genuine, for it to be a love for the real world, the world in its concrete reality, it must go hand in hand with an effort to overcome the tendency toward evil which is a feature of human history and which is present, first, in one's own heart: it must be combined with asceticism and detachment. "Be men and women," he counsels in *The Way*, "of the world, but don't be worldly men and women."[80] Unlike the noun *mundo* (world), which as I have said has a predominantly positive meaning in Monsignor Escrivá's writings, the adjective *mundano* (worldly) is one he uses in a pejorative sense (associated with being selfish, lukewarm, frivolous, mediocre, superficial, shortsighted, over-prudent, suspicious . . .),[81] and this distinction is no accident: St. Josemaría uses it to structure his thinking on this theme.

The dialectic to which the founder of Opus Dei refers in his writings is not a dialectic between presence in the world (or, better, belonging to the world) and distancing oneself from the world; it is a dialectic between a worldly attitude and a Christian attitude, always presupposing (he is speaking to ordinary Christians) that one is in the world and of the world, fully aware that that is where God wants one to be and where one's Christian vocation should take shape. In other words, a dialectic between selfishness and self-surrender, between ambition and service, which implies continuous interior tension and means that one needs to be discerning and sometimes has to exercise true detachment and renunciation—in fact, radical detachment if one's Christian authenticity is put at risk—but that should never lead one "to deny the goodness of God's works. On the contrary, it should bring him to recognize the hand of God working through all human actions, even those which

---

[78] For a first approach to Monsignor Escrivá's soteriology, see L. F. Mateo-Seco, "Sapientia Crucis. El misterio de la Cruz en los escritos de Josemaría Escrivá de Balaguer," in *Scripta Theologica* 24 (1992) 419–38.
[79] *Christ Is Passing By*, no. 114.
[80] *The Way*, no. 939; and a similar point in *The Forge*, no. 259.
[81] See, e.g., *The Way*, nos. 18, 148, 414, 737, and *Furrow*, nos. 306, 814, 940.

betray our fallen nature." [82] A person really loves the world only if he approaches it and "lives it" from the viewpoint of God and with that attitude of self-giving to others which God invites us to have: worldly attitudes lead to losing God and, therefore, losing the world; those who think and live in a worldly way "do not love this world of ours; they exploit it by trampling on others." [83]

4. *Work, detachment, service*

It would not be difficult to go through Monsignor Escrivá's writings to show that the principles concerning love of the world which we have just discussed are applied and related to all the many facets of human life. To keep this essay within limits, I shall simply discuss two basic points (everyday work and the use of material goods) by way of example.

Discussing everyday work, the engaging in a profession or trade which gives one a place in society and is how one contributes to society's development,[84] implies discussing such things as technical standards, ability to do one's job, professional competence, and, paralleling that, social standing, recognition by society of one's competence and ability. Neither of the two—neither technical competence nor professional prestige—is, Monsignor Escrivá will say, a purely neutral thing, much less a negative thing: both are things everyday work needs to have, and therefore they have to be seen in a positive light. The Christian should strive not only to be technically competent, but to become better and better at his job: if he were to turn his back on improvement, and on the scope that skills give him, he would be depriving society of something which could really help its development; he would be giving up "rights that are really duties." [85] And the same is true of professional prestige, which is the natural outcome of doing one's job well; society is to a degree structured on status of this kind, and for an ordinary Christian it is part of his " 'bait' as a 'fisher of men,' " [86] that is, of his way of bearing witness to the power and human attractiveness of the Gospel.

The self-forgetfulness and humility a Christian is asked to have

---

[82] *Conversations*, no. 70.

[83] *Furrow*, no. 304.

[84] On the concept of "professional" work, see J. L. Illanes, *La santificación del trabajo*, pp. 37–44.

[85] *The Way*, no. 603; hence another point of *The Way* (no. 332) will say, "There is no excuse for those who could be scholars and are not."

[86] *The Way*, no. 372.

do not (except in very special circumstances) require him to give up his competence and standing; rather, they require him to have an attitude (always presupposing competence, and to a greater or less degree prestige) which leads him to refer everything to God[87] and to the mission God has given him, that is, to evaluate one's job not in relation to oneself but in terms of the contribution it makes to others. It is a matter, really, of always remembering that the value of one's work is not primarily a function of mere technical efficiency but of its reference to man, for the dignity of work "is based on Love."[88] The great privilege the human being has, what makes him a human being, is really love, the power "to love others, the power to pronounce a 'you' and an 'I' which are full of meaning," and it is here that work and every other human reality acquires its full meaning; therefore, the homily I am quoting concludes, "Man ought not to limit himself to making things, to material production. Work is born of love; it is a manifestation of love and is directed toward love."[89] "A man or a society that does not react to suffering and injustice and makes no attempt to alleviate them," says another sermon, "is still distant from the love of Christ's heart."[90]

Living in human society implies spheres of autonomy, standards of living, quality of life, deciding on how to use the fruits acquired through work or other legitimate ways, and this brings us to the second of the two points to which I referred: the use of material goods. "We are," says Monsignor Escrivá in a homily dedicated to the virtue of detachment, "people walking in the street, ordinary Christians immersed in the bloodstream of society." Starting from

---

[87] "There are some," we read in a letter the founder addressed to members of Opus Dei, "who do not have a particularly lay approach and understand humility to mean a lack of aplomb, an indecisiveness which inhibits action, a surrendering of rights"; "the humility which the Work requires (which it encourages, offering a positive form of teaching) is something very interior, something which derives directly from the contemplative conversation we hold with our Lord *sine intermissione* (1 Thess 5: 17). It is a deep conviction that God our Father is the one who does everything, using us as the poor instruments we all are" (letter, May 6, 1945, no. 31).

[88] *Christ Is Passing By*, no. 48.

[89] Ibid.

[90] *Christ Is Passing By*, no. 167. And in *The Way*, with the vibrant tone typical of that book: "Selfish. Always looking after yourself. You seem incapable of feeling the fraternity of Christ. In those around you, you do not see brothers: you see stepping stones"; "You will never be a leader if you see others only as stepping stones to get ahead. You will be a leader if you are ambitious for the salvation of all mankind. You can't turn your back on your fellow men: you have to be anxious to make them happy" (nos. 31 and 32).

there he goes on to outline the panorama of an ordinary, normal life, involving nothing odd or exaggerated, yet a life which in all sorts of small, unobtrusive ways reflects a deep Christian sense of evangelical poverty, that is, an awareness that man is above things; this leads one to have a deep sense of interior freedom and a genuine detachment from material things that is the touchstone of that freedom. The homily later refers to the intimate connection there is—in everyone, particularly those who are called to live and sanctify themselves in the world, by being fully involved in the progress of the world—between detachment, attitude of service, and generosity. "True detachment leads us to be very generous with God and with our fellow men. It makes us actively resourceful and ready to spend ourselves in helping the needy. A Christian cannot be content with a job that only allows him to earn enough for himself and his family. He will be big-hearted enough to give others a helping hand both out of charity and as a matter of justice." [91]

A paragraph in one of his Letters will round off the point I am making: "The spirituality of Opus Dei, centered on work, impels us to love the poverty Jesus practiced: he was rich but he made himself poor: *egenus factus est cum esset dives* (2 Cor 8: 9). Each of us has the attitude (and makes the intellectual and financial effort) of a good father of a poor family with many children. In the spirit of the Work it is essential for us to feel the responsibility of poverty. That is why we have to take our work seriously." [92] I should like to underline the reference to a *father (or mother) of a poor family with many children*. This graphic phrase sums up a teaching found in a lot of Monsignor Escrivá's preaching; it contains two basic ideas: recognition of the value of material goods, which are indispensable for the advancement of both family and society; and assertion of the primacy of generosity and self-forgetfulness, because parents live not for themselves or their own convenience, but for their children.

These are the same two qualities we met earlier, and here too they go to make up an ethical-spiritual attitude which works in two directions: encouragement to produce work well done and a call to set one's contact with material goods in a context of personal detachment, of attention to the needs of others, of generosity—in

---

[91] *Friends of God*, nos. 120 and 126. "Naturally," we read in *The Forge*, "you have to use earthly resources. But put a lot of effort into being detached from everything of the earth, so as to use it with your mind always focused on the service of God and of your fellow men" (no. 728).

[92] Letter, Sept. 29, 1957, no. 74.

other words, a context of unlimited spirit of service. For (as the passages quoted above show, and it is worth stressing at this point) the *poor family with many children* refers not only to one's own home but to the society in which one is living, to all mankind, in fact: everyone's heart should be open to the whole world, and that applies especially to the Christian.

The two points I have just been looking at, and the attitudes they involve, help to show the implications of something we looked at earlier: in St. Josemaría Escrivá's teaching (and, I might add, in any theologically developed approach) secularity refers not just to being and living in the world but to being and living in the world *in a Christian way*, that is, knowing it and loving it as Christ does. This means, and this is worth stressing, knowing it and loving it not in a detached or theoretical way, but in all the fullness God has designed for it, and thus feeling invited to make the light and power of the Gospel present within it. Therefore the tension between detachment and love necessarily and spontaneously results in action, in work, in a positive effort to give the world (from within and recognizing and respecting the laws proper to it) the spirit of Christ.[93] Christian secularity, then, necessarily means seeing love for the world and faithfulness to Christ as making up one single thing; to be more specific, it means that particular kind of fidelity to Christ which a person should practice who is called by God to live in the world; he should live in such a way that his witness and his action help to make Christ present in that world and therefore imbue social structures with a Christian spirit, and should be well aware that by acting in this way he is orienting the world to its end and therefore to its perfection.[94]

5. *Personal freedom and personal responsibility*

To speak of secularity necessarily and logically means to speak of variety and freedom.

[93] Secularity is connected with understanding and appreciating the autonomy of earthly realities as explained in *Gaudium et spes*, that is, as an assertion of the consistency of Creation and of its ordination to God, in such a way that the imbuing of earthly activities with the spirit of the Gospel does not destroy their nature but, on the contrary, enhances it by directing them to the service of truth and of man's destiny as revealed to us in Christ (*Gaudium et spes*, no. 36; in connection with the preceding text, particularly no. 22).

[94] A very fine summary of St. Josemaría Escrivá's teaching on the intimate connection between love for the world and fidelity to Christ is to be found in the homily the prelate of Opus Dei, Bishop Alvaro del Portillo, gave at the University of Navarre on Sept. 7, 1991, published in *Romana* 7 (1991), 259–62.

Of variety and difference, because secular society is plural and takes many shapes; it is the result of the interplay of a whole range of roles and situations, which are not only different from one another, but also change over the course of time. The ideal of a Christian sanctification in a secular setting brings us up against this variety of situations and therefore of jobs and ways of life: indeed, there are as many situations as there are people, and each person is called to sanctify his or her own life, which is never the same as anyone else's.[95]

Speaking of secularity involves speaking of freedom, because in secular occupations and settings an individual, and therefore a Christian, acts in his own name, in line with his personal opinions and preferences, and therefore on his own responsibility and no one else's. This brings us to a matter of key importance, which it is worth exploring in some detail.

Freedom in temporal or secular affairs (the freedom of any person, and in the case we are discussing, any Christian), although it has features of its own, is really only an aspect of something much broader: freedom as such, and, more specifically, the decisive importance Christianity gives to freedom. According to Christian dogma, the ultimate substance of the cosmos and of history is not necessity but freedom. The world and everything that goes to make it up is the outcome not of a transcendental and eternal necessity, but of a free decision of God's. In fact, it is the result of a love-inspired free decision: God calls things into existence because he loves, because he wants human beings to share in his own abundance and happiness; so he gives them existence and endows them with freedom, that is, the capacity to appreciate love and to respond to love. God's freedom and our freedom explain and sustain the events of history. Every human life (and history in its entirety) is the outcome of the interconnection of the freedom of God, who loves each individual and addresses and calls that person, and the freedom of each man and each woman, who, perceiving that divine invitation in some way or other, react to it, thereby deciding their destiny.[96] As in every case where different free agents meet, there is here a constant (the love that is offered and

[95] This is why, as already pointed out in chapter one, section IV, and particularly in chapter two, section IV, St. Josemaría Escrivá always put such emphasis on the non-specialized nature of the apostolate of Opus Dei, describing it on occasions as "an unorganized organization" in which unity of spirit and of apostolic zeal is diffracted in a plurality of lives and involvements, which do not admit of any type of rigid plan.

[96] On the connection between vocation and freedom, which as we have just said is a very close one, see chapter three, section I.

accepted or rejected) and also a variable—initiative, creativity, resourcefulness.[97]

It is in this context of a general affirmation of human freedom that freedom in temporal affairs fits, although, as we have said, that particular aspect of freedom has features of its own, because the world of the temporal or secular is not only the scenario in which free people live out their lives: it is something markedly diverse and indeterminate. That is why it is, by its very nature, the sphere of change (at the level of planning or acting), autonomous decisions, diversity, and clash of opinions—the sphere of pluralism.[98] The Statutes of the Opus Dei prelature echo this fact, making it quite clear that in all temporal matters (social, cultural, professional, etc.) its members enjoy the same full freedom as any other Catholic. "Opus Dei," says one of the sections of the chapter on training, "has no corporate opinion or school on those theological or philosophical questions which the Church leaves open to the free opinion of the faithful"; "as far as professional activity is concerned, and in matters social, political, etc., each of the faithful of the prelature has the same complete freedom as other Catholic citizens, within the bounds laid down by Catholic teaching on faith and morals."[99]

[97] St. Josemaría's fullest discussion of the freedom–love dialectic is to be found in his homily "Freedom, a Gift from God," published in *Friends of God*, nos. 23–38. There is no need to comment on it here; however, I would point out that the sense of freedom as a basic dimension of the human being was something very deep-rooted in him and in his work; he constantly stresses that man is capable of great things, especially of *the* great thing, love, for the very reason that he is free, can decide what he does with his life, can shape himself, can give himself to another. "Because I want to", "because I feel like it," he often said (e.g., in the homily just referred to, *Friends of God*, no. 35), is the most profoundly human and also, therefore, the most profoundly supernatural motive we can have. For a commentary on his teaching in this regard: C. Fabro's "El primado existencial de la libertad" and his "Josemaría Escrivá de Balaguer, teacher of Christian freedom" in *Irish Theological Quarterly* 47 (1980: 1); also *Mons. Josemaría Escrivá de Balaguer y el Opus Dei*, pp. 341–56, and A. Garcia Suárez, "Existencia secular cristiana," *Scripta Theologica* 2 (1970) 145–64, and R. Garcia de Haro, "Homilías: Es Cristo que pasa," in *La vocación cristiana. Reflexiones sobre la catequesis de Mons. Escrivá de Balaguer*, pp. 195–216.

[98] See the seminal statements on this in *Gaudium et spes*, nos. 36 and 43.

[99] *Statuta*, no. 109 and no. 88 § 3. Very similar language is used in the Declaration of the Congregation for Bishops, Aug. 23, 1982, on the occasion of the establishment of Opus Dei as a personal prelature: "As regards their choices in matters professional, social, political, etc., the lay faithful who belong to the prelature enjoy (within the limits of Catholic faith and morals and of Church discipline) the same freedom as other Catholics, fellow citizens of theirs": *Praelaturae Personales* II, d; AAS, 74 (1983), 465.

The founder of Opus Dei referred very often to this matter, as one might expect, given its importance and the interest public opinion takes in cultural and political affairs. There is no need to quote him here (the texts from the Statutes which I have just cited should suffice),[100] so I shall go on to examine the anthropological and social background to Monsignor Escrivá's statements in this connection; this will make for a better understanding of secularity. On this, as on other points, Monsignor Escrivá's foundational charism and his experience in establishing and promoting Opus Dei helped him to develop his thinking to an important degree.

We can say that his affirmation of the freedom of the Christian in temporal affairs, specifically, the Christian called to sanctify himself or herself in and through temporal tasks and occupations, can be summed up in four basic ideas:

(a) In the first place, and above all, a deep sense of the value of freedom as the key expression of the dignity of the person and therefore of responsibility as the intrinsic correlation of the ability to make free choices. For the very reason that man is free, is in charge of himself, the actions he performs are his, they belong to him: they are therefore actions for which he should assume total responsibility, recognizing them as expressions of his own will; he is also responsible for the consequences that flow from them. All this follows from the way things are and from his dignity as a man and a Christian. Freedom and responsibility are, in fact, terms which, in the writings of St. Josemaría Escrivá, often appear together, like two sides of the same coin or, to be more exact, two dimensions of a single reality which embraces all human existence, including particularly the sphere of the secular, where every human being (and every Christian) acts in his own name, following his conscience and his own lights.[101]

(b) In the second place, an acute awareness of the legitimacy of pluralism, as an expression of the fact that people are different and therefore have different experiences, attitudes, and opinions. In all spheres, including that of temporal affairs which we are now discussing, human actions involve analyzing reality, an intellectual

---

[100] I shall simply mention, by way of example, the texts in *Conversations*, in which, in reply to journalists' questions, he emphasizes this temporal freedom in no uncertain terms: nos. 28–29, 38, 48, 50, 65–67. Other quotations, with commentary, are given in J. Herranz, "Libertad y responsabilidad," in *Cristianos corrientes. Textos sobre el Opus Dei* (Madrid, 1970) pp. 70–90; D. le Tourneau, *What is Opus Dei?*, pp. 38ff.; R. Gómez Pérez, *El Opus Dei*, pp. 88–97.

[101] See, for example, passages in which the connection between freedom and responsibility comes out: *Conversations*, no. 28; *Christ Is Passing By*, no. 184; *Friends of God*, no. 11.

effort to understand the laws that make it work and the requirements deriving from those laws; an effort which each person
should make and which can and in fact will produce a variety of
viewpoints and opinions. Freedom, then, implies not only personal
responsibility but also diversity and, as a consequence, a right to
follow one's own opinion and an obligation to respect the opinions
of others: that is, it implies dialogue and harmony.[102]

(c) Diversity of opinions on temporal matters is linked not only
to the limitations of the human mind and the variety of knowledge
and judgment it produces, but also to another factor to which
Monsignor Escrivá was very sensitive—the flux of history. Man is a
being located in history, that is, in a process open to the future, and
the future has largely to do with the indeterminate, with what has
not yet come into being and which can end up in many different
ways. "God in creating us has run the risk and adventure of our
freedom. He opted for a [human] history which would be a true
one, the outcome of genuine free decisions—not a fiction or some
sort of game";[103] a history, then, whose development cannot entirely be foreseen even with the help of experience or of the Christian faith; for "there are no dogmas in temporal matters,"[104] and
everyone (and every Christian) should form his own views, autonomously, and be personally responsible for them.[105]

(d) Finally (although of primary importance from many points
of view) a different but complementary perspective—the ecclesiological—gives rise to a further insight—that deep understanding of
the mission and vocation of the lay person or ordinary Christian,
which characterized the founder of Opus Dei. By virtue of being a
Christian, the lay member of the faithful is called to sanctify
earthly realities; indeed, to sanctify them acting in his own name

[102] On pluralism not only as a phenomenon but as a natural and therefore positive
part of social life, see *Conversations*, nos. 12, 67, 98.

[103] "Las riquezas de la fe," an article first published in *ABC* (Madrid), Nov. 2,
1969, contains much more on this subject; an English version was published in
booklet form in New York in 1974 under the title "Life of Faith."

[104] *Conversations*, no. 77.

[105] This is emphasized in the article referred to in note 103 and in other texts,
including one with autobiographical flavor in which Monsignor Escrivá, after re-
calling his experience as a priest trying to get individuals to face up to their responsibilities, helping each "to discover what God wants from him in particular—without in any way limiting that holy independence and blessed personal responsibility
which are the features of a Christian conscience," adds, as if explaining his argument, "this way of acting and this spirit are based on respect for the transcendence
of revealed truth and on love for the freedom of the human person. I might add that
they are also based on a realization that history is undetermined and open to a
variety of human options—all of which God respects": *Christ Is Passing By*, no. 99.

and therefore autonomously, thus contributing to the presence of Christ in history. The ordinary Christian's consciousness of his vocation, and the recognition of his temporal freedom by the Christian community as a whole, are key factors in making the Church's mission succeed, and are necessary parts of any valid ecclesiology.[106]

A sense of personal freedom and responsibility; an appreciation of pluralism and living in harmony with others; an awareness of the fact that the future is undetermined; full recognition of the lay person's mission and the lay manner of making the Church present in the world. The whole range of ideas involved in the Christian's exercise of his temporal freedom shows the wealth and complexity of this concept, and explains the key importance it has for a correct understanding of secularity and therefore of the condition proper to the ordinary Christian. The lay person, the Christian called to follow Christ and share in his mission while living in the world, has to face up to life with personal freedom and responsibility; at one and the same time he or she has to have:

—a sense of mission and therefore a real concern to identify himself with Christ and to act according to his mind, with all that that involves in terms of formation of conscience, consistency between belief and action, being interiorly in tune with Christ himself;[107]

—awareness that it is he himself, as an individual and with full

[106] See *Conversations*, nos. 12 and 59, where Monsignor Escrivá spells out some of the ecclesiological and pastoral consequences of this principle and underlines the fact that unless the freedom of the Christian in temporal affairs is properly recognized, the lay person becomes "shrunk," that is, he is hindered or even prevented from fulfilling his mission; and this leads to clericalism and all the harm that follows from it. For further discussion on this subject apropos of Monsignor Escrivá's teaching, see A. del Portillo, *Faithful and Laity in the Church* (Shannon, 1972) and the 3rd rev. Spanish edition, *Fideles y laicos en la Iglesia* (Pamplona, 1991).

[107] The need for a deeply lived Christianity and the importance of training one's conscience are things Monsignor Escrivá touched on in practically all the passages where he deals with freedom in temporal matters, thereby showing the close connection between the two subjects (as can be seen by consulting the references given in the previous notes). Besides, this teaching is part of the ordinary tradition of the Church, as can be seen (just to give an example) from the emphasis John Paul II has put on the value of the social teaching of the Church, seen as a body of principles and guidelines that really help one look at social life from the viewpoint of the true meaning of man as found in the Gospel (see, especially, his three social encyclicals, *Laborem exercens, Sollicitudo rei socialis* and *Centesimus annus*); for an analysis of the social teaching of the Church and a commentary on its connection with the truth concerning man, see my essays, "La doctrina social de la Iglesia como teología moral," in *Scripta Theologica* 24 (1992) 839–75, and "Verdad del hombre y cuestión social," in *Estudios sobre la Centesimus annus* (Madrid, 1992).

personal responsibility and autonomy, who has to face up to history and the tasks it entails.

In St. Josemaría's language this teaching produces an expression which is very useful for understanding secularity—*lay outlook*. I shall quote in full a passage in which he explains its scope and meaning: "You must foster everywhere," he said, in a homily addressed to a large gathering of people, mostly of academics and students, "a genuine 'lay outlook,' which will lead to three conclusions: be sufficiently honest, so as to shoulder one's own personal responsibility; be sufficiently Christian, so as to respect brothers in the faith who, in matters of opinion, propose solutions which differ from those we personally support; and be sufficiently Catholic so as not to use our Mother the Church, involving her in human factions." [108]

This text contains many of the ideas described in the previous paragraphs, running them together and linking them to an outlook, a rooted conviction, which determines the way one evaluates and reacts to things. Secularity implies an appreciation of the world, a sense of freedom, an awareness of one's own limitations, an openness to dialogue with others; however, it implies them not as logical presuppositions but as internalized convictions, so deeply rooted in one's heart that they shape one's mind and therefore the way one acts and behaves. Secularity is, also from this angle, much more than a sociological fact or an abstract quality; it is a component of "what makes a Christian tick."

This is especially true of the Christian called by God to practice his Christianity in the world—which is why Monsignor Escrivá speaks of a *lay outlook*, because it is in the lay person that secularity acquires particular force, becoming a characteristic feature; but it also applies to other Christians, because every Christian needs to adopt the values this outlook implies, and to put them into practice in his own particular way, in line with whatever his or her vocation is.

It is worth pointing out here that, while it is true that St. Josemaría Escrivá sometimes used the expression *lay outlook* on its own (as in the text quoted), very often he linked it to another: *priestly soul*; so much so that the two go hand in hand. [109] *Priestly*

---

[108] *Conversations*, no. 117.

[109] There are the following passages that show the connection between the two expressions:

—"In every thing we do we must all of us (priests and lay people) have a truly *priestly soul and a fully lay outlook*, if we are to understand and use in our personal lives that freedom which we enjoy in the sphere of the Church and in temporal things, *soul*, for him, is closely connected with the common or royal priesthood of the faithful; it *is* that priesthood at the phenomenological level: priestly soul is the force that impels those who are conscious of being part of Christ and therefore equipped to imbue their entire life with a priestly outlook.[110.]

The combined use of *priestly soul* and *lay outlook* brings us again to that theological backdrop to secularity to which I have referred a number of times. The Christian is thereby depicted as someone who, being incorporated into Christ and conscious of the salvific and priestly mission which that incorporation implies, fulfils that mission in everything he does; he approaches human tasks and obligations fully aware of their density, respecting their autonomy, and he does so in cooperation, dialogue, and solidarity with his fellow citizens. *Priestly soul*, then, refers to the interior force or impulse; *lay mentality* to the actual performance; both together complete the physiognomy of a Christian who recognizes both that he is rooted in Christ and has a place in the world.[111]

---

regarding ourselves at one and the same time as citizens of the city of God and citizens of the city of man": letter, Feb. 2, 1945, no. 1.

—"On Oct. 2, 1928, the feast of the Guardian Angels, God our Lord brought Opus Dei into being so that its members—with a priestly soul and lay outlook— should dedicate themselves to the service of God and try to attain Christian perfection in the world and carry out apostolate, each in his own place; so that by staying there where they carry out their professional activities, they act as a supernatural leaven": letter, Feb. 14, 1950, no. 3.

—"Because the Work of God is eminently lay and imbued by the spirit of the priesthood; if the apostolate of the lay people and that of the priest complement one another and each makes the other more effective, our vocation requires that all the members of the Work should also manifest this intimate connection between the two elements, in such a way that each of us has a *truly priestly soul and a fully lay outlook*": letter, March 28, 1955, no. 3.

[110] This is reflected very well in a point in *Furrow*: "You say that you are gradually realizing what 'priestly soul' means. Don't be annoyed with me if I tell you that the facts show that you understand it only in theory. Every day the same thing happens to you: at night time, during the examination, it's all desire and resolutions; during the morning and afternoon at work, it's all objections and excuses. Is that how you are practising the 'holy priesthood, to offer spiritual sacrifices, acceptable to God through Jesus Christ'?" (no. *499*). For a theological reflection on this subject, see M. M. Otero, "El 'alma sacerdotal' del cristiano," in *Mons. Josemaría Escrivá de Balaguer y el Opus Dei*, pp. 293–319.

[111] As the text of the letter of March 2, 1955, already quoted, points out, this distinction also highlights how the various ecclesial positions complement and influence one another: they all are expressions of the values of the Christian condition they have in common; they also serve to remind each other of these values, particularly those to which each gives special emphasis.

6. *Contemplatives in the midst of the world*

"You have got to be a 'man of God,' a man of interior life, a man of prayer and sacrifice";[112] "Opus Dei's weapon is not work; it is prayer. That is why we turn work into prayer, and why we have a contemplative soul."[113] These two statements by St. Josemaría bring us to something we have already referred to a number of times, because it forms the existential background which gives secularity its theological significance: the theological meaning of Christian living and therefore the need for, in fact the primacy of, prayer.

As a Christian and as founder of Opus Dei, Monsignor Escrivá was very aware that everything in the Christian order of things depends on one's having a living connection with God. As one might expect, given the background inspiration of all his work as a priest and a founder, the Statutes of the prelature include a section dealing with the spiritual life. Nor is it surprising that this section is given a place of honor (it comes first in the title dealing with the life and formation of members of Opus Dei) and that its purpose is to outline the main features of a journey toward deepening in the faith, toward an awareness of the nearness of God which should steadily increase until it imbues everything one does.

The basis of this spiritual attitude, the Statutes tell us, is "a sincere and humble sense of divine filiation," born of "the need and, as it were, the supernatural instinct to purify all one's actions, raising them to the level of grace, sanctifying them and making them an opportunity for personal union with God, fulfilling his will, and as a means of apostolate";[114] that is, a Christian enlivening of all existence, which begins with a clear perception of the reality of God and of the fact that he truly loves us; it leads to actively seeking his presence and sincerely striving to do his will. To develop this disposition of soul one obviously needs to exercise faith and to adopt with the help of grace a definite plan or program which will help one toward a growth in theological virtue and a real union with God in work and in other things which go to make up human existence. The founder of Opus Dei did this and taught it, to the point of establishing a plan of spiritual life along these lines:

(a) an intense sacramental life through daily sharing in the sacrifice of the Mass, the center and source of the spiritual life; and

---

[112] *The Way*, no. 961.

[113] RHF 10068, p. 9.

[114] *Statuta*, no. 80 § 1 and 2.

also, if possible, daily communion; and the practice of weekly confession;[115]

(b) an equally intense life of prayer, fostered through definite times for meditation, reading of sacred scripture and of books of spirituality; visits to the Blessed Sacrament; the saying of the Rosary, and other devotions to the Blessed Virgin; all this extended by frequent consideration of divine filiation in Christ and a straightforward dialogue with God the Father, by means of ejaculatory prayers, acts of love, of atonement, of thanksgiving, etc., scattered throughout the day;[116]

(c) the daily practice of mortification and penance, as an expression of that Christian asceticism indispensable for personal purification and for the carrying out of effective apostolate; this spirit of penance does not exclude traditional ascetical practices (in fact, it presupposes them) but, as the text of the Statutes makes clear, it should mainly take the form of doing one's duties, being orderly and dedicated in one's everyday work, and serving others in a pleasant cheerful way: in other words, in little things, in the minutiae of self-surrender which daily life demands.[117]

A first glance at this program of spiritual life shows that the various spiritual and ascetical practices that go to make it up belong to the patrimony of the Church: here, as on many other points, Monsignor Escrivá preferred not to invent prayers or practices of his own but rather to draw on spiritual traditions, particularly those devotions and customs most widespread among the general body of the Christian faithful.

From another point of view, and going deeper in our analysis, it must be noticed that the elements which go to make up this program are not (either in the text of the Statutes, or still less in Monsignor Escrivá's preaching and in the practice of Opus Dei) isolated pieces; they are all parts of a whole, which has two axes: awareness of divine filiation, which leads a person to refer everything to a God whom he recognizes as a Father, and work (that is, the ensemble of secular activities and tasks) as something in which that awareness of the nearness of God must acquire historical content and density.

The spiritual life, we can see, then, has direct reference to real life: it has to inspire one's everyday existence and be fused with it. So, the intensity of the call to prayer and a close relationship with God is in no way reduced; but what is excluded radically is any

[115] *Statuta*, nos. 81 and 83 § 2.
[116] Ibid., nos. 82, 83 § 2, 85.
[117] Ibid., nos. 83 § 1, 86, 92.

attitude of distancing oneself from the world, as also any kind of automatism or rigidity (which would imply division between prayer and life); what it does call for is a theological attitude which is nourished by the Liturgy and by the other periods of prayer, and which influences all aspects of one's life. "Our entire plan of life, our Norms and Customs," Monsignor Escrivá writes, "are designed for men and women who work in the midst of the world, carrying out ordinary everyday jobs. They are not rigid rules, which presuppose a life apart [from the world], but a flexible method, which has a wonderful capacity to adapt to any life of intense professional work, the way a rubber glove molds itself perfectly to the hand using it. In fact, our interior life (contemplative life, in all situations) avails itself of and is nourished by that external life of work proper to each of us." [118]

What the teaching of St. Josemaría Escrivá and the spirituality of Opus Dei propose is (to sum up) a prayer which, by encouraging a person to ground his life more on faith, incorporates into the dynamic of the experience of the faith the totality of life, including (we are discussing ordinary Christians living in the midst of the world) the full range of earthly experiences and realities. Perhaps Monsignor Escrivá never expressed this teaching as clearly as he did in a homily he gave in 1967, later published under the title of "Toward Holiness." [119] "We begin," he says, in connection with the path of the spiritual life, "with vocal prayers which many of us have been saying since we were children. They are made up of simple, ardent phrases addressed to God and to his Mother, who is our Mother as well." It is a simple, almost common or garden beginning, the experience of millions of Christians, but if it really is a beginning (that is, the first step in a journey in which one persists) it leads to an ever deeper relationship with God. "First," the text goes on, "one brief aspiration, then another, and another... till our fervor seems insufficient, because words are too poor ...: then this gives way to intimacy with God, looking at God without needing rest or feeling tired." [120]

Prayer and life tend to become more and more intermixed. In the celebration of the Eucharist (in which is perpetuated "the love of the Blessed Trinity for man")[121] and by meeting Jesus in the Tabernacle, one's awareness of the nearness of God and of the fact that he gave up his life for men becomes deeper and deeper. At

[118] Letter, Oct. 15, 1948, no. 22.
[119] Published in *Friends of God*, nos. 294–316.
[120] *Friends of God*, no. 296.
[121] *Christ Is Passing By*, no. 85.

these points and in other periods of prayer one examines one's own life, including its events, problems, and interests, and sets it before Christ and talks to him and to the Father and the Holy Spirit about the day ahead or the day gone by.[122]

The familiarity with God one acquires in this way naturally influences one's daily life, so that often in the course of the day one feels a desire to address him, to tell him what is happening, or simply to draw support from his presence, even if one does not formulate this in words. "We begin to live as captives, as prisoners. And while we carry out as perfectly as we can (with all our mistakes and limitations) the tasks allotted to us by our situation and duties, our soul longs to escape. It is drawn toward God like iron drawn by a magnet." [123]

"Asceticism? Mysticism?" Monsignor Escrivá asks, a little further on, after describing this panorama of union with God. "I don't mind what you call it. Whichever it is, asceticism or mysticism, does not matter. Either way, it is a gift of God's mercy. If you try to meditate, our Lord will not deny you his assistance. Faith and deeds of faith are what matter: deeds, because, as you have known from the beginning and as I told you clearly at the time, the Lord demands more from us each day. This is already contemplation and union. This is the way," he concludes, "many Christians should live, each one forging ahead along his own spiritual path (there are countless paths) in the midst of the cares of the world, though he may not even realize what is happening to him." [124]

"Contemplatives in the midst of the world," united to God and conscious of his presence in and through all the various occupations and situations of the world: this is, in summary, the idea which Monsignor Escrivá proposes as the goal of the life of prayer.[125] We spoke earlier of the "primacy of prayer" in Christian life; perhaps in the light of what has just been said, it would be more exact to speak of the "centrality of prayer," because the word primacy can suggest simply a ordering of activities which are alongside each other but have little to do with each other; but

---

[122] "The theme of my prayer is the theme of my life," he says in another homily (*Christ Is Passing By*, no. 174). And in *The Way*: "You write: 'To pray is to talk with God. But about what?' About what? About Him, about yourself: joys, sorrows, successes and failures, noble ambitions, daily worries, weaknesses! And acts of thanksgiving and petitions: and Love and reparation. In a word: to get to know him and to get to know yourself: 'to get acquainted!'" (no. 91).

[123] *Friends of God*, no. 296.

[124] *Friends of God*, no. 308.

[125] Similar passages in which "contemplatives in the midst of the world" are mentioned include those quoted in my *La santificación del trabajo*, pp. 110–14.

prayer is not just one activity among many, it is a component or a dimension that gives every activity its fullest meaning. And in the ordinary Christian, who lives in the midst of the world, this expansion of the soul reaches out to and embraces the world.

In prayer, the Christian, every Christian, enters, under the influence of grace, into living, existential communion with God, recognizing him as the center of everything and therefore the center of his own life. In the Christian who lives in the world, the Christian whom God wants to live in the world, this action of prayer implies recognizing that the world makes sense by integrating it with God and God with it: recognizing that through the world God is speaking to man and that it is through the world, using the world, that man should respond.[126] It is true that prayer involves going deep down into oneself and even interrupting the rhythm of one's day so that, with peace of mind, in any quiet atmosphere, one lets faith seep into one's soul and give one a more intense sense of the presence of God; but in no sense does this mean a flight from the world; rather, it means delving into the world, to grasp its meaning better and to understand better what God wants one as a concrete individual to be doing there. Prayer and secularity are therefore (although this might at first sight seem paradoxical) intimately connected, because only in prayer are the world and secular realities seen for what they really are—not just the setting in which life takes place, but something which has a share in our destiny and through which our destiny takes shape until it attains its definitive value and goal.

(iii)

CHRISTIAN COMMITMENT AND SECULARITY IN OPUS DEI

1. *Implications of membership of the Opus Dei prelature*

The Church can be regarded as having two aspects, which form a deep unity: it is a community of believers, and an instrument of salvation. It is the community of those who believe in Christ and share in his life; a brotherhood made up of those who, having received Christ's Spirit, recognize each other as brothers and sisters; a family of the children of God which by its very existence bears witness to the world that Christ has won our reconciliation.

---

[126] On this see also my essay "El trabajo en la relación Dios-hombre," in *Dios y el hombre* (Pamplona, 1985), pp. 717–25.

But the Church is not just the product of the action of Christ's grace and a testimony to his truth; it is also the means God uses to save the world, the community to which he has entrusted the word and the sacraments, thanks to which salvation is proclaimed and communicated.

These ideas have been a constant reference point in this chapter and throughout the course of chapter I with a view to explaining the ecclesiological physiognomy of Opus Dei, as a family or grouping of Christians who, having recognized the universal call to holiness, and specifically to holiness in the midst of the world, make this truth the center or basis of their lives, thereby contributing to the spread of this awareness and this call among those who live alongside them in the various ambiences of human society.[127]

Therefore, in regard to Opus Dei (as, with due respect, in regard to the Church) one can make a distinction between the reality of Christian life and the institution at the service of that reality; but one should do so only provided one remembers that in Opus Dei pastoral phenomenon and institution form a profound unity (again analogous to the case of the Church); certainly the message and the pastoral phenomenon go beyond the institution and its direct activity, but the institution is not made of different stuff from them; on the contrary, the actual life of the members of Opus Dei is what bears witness to a calling to holiness in the midst of the world and what makes for the spread of that call.

In earlier pages we have examined this life, analyzing it from an angle which can throw light on its characteristics and its ecclesial importance: secularity. Bearing in mind the decisive importance (for an understanding of Opus Dei) of the ordinary life in the midst of the world of all and each of its members we should now focus our attention on Opus Dei as an institution, and, in this context, on the obligations contracted by those who join it.

To do this we need to change our methodology or (to put it more accurately) the tone and style of our exposition, because it brings us into an area which while still being that of theology does impinge on institutional and legal matters. But it is worth taking that step; otherwise we would be neglecting the institutional source which the members of Opus Dei draw on, and we would fail to deal with important aspects of their Christian commitment and therefore of their life, because, as we noticed, the members of Opus Dei are not just Christians who, becoming aware of the implications and richness of the vocation baptism gave them, try to

---

[127] See particularly chapter one, above, sections III and IV.

live in a manner consistent with that vocation; they are Christians who are conscious of being called to live that vocation in connection with Opus Dei, or to put it more accurately, by joining that prelature and sharing in its mission.

Previous chapters have also dealt with these institutional aspects but from a different perspective. We are not concerned here with the ecclesiological meaning of membership of Opus Dei (which was looked at in chapter one, above)[128] or with the connection between unity of vocation and diversity of concrete situations (analyzed in chapter two, above),[129] but with the content of the commitment a person acquires on becoming a member of the prelature—which we shall examine both in general and in relation to secularity. This distinction of perspective is easy to see, although obviously there are close connections between the various approaches; therefore, everything I shall say now takes as read what was discussed in the two earlier chapters—specifically, the ecclesiological fact that Opus Dei is an institution with an internal texture of faithful and ministerial priesthood for the purpose of spreading Christian life throughout the world, a mission which is the joint responsibility of all the members, priests and laity. This should be borne in mind when reading the following pages.

However, let us broach our subject—incorporation into Opus Dei and what it implies. First, we must ask a question: What is the nature of the "formal [and mutual] declaration" which gives rise to the bond or link between the faithful and the prelature? or, to put it more exactly, what elements go to make up the act of incorporation, on the side of the individual lay person and on the side of the prelature? The Statutes provide the answer in a very nuanced text which lays down that, at the point when he is being incorporated in the prelature, the person will:

—express his firm resolve to devote his best energies to seeking holiness and carrying out apostolate according to the spirit and practice of Opus Dei; and

—undertake, from the moment of his incorporation and as long as that incorporation lasts, to stay under the jurisdiction of the authorities of the prelature as regards everything to do with its particular purpose, to fulfill all the duties implied by being a member, and to keep in line with the lawful norms and prescriptions emanating from the authorities of the prelature.[130]

As we can see, there are two aspects or points which, while they

---

[128] See chapter one, above, section IV, 1.
[129] See chapter two, above, section IV.
[130] See *Statuta*, no. 27 § 3.

are very closely connected, can and should be conceptually distinguished:

(a) in the first place, a decision to seek holiness and carry out apostolate according to the spirit of Opus Dei, which the person makes in his heart (in response to the divine call) and *expresses* to the representatives of the prelature at the point when he is incorporated into it;

(b) in the second place, certain duties in respect of the prelature and its lawful authorities which the person *undertakes* to obey; parallel with these are certain duties the prelature takes on;[131] the result is a mutual bond.

Focusing attention on the obligations a person takes on when being incorporated in the prelature, we can fill out what has already been said by noticing that these obligations are of two types:

(a) on the one hand, the obligation to make a real effort to seek holiness and carry out apostolate in the midst of the world, and, therefore, the obligation to receive the spiritual training offered by the prelature to equip one to sanctify ordinary life;

(b) on the other, the obligation to take part in the activities the prelature organizes to attain its goals—both as regards the extension of the apostolate and in connection with the training of other members of the prelature itself.[132]

These two aspects are obviously deeply interconnected, both in fact and in the mind of a person who draws near to Opus Dei and ends up becoming a member; because, as was shown at length in the earlier chapters, all the faithful of the prelature have an active role. Accepting this close connection, we shall, however, go on to discuss them separately.

2. *A commitment to sanctification in ordinary life, and the role of the prelature in the formation of its faithful*

We shall begin with what is clearly the basic thing: the decision to sanctify one's life in the world; the faithful of the prelature express

---

[131] *Statuta*, no. 27 § 2, mentions these duties. All that *Statuta*, no. 27 § 2 and 3, does is to detail, with reference to the moment of incorporation, what is laid down in general terms in no. 6.

[132] This distinction between two types of obligation is connected, though this is not said, with the distinction between two stages in the activity of the prelature which, glossing a note from the Congregation for Bishops of Nov. 14, 1981, is commented on above, in chapter one, section III, 1; that is, the activity that the prelate engages in to give pastoral attention to the faithful of the prelature, and the activity that the faithful of the prelature as a whole carry out, in union with their prelate, to spread holiness and apostolate in all kinds of environments.

this decision when they join; and they combine it with a commitment to receive the training and spiritual help which enables them to live in accordance with this stated decision.

This point has been already examined in the previous pages in sufficient detail, at least as far as concerns the attitude of soul and the attitude to life it implies. From the angle that now concerns us, the decisive element is the perception of a divine call or invitation, which leads to a decision which, formulated and expressed at a particular moment (when one accepts the call and when one later becomes incorporated in Opus Dei), affects one's whole life and is to be seen in an ongoing effort, constantly supported by grace, to give a Christian meaning (that of holiness and apostolate) to everything one does.

The very nature of this effort to sanctify one's ordinary life means that we cannot make universally valid generalizations about it, given the fact that one would have to look at each individual life: vocation to Opus Dei (like Christian vocation, its backdrop) covers everything.[133] The decision and commitment to sanctification and apostolate we are examining here cannot, therefore, be reduced to a mere list of obligations and duties; it is more of the nature of an interior energy or impulse that vivifies all one's actions from within, setting in motion a dynamic (unity of life)[134] which leads one to refer them to God and to perceive all the opportunities they offer for the service of others and for apostolate.

This, of course, does not water down the decision and commitment to holiness and apostolate into an empty, formal or generic attitude; we are dealing with something that cannot be described in abstract terms: in every case it is something extremely concrete and specific—one's own life, one's own work, one's family, one's society, one's ambience, whose Christian potentiality one tries to perceive, identify, and realize. This is where the *pastorale* in the prelature comes into play—a range of activities designed to provide its members and those who take part in its apostolate with spiritual insights and helps to see the Christian dimensions and requirements of their lives.

(a) *The contribution of Opus Dei as an institution: formation and spiritual direction.* What are these activities? What does Opus Dei as an institution contribute to the ideal of Christian life in the world to which its members feel called and to which they commit themselves joining part of the prelature?

We must answer this question by simply repeating what we have

---

[133] See what is discussed above, in chapter two, section III.

[134] See earlier the present chapter, section II, 1.

just said or by reaffirming it by using an expression of St. Josemaría: Opus Dei's activity is just "one big catechesis," a constant proclamation of the Gospel message, showing how it applies as regards the sanctification of work and of earthly realities generally.[135] We might distinguish two stages:

(i) Primarily, an activity aimed at the spreading of the Gospel which leads a person not only to recognize the truth of the universal call to holiness, but also to experience it in a precise way; in other words, Christian preaching and dialogue which brings people to consider the need for personal conversion and a real commitment to Jesus Christ. The basic, essential task of Opus Dei, the purpose for which it came into being and which inspires it, is (I repeat) to spread among people in all environments the call to holiness and apostolate in the world; to awaken or revive in them their Christian faith so as to lead them to recognize the light and power which Christ projects over all existence. That is, clearly, the primary and fundamental purpose of the apostolic work of Opus Dei.

(ii) But, obviously, the pastoral action of Opus Dei does not end there. For all who are in contact with its apostolate and particularly for those who form part of the prelature, this pastoral action extends to a series of services or aids designed to help that first conversion or decision to develop into a response to the divine calling which gradually extends to all the activities and situations that life produces. The prelature, we read in the Statutes, on receiving someone as a member, undertakes to give that person "a careful religious-doctrinal, spiritual, ascetic, and apostolic formation, as also specific pastoral assistance from the priests of the prelature."[136] The activity proper to Opus Dei, Monsignor Escrivá explained in a 1967 interview, "consists in offering its members, and others who so wish, the spiritual resources they need to live as good Christians in the midst of the world. It helps them to learn Christ's doctrine and the Church's teachings. Its spirit moves them to do their work well for the love of God and as a service to others"; in other words, "it helps them to behave like real Chris-

---

[135] As already pointed out in chapter two, section III, Monsignor Josemaría Escrivá always made it very clear that Opus Dei's only activity consists in giving formation to its members and to such others as come in contact with its apostolate. To convey this idea, he sometimes described Opus Dei as "one big catechesis," a phrase he used as far back as 1932 ("Apuntes intimos," no. 548). Basically Opus Dei's activity consists "in offering its members, and others who want it, the spiritual resources they need for living as good Christians in the midst of the world": *Conversations*, no. 27.

[136] *Statuta*, no. 27 § 2.

tians: living in harmony with others, respecting the legitimate freedom of all, and trying to make our world more just." [137]

To put it another way and commenting on the passages I have quoted, we can say that the spiritual help that Opus Dei offers people for sanctifying their activities in the world involves:

(a) in the first place, a spirit, that is, a *spiritual teaching*, a lively appreciation of the Gospel, based on that sense of divine filiation which is the keynote of Opus Dei spirituality; this helps them see everything in a deeply theological way, as an encounter with God, a way to follow Christ and carry out the mission of the Church;

(b) second, a doctrinal-theological formation which provides a deep knowledge, appropriate to their circumstances in the world, of Christian faith and morals that allows them truly to sanctify those circumstances and involvements, by evaluating things in a genuinely Christian way;

(c) third, personal spiritual help, that is, spiritual direction, as it is traditionally called or, in the language sometimes preferred by modern pastoral theologians, *spiritual guidance and support*, with all that that direction or guidance implies: encouragement in the practice of virtue and to act sincerely in accordance with one's conscience; support or consolation in times of anxiety; reminders about the criteria or principles which can help one decide on the best course of action; etc.;

(d) finally, encouragement and apostolic orientation, sometimes by proposing specific lines of apostolic action, but normally simply by opening apostolic horizons, that is, by exhortations and suggestions which help one to see the apostolic opportunities one's work and ambience offer.

This doctrinal-theological help is given by Opus Dei through courses or sessions of spiritual formation, person to person conversations, meetings for the interchange of experience, etc.; all this is done in a way that fits in with the secular condition of its members, and therefore at times and places which suit one's social background and the time one can make available. To go into this in detail would require describing the whole range of situations involved; but I feel there is no need to do so, given the space limitations of this essay.[138]

However, it is worth stressing that we have here what is commonly described as a right-duty, that is to say, the faithful of the

---

[137] *Conversations*, no. 27.

[138] For a more detailed description of these facilities, see all title III of the Statutes (nos. 79ff.), particularly nos. 82, 2° and 3°; 83 § 2; 91; 96-101; 107; 110; summaries in *El itinerario jurídico*, pp. 474ff., and R. Gómez Pérez, *El Opus Dei*, pp. 134–37.

prelature have the right to these spiritual aids, but they are also under an obligation to avail themselves of them: incorporation in the prelature implies a commitment to Christian life which includes (as we said at the start of this section) a duty to avail oneself of the facilities for formation which Opus Dei offers.[139]

(b) *Formation and autonomy in temporal matters.* It should also be noted that all this formation and spiritual help is offered by the prelature, and availed of by its faithful, fully in keeping with their secular status and the spontaneity which that involves. We should remember the basic fact: the members of Opus Dei, ordinary Christians, aspire to sanctify their own state in life, thereby manifesting, from within the world, that the whole universe is ordained to God and that the grace of Christ can vivify all human situations. And this, from the viewpoint we are taking here, implies that the training or formation involved has to be structured in a way that harmonizes two principles which at first sight seem opposed to one another but which in fact imbue each other deeply: the all-embracing nature of the Christian spirit, and the autonomy of earthly realities and activities.

I shall explain this by three complementary statements:

1. I begin with a statement which is negatively couched: incorporation in Opus Dei does not imply, as far as family, social, cultural, and professional matters are concerned, any obligations other than those which that family, social, cultural, and professional situation itself involves; nor does it duplicate those obligations by any additional moral imperative. A university professor, a construction worker, a parent, a trade-unionist, a housewife, or a farmer, to refer to a few of the sorts of people who belong to Opus Dei, has exactly the same professional and social obligations (and rights) as anyone else of the same profession or position in society: being a member of Opus Dei does not mean any change of state, occupation, or position in society, and therefore does not take anything from or add anything to the rights and duties which that state, occupation, or position involves.[140]

---

[139] See the previously cited no. 27 of the Statutes. Obviously a duty in conscience is involved, neglect or disregard of which could be a grave fault; we are at one of the points here connected with the *graves et qualificatae obligationes* referred to in *Praelaturae personales* issued by the Congregation for Bishops, already cited.

[140] To the passages from the writings of Opus Dei's founder already cited in the first part of this chapter, we will add a further one, taken from a letter in which, after referring to the diversity of situations and professions in civil society, he says: "Anyone can belong to the Work, if God calls him; his vocation does not have to involve any change of state and therefore no external change of any kind. Each person will

2. But, while becoming a member of Opus Dei does not change those rights and obligations, it does bring with it a refinement of conscience and spiritual assistance which help to make a person alert to recognize those obligations and to face up to them, and it also gives them a spirit which (like the Christian spirit, of which it is a specification) can and should involve all their activity, giving it a deeper meaning. The Christian vocation takes up a person's human vocation and occupations, infusing into them a spirit (awareness of the dignity of every human being, a sense of responsibility, a spirit of service, solidarity, a capacity for understanding and dialogue, etc.) which, so to speak, changes them from within, that is, vivifies them without adulterating them or denaturalizing them. Vocation to Opus Dei leads a person to become very aware of this—its spirit places the accent on the sanctification of everyday work and of ordinary life—and, given this, the main thrust of the prelature's activity is directed to strengthening in all its members the Christian spirit with which they should imbue all their actions; it sets them directly before God and the Catholic faith, without any type of interference or regulation which would reduce their complete freedom and the consequent responsibility each has for the professional and social options he or she makes, yet urging them to take their Christianity very seriously.

3. To sum up, and this is the last of the three statements I want to make, membership of Opus Dei leaves unchanged that freedom which its members, together with other Catholics, enjoy in all professional and social matters; the training and spiritual help they are given by the prelature, therefore, always presupposes and respects that freedom. The work of the prelature has to do only with formation and spiritual guidance: formation in the faith and encouragement to act in a responsible way and in a manner inspired by charity and a spirit of service, but without ever trespassing (on the contrary, respecting) boundaries of that sphere in which everyone forms his own opinions and decides how to approach his temporal activities. "As far as professional activity is concerned, and in matters social, political, etc., each of the faithful of the prelature, within the limits of Catholic doctrine on faith and morals," the Statutes declare, in a passage from which I have already quoted, "has the same complete freedom as other Catholic

---

stay in the place he has in the world, with his work, his outlook, his duties of state, his professional commitments, his duties to society: because all these connections are channels for his apostolic work as a Christian" (March 11, 1940, no. 37).

citizens. The authorities of the prelature must abstain totally from even giving advice on these matters."[141]

The members of Opus Dei, ordinary Christians, men and women working in all kinds of jobs, conscious of their secularity, know that in temporal matters, professional, cultural, social, and political, they have complete autonomy: as regards decisions to do with their temporal activities, the members of Opus Dei owe no obedience to the authorities of the prelature: they consult only their own consciences, and therefore the Gospel, the teaching of the Church, and, ultimately, God. The spirit of Opus Dei has made them aware of their responsibility, and the formation they receive helps them think and act in line with Christian standards, but it is up to each individual to make free and responsible decisions about his own work and lifestyle.

This is really, as we already said, the identifying mark of the ordinary Christian: to act in his own name and, conscientiously taking responsibility for his actions, to bear witness to Christ, to enter into a dialogue with his fellow citizens, and to help by word and action to have the Gospel imbue human history.[142]

---

[141] *Statuta*, no. 88 § 3. This brings us to a central point in the spirit and life of Opus Dei, about which its founder often spoke; countless instances could be cited. I shall simply take a paragraph from an interview published in *Conversations*: all the work of the centers of government in Opus Dei "is directed fundamentally to one task: to provide the members with the spiritual assistance necessary for their life of piety, and an adequate spiritual, doctrinal, religious and human formation. And then, *off you go!* That is to say, Christians, sanctify all the paths of men, for all bear the imprint of the footsteps of God. Having reached this point, the Association as such has done its job, the job precisely for which the members of Opus Dei have come together. The Association has nothing else to do. It neither can nor should it give any further indications. Here begins the free and responsible personal action of each member. Each one does his apostolate spontaneously, working with complete personal freedom. Autonomously forming his own conscience regarding the concrete decisions he has to take, he endeavors to seek Christian perfection and to give Christian witness in his own environment, sanctifying his own work, whether it be professional, intellectual, or manual" (no. 19). See also D. le Tourneau, *What Is Opus Dei?*, pp. 43–58, and R. Gómez Pérez, *El Opus Dei*, pp. 38ff.

[142] For more on this, see section III, 5, above, and the quotations from Monsignor Escrivá therein. I might recall—though it may be unnecessary to do so—that both the assertion of the theological value of human activity and of the Christian conscience's link with God and the proclamation of the temporal freedom of the Christian appear throughout the teaching of Vatican II and subsequent popes; e.g., *Lumen gentium*, nos. 3–37; *Gaudium et spes*, nos. 36 and 43; *Christifideles laici*, nos. 36 and 42.

3. *Availability of members of Opus Dei for tasks of formation and apostolate*

Earlier at the beginning of the third and last section of this essay, I pointed out that Opus Dei is a deeply integrated reality in which two aspects can be distinguished—Christian life in the midst of the world (men and women of all kinds of professions and walks of life who by their day-to-day lives bear witness to and spread the universal call to holiness and apostolate), and an ecclesial structure designed to assist that spread of the Christian life in all spheres of society. What I have written demonstrates the way these two aspects are intimately connected: it is, in effect, impossible to speak about members of Opus Dei, their life and apostolate, without mentioning, however briefly, the encouragement and spiritual help they receive, and therefore without referring to Opus Dei as the source of that encouragement and help. The point has now come, however, to focus our attention more directly on this, that is, to look at that pastoral activity which Opus Dei carries out and at the responsibilities members of the prelature have for it.

From the beginning, that is, from October 2, 1928, its founder saw Opus Dei as an institution made up of priests and lay people working closely together. The Statutes recognize this when they state: "Opus Dei is a personal prelature which comprises clergy and laity in order to carry out special pastoral work under the rule of the prelate."[143] These words have been quoted a number of times in this book. However, they are worth bearing in mind because they give a very clear summary of something dealt with in detail in chapter 1, to which reference should be made.[144] I refer to the fact that Opus Dei is a personal prelature, that is, a jurisdictional structure made up of priests and lay people and charged with a mission; this obviously presupposes not only that all the members warmly support one and the same ideal, but also that they actively play a part in that mission and do what they can to promote it. Opus Dei, then, is a living community, made up of a prelate, a presbyterium, and a laity, who all share the same vocation and mission. And "this Christian community, organic and undivided, is [all of it, we might add] ordered to the purpose of the prelature in line with the principle of co-responsibility and in keeping with the active position of all those who make it up."[145]

---

[143] *Statuta*, no. 5 § 5.

[144] See earlier in the present chapter, particularly sections III and IV.

[145] See J. Hervada, "Aspectos de la estructura jurídica del Opus Dei" in *Lex nova* 5 (1991) 315.

This implies that on joining the prelature a member not only commits himself to receive formation and spiritual help toward sanctifying his life, but also, and inseparably, to contribute in a way appropriate to his circumstances to this work of formation and things connected with it. The Statutes spell this out when, after indicating that the faithful of the prelature commit themselves to sanctifying their own state in life, they immediately add that they also undertake "to carry out the apostolic tasks the prelate entrusts to them."[146] There can be and in fact are in Opus Dei (as in the Church) different roles and tasks, but throughout the prelature the basic position is the same: all its members have and feel joint responsibility for everything to do with the prelature's mission, and, to the extent they can, play an active part in the formational activities and other things necessary for it to perform its mission.

Without going into other matters which have been sufficiently explored elsewhere,[147] let us ask this question: How does Opus Dei carry out the work of formation and spiritual help proper to it? and, therefore, what tasks and apostolic activities (in addition to his personal effort to sanctify his ordinary life in the midst of the world) does a member of the Opus Dei prelature commit himself to as soon as he becomes a member?

We could say that these activities fall into two areas:

(a) We should remember, in the first place, as we saw in the previous section, that Opus Dei offers its members and those who come into contact with it a doctrinal-religious formation and spiritual assistance and guidance; in practice this is provided, bit by bit, through a wide range of activities: study circles, recollections, theology courses, specialized training courses, etc., to some of which we have already referred; all this necessarily presupposes the existence of or the search for resources and physical facilities where these activities can be carried out.

(b) Second, the authorities of the prelature can decide that it is good to provide pastoral help to specific works of apostolate which have been initiated by its faithful and are closely connected with its purpose of spreading the Christian calling in the world. Opus Dei's basic work is and should always be the spiritual formation of people in all walks of life; this will give rise both to a dynamic personal apostolate of friendship and trust directed toward relatives, friends, and colleagues and to a wide range of apostolic initiatives which its members feel called to promote either as indi-

---

[146] *Statuta*, no. 3 § 2; also no. 27 § 3.

[147] Specifically, the ecclesiological dimension of this commitment and this activity, already examined in chapter one, section IV.

viduals or in cooperation with others.[148] When it seems advisable, the prelature can give pastoral help to some of these activities; relatively few activities will be supported in this way (because as I have already said, the accent will always be put on the personal formation of individuals and on their apostolate in all kinds of environments), but they are seen as useful because, on the one hand, they do contribute to the work of formation already mentioned and, on the other, they show in a graphic, tangible way certain features of the spirit of Opus Dei and its solicitude for the problems of the society in which it is set.[149]

There are differences between the two areas just mentioned but both of them involve a series of educational, apostolic, and spiritual undertakings in which the prelature as such engages. As regards these, what obligations do the members of Opus Dei take on with respect to the development of specific apostolic activities? The main obligation has to do with a spiritual and affective attitude: they are conscious that these educational and apostolic activities, whoever actually runs them, affect all members of Opus Dei (they all help to promote the aim of the prelature, an aim all members share) and therefore they should be appreciated and valued. Members also have precise responsibilities along these lines:

(a) they are ready to accept such arrangements as the prelate or other authorities of the prelature may give them, unless other duties (family, professional, or social) make it really impossible for them to do so;[150]

(b) they have a duty to give financial support to these apostolic undertakings, to the degree that they can.[151]

In both cases these are genuine obligations, but what they mean in practice obviously depends on a person's circumstances.[152] The qualifications "unless other duties make it really impossible" and "to the degree that they can" (taken from the text of the Statutes) indicate that realism has to operate.

[148] For a description of this apostolic panorama, a veritable "sea without shores," as St. Josemaría Escrivá himself put it, see *Conversations*, nos. 57 and 120.

[149] On this pastoral help given to particular apostolic undertakings, see *Statuta*, no. 121 § 1–2; for a more general account, see the passages quoted from Monsignor Escrivá at the end of section I, 4, of this chapter, and bibliography indicated.

[150] See *Statuta*, no. 3 § 2.

[151] See *Statuta*, no. 94 § 2.

[152] This too is an instance of the *graves et qualificatae obligationes* mentioned in the declaration by the Congregation for Bishops, May 23, 1982. As regards the first case mentioned (cooperating in apostolic undertakings) this is an obvious exercise of the power of jurisdiction of the prelate (or of vicars and associates acting in his name) which involves a strict duty of obligation.

As far as sanctification of one's state in life and of one's profession is concerned, no such restrictive clauses can apply. Obviously, as one's life goes on changes can take place, new circumstances (unforeseen and undesired) can arise which may alter one's circumstances, even very considerably, but that in no way lessens one's commitment to sanctification; on the contrary, both foreseen and unforeseen circumstances are part of the "real life" that each person should sanctify.

As regards the commitment to help in specific apostolic or formational tasks, the same does not hold: presupposing the same disposition of soul and the same self-surrender to the will and love of God, it can happen that genuine incompatibilities arise; in each case an effort needs to be made to devise a solution which does not reduce one's basic availability for apostolic work or one's genuine human and Christian readiness to cope with family, professional, and social obligations.[153]

4. *The same apostolic zeal, and diversity of scope for apostolate*

What I have just said might appear to be the end of the matter; however, I should make one further point: the objective circumstances to which I have referred, and the effect they may have in practice on one's availability for such tasks, is not something that applies in Opus Dei only *a posteriori*, that is, as circumstances present themselves; it is also something that applies *a priori*, something that is foreseen. The reason for this has to do with an essential element in the makeup of Opus Dei, an element which belongs to its foundational charism: the presence of members of the prelature who join it with a commitment of celibacy.

Both this fact and the distinction among Numerary, Associate, and Supernumerary members have been commented on earlier, in connection with unity of vocation;[154] here I shall simply make some points which directly concern the subject of this essay, that is, secularity and the commitment which members of the faithful acquire on joining the prelature.

[153] Obviously (though it is worth underlining) the types of incompatibility referred to in the text are objective ones dictated by circumstances: subjectively every member of Opus Dei should be ready to assist these undertakings as far as he or she can. That, for example, is why in matters of finance the members of Opus Dei do not commit themselves to contribute a fixed sum, nor is any distinction made on the basis of what each can in fact contribute: responsibility for these undertakings falls on everyone, and each contributes what he can, after maintaining himself and attending to family, professional, and other commitments.

[154] See chapter two, section IV, 2.

The key question in this regard (that is, the obligations which different members take on joining Opus Dei) can be dealt with as follows:

(a) Some members of the prelature, by practicing celibacy, are very available to look after the apostolic undertakings and the formation of the other faithful of the prelature, to which they commit themselves especially. In fact, they have to be ready to change jobs at any particular time in order to look for alternative work which will allow them more easily to attend to some specific apostolate; and they may even have to give up their present job (normally only for a period of time) in order to devote themselves to the prelature's functions of formation and government. Supernumeraries should have the same sense of responsibility for the apostolate, but their availability in practice is naturally restricted by their family obligations, which obviously take priority.

(b) Numeraries and Associates, once they have fulfilled their fiscal, financial, social, or family obligations and once they have (in keeping with their professional position, but with sobriety and detachment) covered their maintenance costs, contribute their fees or earnings to support the prelature's apostolic undertakings. Supernumeraries contribute to the support of the apostolate insofar as they can, after attending to their family and other such obligations.[155]

So there are practical differences as regards availability, just as there are differences to do with special obligations, but (I stress it, although it has been dealt with in the previous chapter and I have referred to it again only a moment ago), that diversity of situations and the obligations that result from them do presuppose a radical oneness of spirit, of vocation, and of mission. I shall just make two further points, which although they go in different directions are profoundly complementary, because both hinge on something quite basic: the fact that Opus Dei is an institution ordained to the spreading of holiness and apostolate in the midst of the world through the very life of its members, ordinary Christians of widely different nationalities and conditions.

The first of these points is simply a reaffirmation of the basic fact of unity of vocation. Joining Opus Dei is not (I repeat) the result of a mere desire to cooperate in a worthwhile project (which is a very praiseworthy thing to do, but it does not involve the total commitment of oneself); it is a matter of vocation, of realizing that

[155] As pointed out earlier, in no case does any fixed contribution apply; thus, it is up to each Supernumerary to make a conscientious decision in a spirit of generosity and with the sense of apostolic responsibility every Christian should have, as to how much he or she can and should give at any particular time.

one is being called by God to sanctify one's own life, becoming totally involved in this job of spreading holiness and apostolate in the midst of the world, which is what defines and characterizes Opus Dei. And this fact of vocation is the same in each and every one of those who become members of the prelature. So, diversity of personal situations and occupations does not break this unity; on the contrary, it produces it, allowing people of very different backgrounds to live one and the same spirit and to bear effective Christian witness in the various settings and professions that make up civil society.

All that is equivalent to saying that the distinction between Numeraries, Associates, and Supernumeraries has nothing at all to do with different levels or standards of holiness, with greater or lesser self-surrender, with more or less generosity: it concerns only differences in availability for certain tasks, within a single spiritual and apostolic reality. This is something the Statutes stress: the different kinds of bond or link with the prelature are described by relating them (as can be seen from the summary given above, and seen even more clearly from the text of the Statutes)[156] not to basic attitudes but to availability for specific tasks: Numeraries, Associates, and Supernumeraries all share one and the same spirit and vocation, and all work together at the same mission, striving to sanctify their own lives and contributing, to the extent that circumstances allow, to the development of the pastoral work the prelature carries out, in keeping with the principle of joint responsibility to which I referred earlier.[157]

The second point refers specifically to Numeraries and Associates, although, like the first point, it does affect the central nucleus of Opus Dei and, very directly, secularity. Opus Dei, everything to do with all its members and all its activity, refers to sanctification of the world from within the world itself. In other words, the commit-

---

[156] See above, chapter two, section IV, 2.

[157] In the preaching and writings of the founder of Opus Dei on the subject of the diversity of circumstances in which members of the prelature find themselves, there is not the least trace of that neo-Platonic way of thinking that identifies ranks or degrees of perfection. He always thought and spoke in terms of what is usually called today an "ecclesiology of communion": thus, he always spoke of a multiplicity of situations, roles, and involvements, each endowed with intrinsic dignity, which, on account of their very diversity, complement one another, all contributing to the perfection, and apostolic effectiveness, of the whole. In other words, the universal call to holiness and apostolate, with all that it implies (recognizing in and from all human situations and circumstances an openness to one and the same fullness of Christian life) is accommodated in the very structure of Opus Dei, thereby enabling the prelature to be effective in its mission of proclaiming and spreading that call from within all kinds of earthly realities.

ment of celibacy, which Numeraries and Associates take on, has nothing whatever to do with attitudes of consecration or giving up secular activities. On the contrary, it is set firmly in a context of full, radical affirmation of things secular; in fact, it is a call to testify to the value of things secular in and through temporal tasks and occupations.[158] Numeraries and Associates dedicate themselves, then, with full personal freedom and responsibility, to whatever their occupation is; they take very seriously the obligations involved; they are in every sense ordinary citizens who share the same yearnings, interests, and problems as their fellow citizens, their equals.

It is true that both Numeraries and Associates have to be ready, as I said earlier, to give up whatever job they may have at a particular time in order to look after some apostolic work of the prelature, but that all happens in keeping with secularity, as I have recently pointed out. For we should not forget that:

(a) On the one hand, the apostolic undertakings to which the prelature gives spiritual assistance are always educational or social welfare activities of a secular style, initiated and run by citizens in the exercise of their civic rights: leaving one professional occupation to work in one of these undertakings is the equivalent of changing one's type of work—as people often do for all kinds of reasons.[159]

---

[158] There is a rich corpus of literature, ancient and modern, on Christian celibacy, its features, its meaning, its charismatic origin, etc.; and a rich variety of theories and evaluations of historical data. Without going into this in depth, I would say there are basically two approaches. On the one hand, we find celibacy interpreted as renunciation, more specifically, as an element or *the* element in separation from the world and the ordinary circumstances of human life; this is the approach of early monasticism and it survives in some form or other in the religious tradition initiated by monasticism. On the other hand, we find celibacy (for example, priestly celibacy) seen as a reflection, condition, or consequence of commitment to an ecclesial mission or vocation. The second kind has no direct reference, positive or negative, to secularity; the reference is a function of the vocation to which the celibacy is linked. And, in the case of the celibacy practiced by Numerary and Associate members of Opus Dei, the vocation and mission into which it is set refer directly to things secular.

[159] On the secular character of these apostolic activities, see the quotations cited in previous notes and the bibliography referred to. "Professional vocation," Monsignor Escrivá wrote in one of his letters (developing these ideas about mobility within one's sphere of work to which we have referred), "is something which becomes more definite as life goes on: often enough a person who begins a certain course of study later discovers that he is better gifted for other things and he changes over to them; or he ends up specializing in a field different from the one he had in mind at the start; or he finds when he is already working away at his chosen profession, new work which allows him to improve the social position of his family, or to make a better contribution to society; or for health reasons he has to move

(b) On the other hand, arrangements to do with the formation of other members of the prelature are compatible, as we have seen, with full commitment to a job; it is just like someone devoting some of his time to his family or to some voluntary social work; only in special cases does it involve having to give up one's professional work, and even then it is only for a period of time. Indeed, even in those situations where a definitive break with one's profession is concerned (as normally occurs in the case of Numeraries and Associates who are called to the priesthood and become part of the prelature's presbyterium, devoting all their time to pastoral work), the founder of Opus Dei stressed that people affected in this way should not lose their connection, at least their psychological connection, with the work they had been doing previously: they should keep the "mentality" of their profession.[160]

Celibacy and marriage (as in another sphere, common priesthood and ministerial priesthood)[161] are seen and practiced in Opus Dei with reference to the secular context. At all times the governing criterion is a desire to express the Christian value of earthly realities from within the temporal context, that is, not just proclaiming the universal call to holiness and apostolate, but showing the reality of that call in their concrete lives (which differ from each other but all of which are secular). The ecclesiology of com-

---

somewhere else and do a different kind of work"; a few paragraphs further on he takes up the theme again, applying it not only to changes caused by family and social factors but also to changes made for apostolic reasons. The new task one takes on in this case is also a genuinely professional activity in which one should engage "with the same spirit, with the same commitment (as that with which one worked at one's previous profession): sanctifying the job you are given, sanctifying yourself with that activity, and sanctifying others; putting all your human idealism, all your talents, into that work": letter, Oct. 15, 1948, nos. 33 and 37.

[160] Those lay men, members of Opus Dei, who are called to the priesthood, have previously worked at a job, and this fact, Monsignor Escrivá comments in a letter, influences their outlook and should continue to do so: "If for all members of the Work, professional vocation is an important part of their divine vocation, this is also true for our priests. Therefore, all should try, after they receive Holy Orders, to keep up their interest in their profession and in fact there is no objection to their exercising (always being priests in the fullest sense) the secular profession they had before, insofar as their priestly ministry permits": letter, Feb. 2, 1945, no. 29. Elsewhere he writes: "The Work asks my priest sons to reduce the time they used to give to the professional work they had before ordination and, very often, to give up doing it altogether," but even so, he adds, "while being profoundly priests, you should keep your lay outlook and, insofar as is compatible with your pastoral work, you can continue to exercise the profession you had. Professional vocation is for us all—priests and lay people—an integral part of our way": letter, Oct. 15, 1948, no. 40.

[161] See above, chapter one, especially section III.

munion to which we referred earlier, that is, the complementarity of different situations, all helping to achieve the one goal, can be seen here in all its importance.

5. *Fraternity and family spirit*

When, in the early decades of this century, Romano Guardini decided to take up the challenge issued by writings (clearly inspired by Rationalism and the Enlightenment) which spoke of an "essence of Christianity" and did so with an obvious reductionist purpose, he soon came to a conclusion which at first sight might seem paradoxical: to reply to the challenge one has to say that the question is wrongly posed, because, strictly speaking, Christianity does not have an essence. In other words, Christianity cannot be reduced to an idea, because it is something alive. The essence of Christianity is the living person of Jesus, the very life of God who, in Christ, is communicated to mankind. Christianity is, essentially, life, communicated life, and therefore the Church is community, family.

This is something that is reflected in every Christian institution, and it is deeply reflected in Opus Dei, as has been shown in previous chapters.[162] The various forms it takes, while they are all ultimately one (reference to God in Christ), have different features depending on the spirit and nature of the institution in question. In the case of Opus Dei those features can be reduced to two basic ones: supernatural character and secular character.

"We are a family with *supernatural* ties."[163] These words of Monsignor Escrivá, often repeated by him and cited a number of times in this book, show the source or origin of the family spirit proper to Opus Dei: it is born of an awareness of cooperating together in a divine union, which transcends human differences, and it opens out to everyone with links of true affection over and above differences of race, social status, and ideological views. By speaking in this way the founder of Opus Dei was also saying that this affection is to be found at a *supernatural* level, that is, regarding a person from the viewpoint of his ultimate destiny, and therefore focusing exclusively on the search for holiness and on the spread of apostolate, not allowing other considerations or objectives to blur it.[164]

---

[162] See ibid., section IV, 3, and chapter two, section IV, 3.

[163] Letter, Sept. 29, 1957, no. 57; the italics are mine.

[164] "The members of Opus Dei," its founder stresses in this connection, "have come together *only* for the purpose of following a clearly defined way of holiness and of cooperating in specific works of apostolate. What binds them together is something exclusively spiritual and therefore rules out all temporal interests, because

Secular character, because the paradigm of Opus Dei's sense of family is established by what we might call, to use a phrase of its founder, "a Christian family home." Appreciation for the family, as a basic human and Christian reality, runs in two directions in his teaching. On the one hand it takes the form of a vigorous assertion of the value of marriage and of the family life marriage creates, as a Christian vocation and condition; this finds its institutional expression, within Opus Dei, through the figure of the Supernumeraries particularly, who, as the Statutes say, turn "their own home and their own family involvements"[165] into a means of sanctification and apostolate. On the other hand, it takes the form of relationships between members of the prelature (a relationship which is simple, affable, natural, without the use of formalities of any type), and it is to be seen in the general style of all its activities, including apostolic works and the places where they are run, which are to possess the "tone and ambience" of a normal "Christian family home" as stated by the first regulations, of 1941, which we have quoted.

Monsignor Escrivá always thought it providential that his apostolate in Madrid, in the period prior to the foundation, was something that developed in a spontaneous way and was based on his own home, which he shared with his mother and brother and sister. This gave a simple, ordinary family accent to all the apostolate in that period, and it influenced all Opus Dei's later apostolate, thereby underlining, from this point of view also, its sense of secularity.

St. Josemaría Escrivá had occasion to return to this theme quite frequently, not, indeed, because the members of Opus Dei began to have any doubts or second thoughts, but, on the contrary, because this was one of the points on which, to avoid misunderstanding, it seemed appropriate to show the difference between Opus Dei and the religious state, particularly during the period when there was a strong tendency to see that state (for which Monsignor Escrivá had deep love) as the benchmark for every type of profound Christian experience; this attitude led to an attempt to

---

in the temporal area all the members of Opus Dei are free and so each goes his own way, with aims and interests which are different and sometimes opposite" *Conversations*, no. 67; so, to sum up, there is in Opus Dei no clash between apostolic activity and human purposes and objectives members can legitimately adopt in the exercise of their personal freedom and therefore of their (also personal) responsibility; Opus Dei interferes in no way, and provides no form of support.

[165] *Statuta*, no. 11. On the evaluation of married life in the teachings of St. Josemaría Escrivá, see above, chapter two, section IV, 2.

apply to apostolic activities initiated by Opus Dei criteria or molds which had nothing to do with them, or to confuse the simple family life of those members of Opus Dei who shared the same domicile (a small number compared with the total number of members, who usually live with their families or in places where their occupation takes them) as something quite different: the community life typical of the religious state.

Monsignor Escrivá was always very concerned to show the marked difference between these two lifestyles both in practical, concrete things and in terms of their deep theological significance: "The *family life* [of members of Opus Dei who live in the same place]," he says in one of his Letters, "has nothing to do with the community life of religious." "Canonical common life," he goes on, "is a sign, a testimony, to the separation from the world which religious profess"; the family life of some members of Opus Dei "has no greater social significance than the style of life proper to ordinary Christian families." [166] Canonical common life connotes the very substance of the religious state as envisaged from its very beginning: the establishment of a mode of life which, by differentiating itself from the ordinary, bears witness to the transcendent. Family life in Opus Dei is simply a matter of a few people sharing a domicile and a Christian experience.

Using this theological core as our starting point, we can see the full meaning of the phrases we have just been quoting, to the effect that the Centers of Opus Dei reflect "the tone and ambience of an ordinary Christian family home," "the style of life proper to ordinary Christian families." There is a very close connection between these statements and what we said earlier when speaking of the members of Opus Dei being ordinary Christians; both refer to the same thing: the value of the secular as the setting for a Christian life designed to lead the world toward God (this is in the last analysis the only ultimate meaning of Christianity and therefore of every vocation) but designed to do so within the world itself.

From the point of view of vocation, living in one place or another (with other members, with one's own family, in accommodation beside one's place of work, etc.) is something incidental: what matters is that awareness of vocation and that spirit which makes one conscious of engaging in a mission which each person carries out via his or her own life. [167] I might also add, for complete-

---

[166] Letter, May 6, 1945, no. 22. Similar statements and a fuller treatment of this subject are to be found in *El itinerario jurídico*, especially pp. 108–10, 134, 266ff.

[167] This holds true not only for Supernumeraries, who live in their own home, and for Associates, who normally live with their own families; it also applies to

ness' sake, that in keeping with the basic normality we spoke of earlier (theology here bears out sociology, or to put it another way, the spirit explains the actual facts), in those cases where, for longer or shorter periods, some members of Opus Dei live together, the accommodation used naturally has a secular style, in keeping with the customs of the region or country in question. Their lifestyle will also be simple and ordinary: there will probably be a timetable, to make things go smoothly and to ensure rest, and also a period for family prayer, but in an ambience of spontaneity and freedom, without constraints on life;[168] on the contrary, keeping the tone of a home "where some days one person is missing, some days someone else, as can happen."[169] The sociological and theological dimensions of secularity, as in other ways, are always there, always profoundly influence the spirit and practice of Opus Dei.

Numeraries, who, though they usually live in centers of Opus Dei so as to look after apostolic undertakings or formation programs, can also live, and frequently do live, elsewhere, when family, professional, etc., reasons so require or advise.

[168] Instruction, May 31, 1936, no. 49.
[169] Letter, Dec. 29, 1947/Feb. 14, 1966, no. 22.

CONCLUSION

On the occasion of the beatification of Monsignor Escrivá de Balaguer, Pope John Paul II said, in the course of his remarks:

> With supernatural intuition, Blessed Josemaría untiringly preached the universal call to holiness and apostolate. Christ calls everyone to become holy in the realities of everyday life: hence *work too is a means of personal holiness and apostolate*, when it is done in union with Jesus Christ, for the Son of God, in the Incarnation, has in some way united himself with the whole reality of man and with all creation.
>
> Blessed Josemaría, thanks to God's light, understood this universal call, not only as a doctrine to be taught and spread particularly among the lay faithful, but also, and above all, as the very center of an active commitment in his pastoral ministry.[1]

These words of the Pope can provide the setting for the short epilogue to this book. As we said in the Introduction, our aim in writing was to study some aspects, mainly ecclesiological ones, of Opus Dei and its apostolate. We hope we have helped to show, in a year which has seen both the tenth anniversary of the establishment of Opus Dei as a personal prelature and the beatification of its founder, some of the theological implications of its spirit.

As these two pontifical texts stress, the birth of Opus Dei and the development of its apostolate stem from the theoretical and practical inspiration which was Monsignor Escrivá's guiding light from October 2, 1928, onward. In other words, they are the result of his profound grasp of the universal call to holiness and the outcome of the interior impulse which led him to devote his life to spreading that call, causing it to be accepted and acted on by so many men and women.

[1] The first paragraph comes from the homily preached by John Paul II at the Beatification Mass celebrated in St. Peter's Square, May 17, 1992; the second, from his address in the audience he gave, also in St. Peter's Square, the following day. Both texts appear in *L'Osservatore Romano*, May 18 and 19, 1992, as also in *Romana* 8 (1992) 29ff., 36ff.

This union between theory and practice, between message, pastoral phenomenon and institution, has been one of the axes, if not the main axis of our study. This unity is, in our view, the key to understanding what Opus Dei is, both in terms of its internal structure and as regards its mission.

Its mission in the first place, because Opus Dei (for its founder, and as it has developed over the course of time) has no other reason for being than to foster a genuine search for holiness in all walks of life in the midst of the world. Therefore, its aim fuses with the aim of the Church, of which it forms part, from which it receives its life, and to which it is ordained, conscious as it is, as we quoted Monsignor Escrivá at the start of the first chapter, of being a "little bit" of the greater Christian community.

This unity also explains its internal structure, because, by virtue of its foundational charism, Opus Dei is an institution made up of priests and lay people who aspire to foster the search for holiness and the carrying out of apostolate in the midst of the world, precisely through their own lives. Members strive to bear witness to the fact that that ideal is not a theory or a will-o'-the-wisp, but something which the grace of God makes possible. Hence that wide variety of situations, all in the context of an unambiguous unity of vocation, and that enhanced appreciation of the Christian value of ordinary life and therefore of secularity, which we have analyzed in the second and third chapters.

In his homily at the thanksgiving Mass in St. Peter's Basilica on the morning of May 18, 1992, the prelate of Opus Dei, Bishop Alvaro del Portillo, recalled that according to the Gospel there can be no Christianity except by following Jesus in a fully committed way. And he went on: "Blessed Josemaria responded without hesitation to this demand, and he taught that it is possible to live it fully while staying in the world. Yes, it is possible 'to belong' in the world without being worldly! It is possible for each person to stay in his place, and at the same time to follow Christ and abide in him. It is possible to live "in heaven and on earth,' to be 'contemplatives in the midst of the world,' transforming the circumstances of ordinary life into an occasion for an encounter with God." [2] This is the theological core with which we began this study, and with which we now conclude it.

---

[2] *Romana* 8 (1992) 31.

APPENDIX I.

CONSTITUTIO APOSTOLICA SANCTAE CRUCIS ET OPERIS DEI

OPUS DEI IN PRAELATURAM PERSONALEM AMBITUS INTERNATIONALIS ERIGITUR

IOANNES PAULUS EPISCOPUS
SERVUS SERVORUM DEL
AD PERPETUAM REI MEMORIAM

Ut sit validum et efficax instrumentum suae ipsius salvificae missionis pro mundi vita, Ecclesia maternas curas cogitationesque suas maxima cum spe confert in Opus Dei, quod Servus Dei Ioseph Maria Escrivá de Balaguer divina ductus inspiratione die II Octobris anno MCMXXVIII Matriti inivit.

Haec sane Institutio inde a suis primordiis sategit missionem laicorum in Ecclesia et in humana societate non modo illuminare sed etiam ad effectum adducere necnon doctrinam de universali vocatione ad sanctitatem re exprimere atque sanctificationem in labore et per laborem professionalem in quolibet sociali coetu promovere. Idem pariter efficiendum curavit per Societatem Sacerdotalem Sanctae Crucis quoad sacerdotes dioecesibus incardinatos in sacri ministerii exercitio.

Cum Opus Dei divina opitulante gratia adeo crevisset ut in pluribus orbis terrarum dioecesibus extaret atque operaretur quasi apostolica compages quae sacerdotibus et laicis sive viris sive mulieribus constabat eratque simul organica et indivisa, una scilicet spiritu fine regimine et spirituali institutione, necesse fuit aptam formam iuridicam ipsi tribui quae peculiaribus eius notis responderet. Idemque Operis Dei Conditor, anno MCMLXII, a Sancta Sede humili cum fiducia suppliciter postulavit ut, natura theologica et primigenia Institutionis perspecta ciusque maiore apostolica efficacia considerata, consentanea configuratio ei inveniretur.

Ex quo autem tempore Concilium Oecumenicum Vaticanum Secundum, Decreto *Presbyterorum Ordinis*, n. 10 per Litteras "motu proprio" datas *Ecclesiae Sanctae*, I n. 4 rite in actum deducto, in ordinationem Ecclesiae figuram Praelaturae personalis ad peculiaria opera pastoralia perficienda induxit, visa est ea ipsa Operi Dei apprime aptari. Quapropter anno MCMLXIX Decessor Noster felicissimae recordationis Paulus Sextus petitioni Servi Dei Ioseph Mariae Escrivá de Balaguer benigne annuens potestatem illi dedit Congressum generalem specialem convocandi, cui cura esset, ipso duce, ut studium iniretur de Operis Dei transformatione, eius ipsius indoli et Concilii Vaticani Secundi normis magis consentanea.

Quod omnino studium explicate iussimus Nos ipsi continuari atque anno MCMLXXIX Sacrae Congregationi pro Episcopis, ad quam res suapte pertinebat natura, mandatum dedimus ut, cunctis elementis sive iuris sive facti attente consideratis, formalem petitionem ab Opere Dei exhibitam examini subiceret.

Profecto eadem Congregatio huic negotio vacans quaestionem sibi propositam accurate investigavit ratione cum historica tum iuridica et pastorali ita ut, quolibet sublato dubio circa fundamentum possibilitatem et concretam rationem postulationi obsecundandi, plane pateret opportunitas atque utilitas optatae transformationis Operis Dei in Praelaturam personalem.

Idcirco Nos de apostolicae plenitudine potestatis Nostrae, adsensi interea consilio, Nobis dato, Venerabilis Fratris Nostri S.R.E. Cardinalis Praefecti Sacrae Congregationis pro Episcopis ac suppleto, quatenus necessarium sit, eorum consensu quorum interest vel qui sua interesse existimaverint, haec quae sequuntur decernimus fierique volumus.

I.   Opus Dei in Praelaturam personalem ambitus internationalis erigitur sub nomine Sanctae Crucis et Operis Dei, breviato autem nomine Operis Dei. Simul vero erigitur Societas sacerdotalis Sanctae Crucis qua Adsociatio Clericorum Praelaturae intrinsecus coniuncta.

II.   Praelatura regitur normis iuris generalis et huius Constitutionis necnon propriis Statutis, quae "Codex iuris particuaris Operis Dei" nuncupantur.

III.   Praelaturae iurisdictio personalis afficit clericos incardinatos necnon, tantum quoad peculiarium obligationum adimpletionem quas ipsi sumpserunt vinculo iuridico, ope conventionis cum Praelatura initae, laicos qui operibus apostolicis Praelaturae sese dedicant, qui omnes ad operam pastoralem Praelaturae perficiendam sub auctoritate Praelati exstant iuxta praescripta articuli praecedentis.

IV. Praelaturae Operis Dei Ordinarius proprius est eius Praelatus cuius electio iuxta praescripta iuris generalis et particularis facta Romani Pontificis confirmatione eget.

V. Praelatura a Sacra Congregatione pro Episcopis dependet et pro rei diversitate quaestiones pertractabit cum ceteris Romanae Curiae Dicasteriis.

VI. Praelatus singulis quinquenniis per Sacram Congregationem pro Episcopis relationem Romano Pontifici exhibebit de Praelaturae statu deque modo quo eius apostolatus procedit.

VII. Praelaturae sedes gubernii centralis in Urbe posita est. In ecclesiam praelatitiam erigitur oratorium Sanctae Mariae de Pace apud sedem centralem Praelaturae.

Praeterea Reverendissimus Alvarus del Portillo, die XV mensis Septembris anno MCMLXXV Praeses Generalis Operis Dei rite electus, confirmatur atque nominatur Praelatus erectae Praelaturae personalis Sanctae Crucis et Operis Dei.

Denique ad haec omnia convenienter exsequenda destinamus Nos Venerabilem Fratrem Romulum Carboni, Archiepiscopum titulo Sidoniensem et in Italia Apostolicum Nuntium, dum necessarias ei atque opportunas tribuimus facultates, etiam subdelegandi ad effectum de quo agitur quemlibet virum in ecclesiastica dignitate constitutum, onere imposito ad Sacram Congregationem pro Episcopis quam primum remittendi verum exemplar actus ita impletae exsecutionis. Contrariis quibusvis rebus minime obstantibus.

Datum Romae, apud S. Petrum, die XXVIII mensis Novembris, anno MCMLXXXII, Pontificatus Nostri quinto.

AUGUSTINUS Card. CASAROLI +
a publicis Eccliesiae negotiis
Loco + Plumbi
In Secret. Status tab., n. 101486.

SEBASTIANUS Card. BAGGIO
S. Congr. pro Episc. Praeftctus
Iosephus Del Ton, *Proton. Apost.*
Marcellus Rossetti, *Proton. Apost.*
AAS 75 (1983) 423–425.

APPENDIX II.

CODEX IURIS PARTICULARIS OPERIS DEI

TITULUS I
DE PRAELATURAE NATURA
EIUSDEMQUE CHRISTIFIDELIBUS

CAPUT I
DE PRAELATURAE NATURA ET FINE

1. § 1. Opus Dei est Praelatura personalis clericos et laicos simul complectens, ad peculiarem operam pastoralem perficiendam sub regimine proprii Praelati (cfr. n. 125).

§ 2. Praelaturae presbyterium constituunt illi clerici qui ex eiusdem fidelibus laicis ad Ordines promoventur et eidem incardinantur; laicatus Praelaturae ab iis fidelibus efformatur qui, vocatione divina moti, vinculo juridico incorporationis speciali ratione Praelaturae devinciuntur.

§ 3. Praelatura, quae Sanctae Crucis et Operis Dei, breviato autem nomine Operis Dei nuncupatur, est ambitu internationalis, sedem suam centralem Romae habet atque regitur normis iuris universalis Praelaturarum personalium necnon horum Statutorum, et juxta Sanctae Sedis specialia praescripta vel indulta.

2. § 1. Praelatura sibi proponit suorum fidelium, iuxta normas iuris particularis, sanctificationem per exercitium in proprio cuiusque statu, professione ac vitae condicione virtutum christianarum, secundum specificam ipsius spiritualitatem, prorsus saecularem.

§ 2. Item Praelatura intendit totis viribus adlaborare ut personae omnium condicionum et statuum civilis societatis, et in primis quae intellectuales dicuntur, Christi Domini praeceptis integro corde adhaereant ipsaque, etiam ope sanctificationis proprii uniuscuiusque laboris professionalis, in praxim deducant, in medio mundo, ut omnia ad Voluntatem Creatoris ordinentur; atque viros ac mulieres informare ad apostolatum item in societate civili exercendum.

3. § 1. Media quae, ad hos fines supernaturales obtinendos, christifideles Praelaturae adhibent, haec sunt:

1. impensa vita spiritualis orationis et sacrificii, iuxta spiritum Operis Dei: ipsorum enim vocatio est essentialiter contemplativa, fundatur in humili ac sincero sensu filiationis divinae et subridenti ascetismo constanter sustinetur;

2. profunda ac continua institutio ascetica et doctrinalis religiosa, ad personalia cuiusque adiuncta accommodata atque in ecclesiastico Magisterio solide innixa, necnon constans studium adquirendi et perficiendi necessariam formationem professionalem propriamque animi culturam;

3. imitatio vitae absconditae Domini Nostri Iesu Christi in Nazareth, etiam in sanctificatione proprii laboris professionalis ordinarii, quem, exemplo et verbis, convertere satagunt in instrumentum apostolatus, unusquisque propriam attingens actionis sphaeram, prout sua cuiusque cultura et aptitudo expostulant, sciensque se esse debere tamquam fermentum in massa humanae societatis latens; item, seipsos sanctificent christifideles in perfecta adimpletione huius laboris, peracti quidem in constanti unione cum Deo; necnon per ipsum laborem alios sanctificent.

§ 2. Propterea omnes Praelaturae christifideles:

1. se obligant ad exercitium laboris professionalis vel alterius aequipollentis non derelinquendum, quia per ipsum sanctificationem et peculiarem apostolatum persequentur;

2. quam maxima fidelitate adimplere satagunt officia proprii status necnon actionem seu professionem socialem cuiusque propriam, summa semper cum reverentia pro legitimis societatis civilis legibus; itemque labores apostolicos perficiendos, a Praelato ipsis commissos.

4. § 1. Sub regimine Praelati, presbyterium suo ministerio sacerdotali universum Opus Dei vivificat atque informat.

§ 2. Sacerdotium ministeriale clericorum et commune sacerdotium laicorum intime coniunguntur atque se invicem requirunt et complent, ad exsequendum, in unitate vocationis et regiminis, finem quem Praelatura sibi proponit.

§ 3. In utraque pariter Operis Dei Sectione, virorum scilicet ac mulierum, eadem est unitas vocationis, spiritus, finis et regiminis, etsi unaquaeque Sectio proprios habeat apostolatus.

5. Praelatura tamquam Patronos habet Beatam Mariam semper Virginem, quam uti Matrem veneratur, et S. Ioseph, eiusdem Beatae Mariae Virginis Sponsum. Peculiari devotione christifideles prosequuntur SS. Archangelos Michaëlem, Gabrielem et Raphaëlem, atque SS. Apostolos Petrum, Paulum et Ioannem, quibus

universum Opus Dei eiusdemque singula actionis genera specialiter consecrantur.

CAPUT II
DE PRAELATURAE CHRISTIFIDELIBUS

6. Cuncti christifideles qui Praelaturae incorporantus, vinculo
iuridico de quo in n. 27, hoc faciunt eadem divina vocatione moti:
omnes eundem finem apostolicum prosequuntur, eundem spiritum
eandemque praxim asceticam colunt, congruam recipiunt doctrinalem institutionem et curam sacerdotalem atque, ad finem
Praelaturae quod attinet, subsunt potestati Praelati eiusque Consi-
liorum, iuxta normas iuris universalis et horum Statuorum.

7. § 1. Pro habituali cuiusque disponibilitate ad incumbendum
officiis formationis necnon aliquibus determinatis operis Dei
apostolatus inceptis, fideles Praelaturae, sive viri sive mulieres,
vocantur Numerarii, Aggregati vel supernumerarii, quin tamen
diversas classes efforment. Haec disponibilitas pendet ex diversis
uniuscuiusque permanentibus adiunctis personalibus, familiaribus,
professionalibus aliisve id genus.

§ 2. Quin Praelaturae fideles efficiantur, ipsi aggregari valent
associati Cooperatores, de quibus in n. 16.

8. § 1. Vocantur Numerarii illi clerici et laici qui, speciali motione
ac dono Dei coelibatum apostolicum servantes (cfr. *Matth.* XIX;
11), peculiaribus inceptis apostolatus Praelaturae totis viribus
maximaque adlaborandi personali disponibilitate incumbunt, et
ordinarie commorantur in sedibus Centrorum Operis Dei, ut illa
apostolatus incepta curent ceterorumque Praelaturae fidelium
institutioni se dedicent.

§ 2. Numerariae familiarem insuper administrationem seu
domesticam curam habent omnium Praelaturae Centrorum, in
loco tamen penitus separato commorantes.

9. Admitti possunt qua Numerarii ii omnes fideles laici qui plena
gaudeant disponibilitate ad incumbendum officiis formationis
atque laboribus apostolicis peculiaribus operis Dei, quique, cum
admissionem expostulant, ordinario praediti sint titulo academico
civili aut professionali aequipollenti, vel saltem post admissionem
illum obtinere valeant. Praeterea, in Sectione mulierum, Numerariae Auxiliares, eadem disponibilitate ac ceterae Numerariae, vitam suam praecipue deicant laboribus manualibus vel officiis
domesticis, quae tamquam proprium laborem professionalem
voluntarie suscipiunt, in sedibus Centrorum operis.

10. § 1. Vocantur Aggregati illi fideles laici qui vitam suam plene

Domino tradentes in coelibatu apostolico et iuxta spiritum Operis Dei, curam tamen impendere debent in suas concretas ac permanentes necessitates personales, familiares vel professionales, quae eos ordinarie ducunt ad commorandum cum propria ipsorum familia. Haec omnia determinant simul eorum dedicationem aliquibus officiis apostolatus vel formationis Operis Dei perficiendis.

§ 2. Aggregati, nisi aliud pro eis specialiter caveatur, omnia officia seu obligationes suscipiunt ac Numerarii, et ipsorum identicis mediis asceticis ad assequendam sanctitatem et apostolatum exercendum uti debent.

11. § 1. Vocantur Supernumerarii ii omnes fideles laici, coelibes et etiam coniugati, qui, eadem vocatione divina ac Numerani et Aggregati, peculiarem apostolatum Operis Dei plene participant, ea quidem disponibilitate quoad incepta apostolica, quae sit compatibilis cum adimpletione suarum obligationum familiarium, professionalium ac socialium; quique non solum suam vitam suamque professionem convertunt, sicut et ceteri alii Praelaturae christifideles, in medium sanctificationis et apostolatus, verum etiam, non aliter ac Aggregati, propriam domum propriasque familiares occupationes.

§ 2. Supernumerarii de eodem spiritu vivunt, et pro viribus easdem servant consuetudines ac Numerarii et Aggregati.

12. Inter Aggregatos et Supernumerarios recipi valent etiam chronica aliqua infirmitate laborantes.

13. Numerarii specialiter dicati muneribus regiminis vel formationis residere debent in sede Centrorum quae ad hunc finem destinantur.

14. § 1. Candidatus qui litteras scripserit expostulando admissionem in Opus Dei qua Numerarius vel Aggregatus, cum ipsi ordinarie per competentem Directorem significetur suam petitionem dignam, quae examinetur, habitam fuisse, eo ipso inter Supernumerarios admissus manet, quoadusque eidem concedatur admissio quam exoravit.

§ 2. Si quis ante incorporationem ut Numerarius vel Aggregatus videtur ad hoc idoneitate carere, potest in Opere Dei retineri qua Supernumerarius, modo requisitas condiciones habeat.

15. Possunt Supernumerarii inter Numerarios vel Aggregatos recipi, modo tamen requisitis polleant qualitatibus.

16. § I. Cooperatores, assiduis precibus ad Deum effusis, eleemosynis, et quatenus possibile etiam proprio labore, collaborationem praestant operibus apostolicis et bona spiritualia Operis Dei participant.

§ 2. Sunt etiam qui a domo paterna diversimode longe absunt vel veritatem catholicam non profitentur, qui attamen adiumentum Operi Dei proprio labore aut eleemosynis praestant. Hi iure meritoque Operis Dei Cooperatores nuncupari quoque possunt. Cuncti Praelaturae fideles, oratione, sacrificio, conversatione, ita cum his Cooperatoribus laborare debent ut, Beatissima Virgine intercedente, a misericordia divina indeficiens lumen fidei pro ipsis consequantur, eosque ad christianos mores suaviter et efficaciter trahant.

CAPUT III
DE FIDELIUM ADMISSIONE ET INCORPORATIONE
IN PRAELATURAM

17. Adscriptio tres gradus comprehendit: simplicis Admissionis, quam facit Vicarius Regionalis, audita sua Commissione; incorporationis temporaneae, quae Oblatio dicitur, post annum saltem ab Admissione; incorporationis definitivae seu Fidelitatis, post quinquennium saltem ab incorporatione temporanea transactum.

18. Admissionem postulare valet, habita quidem Directoris localis licentia, quilibet laicus catholicus qui, praeter aetatem et alias qualitates requisitas, de quibus in n. 20, recta intentione moveatur ex vocatione divina ad enixe prosequendam suam sanctificationem, mediante proprio labore vel professione, quin ideo mutet suum statum canonicum, velitque totis viribus incumbere apostolatui exercendo, iuxta fines ac media Operis Dei propria, et ad eiusdem onera ferenda eiusdemque peculiares labores exercendos sit idoneus.

19. Candidatus expostulare tenetur suam admissionem mediantibus litteris ad competentem Praelaturae Ordinarium inscribendis, in quibus manifestet suum desiderium ad Opus Dei pertinendi qua Numerarius Aggregatus vel Supernumerarius.

20. § 1. Ut quis possit ad Praelaturam admitti requiritur:

1. ut aetatem saltem decem et septem annorum compleverit;

2. ut in sanctificationem personalem incumbat, enixe colendo virtutes christianas, iuxta spiritum et praxim asceticam quae Operis Dei sunt propria;

3. ut vitae spirituali prospiciat, per frequentem receptionem Sacramentorum SS. Eucharisti et Paenitentiae et per exercitium orationis mentalis quotidianae aliarumque normarum pietatis Operis Dei;

4. ut antea in apostolatu peculiari Operis Dei, per

dimidium saltem annum, sub ductu auctoritatis competentis sese exercuerit; nihil obstat quominus candidatus iam prius per aliquot tempus ut adspirans habeatur, quin tamen ad Praelaturam adhuc pertineat;

§ 5. ut ceteris qualitatibus personalibus sit praeditus, quibus experimentum praebeat se recepisse vocationem ad Opus Dei.

§ 2. Ab Opere Dei arcentur qui alicuius Instituti religiosi vel Societatis vitae communis fuerit sodalis, novitius, postulans vel alumnus scholae apostolicae; et qui in aliquo Instituto saeculari qua probandus degerit vel admissionem expostulaverit.

§ 3. Praeterea, ne dioeceses priventur propriis vocationibus sacerdotalibus, ad Praelaturam non admittuntur alumni Seminariorum, sive laici sive clerici, neque sacerdotes alicui dioecesi incardinati.

21. Candidati, ex quo admissionem expostulent eisque significetur suam petitionem dignam, quae examinetur, habitam esse ad normam n. 14. § I, ius habent recipiendi congrua formationis media necnon curam ministerialem sacerdotum Praelaturae.

22. Edocendus est candidatus, antequam admittatur, spiritum Operis Dei exigere ut unusquisque vitam agat impensi laboris, utque, mediante exercitio propriae professionis vel actuositatis, sibi procuret media oeconomica: ea nempe quae sunt necessaria non solum ad suipsius et, si res id ferat, suae familiae sustentationem, sed etiam ad contribuendum generose et iuxta propria personalia adiuncta operibus apostolicis sustinendis.

23. Incorporatio, tum temporanea tum definitiva, requirit praeter liberam et expressam candidati voluntatem, opportunam concessionem Vicarii Regionalis cum voto deliberativo sui Consilii; si vero de incorporatione definitiva agatur, necessaria est insuper Praelati confirmatio.

24. § 1. Cuncti Praelaturae fideles necessarias assumere debent assecurationes seu cautiones, quas civiles leges pro casibus defectus vel impossibilitatis laboris, infirmitatis, senectutis, etc., praevident.

§ 2. Quoties, attentis adiunctis, id requiratur, Praelaturae officium est subveniendi necessitatibus materialibus Numerariorum et Aggregatorum.

§ 3. Fidelium, de quibus in paragrapho praecedenti, parentibus forte indigentibus, Praelatura, qua par est caritate et generositate providet, quin ex hoc iuridica quaelibet obligatio umquam oriri possit.

25. Incorporatio temporanea singulis annis ab unoquoque fideli singillatim renovatur. Ad hanc renovationem requiritur et sufficit licentia Vicarii Regionalis, qui, in casu dubii, suam Commissionem

et Directorem localem cum eius Consilio audire potest. Si nullum dubium subsit circa Vicarii renovationi contrariam voluntatem, et nihil ex parte Directoris obsit, licentia iure praesumitur et incorporatio temporanea renovari potest; iure item praesumitur renovationem tacite factam fuisse si fidelis prius non manifestaverit suam voluntatem renovationi contrariam; ipsa vero renovatio subiicitur condicioni resolutivae si Vicarius de ea certior factus, una cum Defensore et audita sua Commissione, contradicat.

26. Quando aliquis Supernumerarius devenerit Aggregatus aut Numerarius, potest totaliter vel partialiter dispensari circa tempus requisitum pro nova incorporatione temporanea vel definitiva, sed a speciali formatione nullatenus dispensatur.

27. § 1. Pro incorporatione temporanea vel definitiva alicuius christifidelis, fiat a Praelatura et ab eo cuius intersit formalis declaratio coram duobus testibus circa mutua officia et iura.

§ 2. Praelatura, quae in casu ab eo repraesentatur, quem Vicarius respectivae circumscriptionis designaverit, a momento incorporationis eiusdem christifidelis eaque perdurante, se obligabit:

1. ad praebendam eidem christifideli assiduam institutionem doctrinalem religiosam, spiritualem, asceticam et apostolicam, necnon peculiarem curam pastoralem ex parte sacerdotum Praelaturae;

2. ad adimplendas ceteras obligationes quae, erga eiusdem christifideles, in normis Praelaturam regentibus statuuntur.

§ 3. Christifidelis vero suum firmum propositum manifestabit se totis viribus dicandi ad sanctitatem prosequendam atque ad exercendum apostolatum iuxta spiritum et praxim Operis Dei, seque obligabit, a momento incorporationis eaque perdurante:

1. ad manendum sub iurisdictione Praelati aliarumque Praelaturae competentium auctoritatum, ut fideliter sese impendat in iis omnibus quae ad finem peculiarem Praelaturae attinent;

2. ad adimplenda omnia officia quae secum fert condicio Numerani vel Aggregati vel Supernumerani Operis Dei atque ad servandas normas Praelaturam regentes necnon legitimas praescriptiones Praelati aliarumque competentium auctoritatum Praelaturae quoad eius regimen, spiritum et apostolatum.

§ 4. Quod attinet ad Praelaturae fideles, potest Ordinarius Praelaturae, iusta de causa, vota privata itemque iusiurandum promissorium dispensare, dummodo dispensatio ne laedat ius aliis quaesitum. Potest quoque, quoad eosdem fideles, adscriptionem alicui tertio Ordini suspendere, ita tamen ut ipsa reviviscat si, qualibet de causa, vinculum cum Praelatura cesset.

CAPUT IV
DE FIDELIUM DISGESSU ET DIMISSIONE
A PRAELATURA

28. § 1. Antequam aliquis temporaliter Praelaturae incorporetur, potest quovis momento libere ipsam deserere.

§ 2. Pariter auctoritas competens, ob iustas et rationabiles causas, valet eum non admittere, aut ei discedendi consilium dare. Hae causae praesertim sunt defectus spiritus proprii Operis Dei et aptitudinis ad apostolatum peculiarem fidelium Praelaturae.

29. Perdurante incorporatione temporanea vel iam facta definitiva, ut quis possit Praelaturam voluntarie relinquere, indiget dispensatione, quam unus Praelatus concedere potest, audito proprio Consilio et Commissione Regionali.

30. § 1. Fideles temporarie vel definitive Praelaturae incorporati nequeunt dimitti nisi ob graves causas, quae, si agatur de incorporatione definitiva, semper ex culpa eiusdem fidelis procedere debent.

§ 2. Infirma valetudo non est causa dimissionis, nisi certo constet eam, ante incorporationem temporaneam, fuisse dolose reticitam aut dissimulatam.

31. Dimissio, si opus sit, fiat maxima caritate: antea tamen suadendus est is cuius interest ut sponte discedat.

32. Dimissio a Praelato vel, in sua circumscriptione, a Vicario, semper cum voto deliberativo proprii Consilii, est decernenda, causis ei cuius interest manifestatis dataque eidem plena respondendi licentia, et post binas monitiones incassum factas, salvo semper iure fidelium ad Praelatum vel ad Sanctam Sedem recurrendi. Si recursus interpositus fuerit intra decem dies, effectus iuridicus dimissionis suspenditur donec responsio a Praelato vel, in casu, a Sancta Sede prodierit.

33. Exitus legitimus ab Opere Dei secum fert cessationem vinculi, de quo in n. 27, necnon officiorum atque iurium, quae ex ipso profluunt.

34. Qui qualibet ratione Praelaturae valedicat vel ab ea dimittatur, nihil ab ea exigere potest ob servitia eidem praestita, vel ob id quod, sive industria sive exercitio propriae professionis, sive quocumque alio titulo vel modo, eidem rependerit.

35. Clericus Praelaturae incardinatus, ad normam n. 36, nequit ipsam deserere donec Episcopum invenerit, qui eum in propria dioecesi recipiat. Quodsi non invento Episcopo exierit, nequit interim suos Ordines exercere, donec Sancta Sedes aliter providerit.

TITULUS II
DE PRAELATURAE PRESBYTERIO DEQUE
SOCIETATE SACERDOTALI SANCTAE CRUCIS

CAPUT I
DE COMPOSITIONE PRESBYTERII
ET SOCIETATIS SACERDOTALIS SANCTAE CRUCIS

36. § 1. Praelaturae presbyterium ab illis clericis constituitur, qui, ad sacros Ordines a Praelato promoti ad normam nn. 44–51, Praelaturae incardinantur eiusque servitio devoventur.

§ 2. Hi sacerdotes, ex ipso suae ordinationis facto, fiunt socii Numerarii vel, iuxta infra dicenda (n. 37, 2), Coadiutores Societatis Sacerdotalis Sanctae Crucis, quae est Associatio clericalis Praelaturae propria ac intrinseca, unde cum ea aliquid unum constituit et ab ea seiungi non potest.

§ 3. Praelatus Operis Dei est Praeses Generalis Societatis Sacerdotalis Sanctae Crucis.

37. § 1. Ut quis sacros Ordines recipere valeat in servitium Praelaturae, requiritur ut sit eidem definitive incorporatus qua Numerarius vel Aggregatus, atque ut periodum formationis compleverit, quam omnes laici Numerarii, necnon Aggregati illi qui ad sacerdotium destinantur perficere tenentur, ita ut nemini immediate in Praelatura qua sacerdos Numerarius vel respective Aggregatus Operis Dei incardinari liceat.

§ 2. Quo aptius a sociis Aggregatis Societatis Sacerdotalis Sanctae Crucis, de quibus in nn. 58 et sequentibus, iure distinguantur, Aggregati laici Operis Dei, qui sacerdotium in servitium Praelaturae suscipiunt, in Societate ipsa Coadiutores seu simpliciter sacerdotes Aggregati Operis Dei vocantur.

38. Hi sacerdotes operam suam prae primis navabunt formationi spirituali . et ecclesiasticae atque peculiari curae animarum ceterorum fidelium utriusque Sectionis Operis Dei.

39. Sacerdotes Operis Dei cum aliis quoque fidelibus ministeria Ordinis sacerdotalis propria exercebunt, semper quidem habitis licentiis ministerialibus ad normam iuris.

40. Si, ratione officii ecciesiastici vel personalis competentiae, hi sacerdotes ad Consilium presbyterale aliaque organa dioecesana invitantur, pro posse participare debent, praehabita tamen licentia Praelati Operis Dei vel eius Vicarii.

41. In cunctis dioecesibus in quibus suum ministerium exercent, hi sacerdotes apostolicae caritatis nexibus coniunguntur cum ceteris sacerdotibus presbyterii uniuscuiusque dioecesis.

42. Praeter clericos de quibus in nn. 36 et 37, ipsi Societati Sacerdotali Sanctae Crucis adscribi etiam valent, ad normam n. 58, tam socii Aggregati quam socii Supernumerarii, quin tamen inter Praelaturae clericos adnumerentur, nam unusquisque pertinere perget ad suum presbyterium dioecesanum, sub iurisdictione unius respectivi Episcopi.

43. Societati Sacerdotali Sanctae Crucis adnumerari etiam possunt, ut associati Cooperatores, alii clerici alicui dioecesi incardinati, qui Societati adiumentum praestant oratione, eleemosynis et, si fieri possit, etiam proprio cuiusque ministerio sacerdotali.

CAPUT II

DE PROMOTIONE AD SACROS ORDINES
ET DE PRESBYTERORUM MISSIONE CANONICA

44. Illi tantum Numerarii et Aggregati Operis Dei ad sacros Ordines promoveantur, quos Praelatus vocatione ad sacerdotium ministeriale praeditos noverit et Operi Dei eiusque ministerus necessarios vel congruentes iudicaverit. Qui autem Ordines appetere exoptant, desiderium suum Praelato exponere possunt, sed eius decisioni acquiescere debent.

45. Ut quis Numerarius vel Aggregatus ad Ordines promoveri valeat, praeter carentiam irregularitatum aliorumque impedimentorum, de quibus in iure universali, requiritur—servato quoque praescripto n. 37—ut sit speciali aptitudine ornatus ad munera sacerdotalia prout in Praelatura exercenda sunt, et sit saltem viginti quinque annos natus antequam presbyteratum recipiat.

46. Ad formationem quod attinet candidatorum ad sacerdotium, accurate serventur normae iuris universalis et proprii Praelaturae.

47. Adscriptio inter candidatos per liturgicum admissionis ritum, ministeriorum collatio necnon promotio ad sacros Ordines Praelato reservantur, post praeviam uniuscuiusque candidati declarationem propria manu exaratam et subscriptam, qua testificetur se sponte ac libere sacros Ordines suscepturum atque se ministerio ecclesiastico perpetuo mancipaturum esse, insimul petens ut ad Ordinem recipiendum admittatur.

48. Litteras dimissorias pro ordinatione dat Praelatus Operis Dei, qui potest promovendos ab interstitus necnon a defectu aetatis his in Statutis requisitae dispensare, non tamen ultra annum.

49. Qui ad sacros Ordines vocantur, non modo requisita a canonibus praescripta habere debent, praesertim specialem in disciplinis ecclesiasticis cognitionem, verum etiam emineant pietate, vitae integritate, animarum zelo, erga SS. Eucharistiam fervido amore, ac desiderio imitandi quod quotidie tractare debent.

50. § 1. Cum sacros Ordines recipiunt, clerici ad nutum Praelati manent quoad primam et ulteriores destinationes ad unam vel aliam Operis Dei circumscriptionem.

§ 2. Missio canonica sacerdotibus confertur a Praelato, per se vel per respectivos Vicarios circumscriptionum, semper quidem iuxta normas a Praelato statutas, ipsis concedendo opportunas licentias ministeriales, Sacrum nempe litandi, Verbum Dei praedicandi atque confessiones excipiendi.

§ 3. Haec facultas audiendi confessiones, quae ab Ordinario Praelaturae presbyteris quibuslibet conferri potest, extenditur ad omnes fideles Praelaturae atque Societatis Sacerdotalis Sanctae Crucis socios secundum tenorem ipsius concessionis, necnon ad illos omnes qui in Centris Operis Dei diu noctuque degunt.

51. § 1. Sacerdotes presbyterii Praelaturae munia et officia ecclesiastica quaelibet, etsi cum propria condicione et munere pastorali in Praelatura compatibilia, absque Praelati Operis Dei expressa venia admittere non valent.

§ 2. Non tamen ipsis prohibetur exercere actuositatem professionalem sacerdotali characteri, ad normam iuris Sanctaeque Sedis praescriptorum atque instructionum, non oppositam.

52. Sacerdotum Praelaturae ius est et officium, cum periculum mortis immineat, infirmis Numerariis Sacramenta ministrare, quod etiam facere possunt Aggregatis necnon omnibus in Centris Operis Dei versantibus. Agonia autem superveniente, commendatio animae fiat, adstantibus, quoad fieri possit, omnibus fidelibus Centro adscriptis, et orantibus ut Deus infirmum soletur, ei festivus occurrat eumque in Paradisum perducat.

53. Iusta funebria tam pro Numerariis quam pro Aggregatis et Supernumerariis ex regula in paroecia, ad normam iuris, persolvantur. Celebrari autem possunt per exceptionem in sede alicuius Centri, saltem quando ipsum habeat ecclesiam adnexam, vel agatur de Centro maiore.

54. Post receptam sacram Ordinationem, sacerdotes periodice frequentabunt cursus theoreticos et practicos de re pastorali, collationes, conferentias aliaque id genus, atque statuta examina post presbyteratum et pro licentiarum ministerialium prorogatione subibunt, iuxta normas a Praelato determinatas.

55. Praelato officium est providendi, mediantibus opportunis normis, honestae sustentationi clericorum qui sacros Ordines receperint in servitium Praelaturae, necnon congruae eorum assistentiae in casibus infirmae valetudinis, invaliditatis et senectutis.

56. Praelatus eiusque Vicarii fovere enitantur in omnibus Praelaturae sacerdotibus fervidum spiritum communionis cum ceteris sacerdotibus Ecclesiarum localium, in quibus ipsi suum exercent ministerium.

CAPUT III
DE SOCIIS AGGREGATIS ET SUPERNUMERARIIS
SOCIETATIS SACERDOTALIS SANCTAE CRUCIS

57. Societas Sacerdotalis Sanctae Crucis, de qua in n. 36, constituitur in Associationem, quo melius suum sanctificationis sacerdotalis finem etiam inter clericos ad Praelaturam non pertinentes prosequatur iuxta spiritum et praxim asceticam Operis Dei.

58. § 1. Socii Aggregati ac Supernumerarii Societatis Sacerdotalis Sanctae Crucis, qui quidem membra non efficiuntur cleri Praelaturae, sed ad suum cuiusque presbyterium pertinent, sunt sacerdotes vel saltem diaconi alicui dioecesi incardinati, qui Domino in Societate Sacerdotali Sanctae Crucis iuxta spiritum Operis Dei, peculiari superaddita vocatione, sese dicare volunt, ad sanctitatem nempe in exercitio sui ministerii pro viribus prosequendam, quin tamen eorum dioecesana condicio plenaque proprio uniuscuiusque Ordinario subiectio quoquo modo ex hac dedicatione afficiantur, sed contra, iuxta infra dicenda, diversis respectibus confirmentur.

§ 2. In Societate Sacerdotali Sanctae Crucis non sunt Superiores interni pro Aggregatis et Supernumerariis, quapropter, cum ipsi oboedire tantum debeant proprio loci Ordinario, ad normam iuris, nulla omnino exsurgit quaestio de duplici oboedientia: nulla enim viget oboedientia interna, sed solummodo normalis illa disciplina in qualibet Societate exsistens, quae provenit ex obligatione colendi ac servandi proprias ordinationes; quae ordinationes, hoc in casu, ad vitam spiritualem exclusive referuntur.

59. § 1. Qui admitti volunt, eminere debent in amore dioeceseos, oboedientia ac veneratione erga Episcopum, pietate, recta in scientus sacris institutione, zelo animarum, spiritu sacrificii, studio vocationes promovendi, et desiderio adimplendi cum maxima perfectione officia ministerialia.

§ 2. Pro incorporatione in Societatem Sacerdotalem Sanctae Crucis nullus viget limes maximus aetatis, et admitti quoque possunt clerici chronica aliqua infirmitate laborantes.

60. § 1. Alumni Seminariorum nondum diaconi non possunt in Societatem recipi. Si vocationem persentiunt antequam ordinentur, ut Adspirantes haberi et admitti valent.

§ 2. Iure etiam a Societate arcentur qui alicuius Instituti religiosi vel Societatis vitae communis fuerit sodalis, novitius, postulans vel alumnus scholae apostolicae; et qui in aliquo Instituto sæculari qua probandus degerit vel admissionem expostulaverit.

61. Ut quis qua Aggregatus admittatur, divina vocatio requiritur sec um ferens totalem et habitualem disponibilitatem ad sanctitatem quaerendam iuxta spiritum Operis Dei, qui exigit:

1. imprimis studium perfecte adimplendi munus pastorale a proprio Episcopo concreditum, sciente unoquoque se soli Ordinario loci rationem reddere debere de huiusmodi muneris adimpletione;

2. propositum dedicandi totum tempus totumque laborem ad apostolatum, spiritualiter praesertim adiuvando confratres sacerdotes dioecesanos.

62. Ut quis recipi possit qua Supernumerarius, eadem vocatio divina requiritur ac pro Aggregatis, necnon plena disponibilitas ad sanctitatem quaerendam iuxta spiritum Operis Dei, licet Supernumerarii, propter suas condiciones personales, familiares aliasque id genus, habitualiter in activitatem apostolicam incumbere non valent totaliter et immediate.

63. Admissio petitur litteris ad Praesidem Generalem inscriptis, in quibus candidatus manifestet suum desiderium sese incorporandi Societati Sacerdotali Sanctae Crucis qua socius Aggregatus vel Supernumerarius.

64. Pro admissione ac incorporatione clericorum inter Aggregatos vel Supernumerarios Societatis Sacerdotalis Sanctae Crucis, eaedem normae et agendi ratio servari debent, quae pro admissione et incorporatione Aggregatorum et Supernumerariorum Operis Dei praescribuntur, etiam relate ad tempus peculiaris formationis spiritualis et ad media quae candidatis praebentur, ut eorum spiritualis vita alatur.

65. Qui admissionem qua Supernumerarii expostulaverint, possunt postea inter Aggregatos recipi, modo tamen requisitis polleant qualitatibus.

66. Si quis ante incorporationem ut Aggregatus videtur necessaria disponibilitate carere, potest retineri qua Supernumerarius, modo requisitas condiciones habeat.

67. Quoad egressum et dimissionem, eadem vigent ac tenenda sunt, congrua congruis referendo, quae pro egressu et dimissione Aggregatorum ac Supernumerariorum Operis Dei statuuntur.

68. Praeter finem Operis Dei, quem hi socii in propria condicione suum faciunt, hunc ut peculiarem propriumque vindicant, scilicet: sanctitatem sacerdotalem atque sensum plenae deditionis ac subiectionis Hierarchiae ecclesiasticae in clero dioecesano impense promovere; et inter sacerdotes cleri dioecesani vitam communem fovere, prout Ordinario loci expedire videatur.

69. Spiritus quo Aggregati et Supernumerarii Societatis Sacerdotalis Sanctae Crucis informari in omnibus debent, his praeprimis continetur:

1. nihil sine Episcopo agere, quod quidem complecti debet omnem ipsorum vitam sacerdotalem atque animarum ministeria;

2. propriam condicionem dioecesanam non derelinquere, sed contra, ipsam maiore semper Dei amore exercere;

3. maxima quidem semper et ubique naturalitate inter confratres sacerdotes se gerant, et nullo modo secretos sese exhibeant, cum nihil in ipsis inveniri debeat quod ita celari oporteat;

4. a confratribus sacerdotibus nullo modo distingui velint, sed totis viribus uniri cum ipsis nitantur;

5. cum ceteris membris presbyterii cuiusque proprii ita fraterna caritate pleni sint, ut quamlibet prorsus divisionum umbram vitent, specialibus apostolicae caritatis et fraternitatis nexibus coniungantur, et inter omnes omnino sacerdotes maximam unionem studeant.

70. Aggregati et Supernumerarii Societatis Sacerdotalis Sanctae Crucis, praeter clericorum obligationes in iure universali statutas aliasque quas pro omnibus suis sacerdotibus singuli Episcopi praescribere possint, pietatis officia colunt praxis asceticae Operis Dei propria; cursus vero recessus spiritualis ipsi peragere debent cum ceteris suae dioecesis sacerdotibus, loco et modo ab Ordinario proprio determinatis.

71. Sacerdotes Aggregati et Supernumerarii ad christianas virtutes tam theologales quam cardinales specialiter colendas dicantur, unusquisque in proprio labore et munere pastorali, a suo cuiusque Episcopo sibi concredito.

72. Spiritus Operis Dei fovet, in Aggregatis et Supernumerariis Societatis Sacerdotalis Sanctae Crucis, necessitatem ardenter obsecundandi atque ad effectum deducendi directionem spiritualem collectivam, quam Episcopus dioecesanus suis sacerdotibus impertit litteris pastoralibus, allocutionibus, provisionibus disciplinaribus alisque mediis. Hunc sane in finem, et sine ulla umquam interferentia cum indicationibus dioecesanis vel cum temporibus ad eas adimplendas praescriptis, Societas Sacerdotalis

Sanctae Crucis Aggregatis et Supernumerariis praebet peculiaria media formationis, quorum praecipua sunt sequentia:

1. periodicae collationes, in quibus directio spiritualis personalis recipitur, et studiorum Circuli, quibus praesunt Zelatores ad spiritum sociorum fovendum: quae quidem omnia ita ordinari debent, quoad durationis tempus, absentiam e propria dioecesi diebus festis, aliaque similia, ut sacerdotes omnes eisdem assistentes praeprimis muneribus in dioecesi sibi commissis commode satisfacere valeant;

2. alia omnia media, industriae, instrumenta ascetica piaeque praxes Operis Dei;

3. expolitio atque opportuna, prout in Domino videatur, intensio et ampliatio culturae et formationis scientificae, quatenus ipsae sunt medium ad ministerium exercendum.

73. § 1. Absolute accurateque vitanda est in dioecesi, quoad Aggregatos et Supernumerarios, vel umbra specialis hierarchiae Societatis propriae; quod enim unice quaeritur, hoc esse debet: perfectio vitae sacerdotalis ex diligenti fidelitate vitae interiori, ex tenaci constantique studio formationis, atque ex mente, criterio et ardore apostolicis, quin hi clerici ullo modo subsint potestati regiminis Praelati Operis Dei eiusque Vicariorum.

§ 2. Ad Aggregatos et Supernumerarios Regionis adiuvandos, Vicarius Regionalis utitur ministerio Sacerdotis Rerum Spiritualium Praefecti, quocum collaborant in unaquaque dioecesi Admonitor et Director spiritualis cum propriis ipsorum substitutis.

74. Pro illis omnibus cum Episcopo locive Ordinario tractandis vel expediendis, quae ad Aggregatos et Supernumerarios in propria uniuscuiusque dioecesi spectant, Societas ex regula Admonitore eiusve substituto utitur, nisi Vicarius Regionalis, vel ipse directo, vel per specialem suum delegatum aliqua negotia agere seu expedire maluerit.

75. § 1. Vicarius Regionalis sacerdotes Admonitores, Directores spirituales eorumque substitutos ad quinquennium designat.

§ 2. Haec munera quamlibet potestatis regiminis formam seu speciem vitare prorsus debent.

§ 3. Designationes factas quantocius opportune Episcopo dioecesano locive Ordinario communicare Vicarius Regionalis satagat.

76. Sacerdotes Aggregati et Supernumerarii Societatis Sacerdotalis Sanctae Crucis in Coetibus componuntur ac ordinantur, qui specialibus Centris personalibus adscribuntur. Unum idemque Centrum diversos huiusmodi Coetus adscriptos, etiam per varias dioeceses, prout magis expedire videatur, distributos, habere valet.

77. Societas nullam peculiarem oeconomicam administrationem habere debet. Ipsa ordinaria fidelium Operis Dei administratione, si qua egeat, utitur.

78. In illis quae hic expresse praescripta non sunt, congrua congruis referendo et dummodo condicioni sacerdotali conveniant, ea omnia sacerdotibus Aggregatis ac Supernumerariis applicantur, quae pro Aggregatis et Supernumerariis Operis Dei ordinata sunt, eorumque bona spiritualia et facultates ipsi participant.

TITULUS III
DE VITA, INSTITUTIONE ET APOSTOLATU FIDELIUM PRAELATURAE

CAPUT I
DE VITA SPIRITUALI

79. § 1. Spiritus et praxis ascetica propria Praelaturae specificos characteres habent, plene determinatos, ad finem proprium prosequendum. Unde spiritus Operis Dei aspectus duplex, asceticus et apostolicus, ita sibi adaequate respondet, ac cum charactere saeculari Operis Dei intrinsece et harmonice fusus ac compenetratus est, ut solidam ac simplicem vitae—asceticae, apostolicae, socialis et professionalis—unitatem necessario secum ferre ac inducere semper debeat.

§ 2. Ut exigentiae asceticae et apostolicae sacerdotii communis et, pro clericis, sacerdotii ministerialis iuxta spiritum Operis Dei in praxim serio et continuo deducantur, utque ita Praelaturae fideles efficax fermentum sanctitatis et apostolatus inter ceteros clericos et laicos saeculares esse possint, intensa vita orationis et sacrificii praeprimis ab omnibus requiritur, iuxta pietatis officia hoc in Codice statuta ceteraque ad traditionem Operis Dei pertinentia.

80. § 1. Fundamentum solidum, quo omnia in Opere Dei constant, radixque fecunda singula vivificans, est sensus humilis ac sincerus filiationis divinae in Christo Iesu, ex quo dulciter creditur caritati paternae quam habet Deus in nobis; et Christus Dominus, Deus homo, ut frater primogenitus ineffabili sua bonitate sentitur a Praelaturae fidelibus, qui Spiritus Sancti gratia Iesum imitari conantur,in memoriam praesertim revocantes mirum exemplum et fecunditatem operosae eius vitae in Nazareth.

§ 2. Hac ratione, in vita fidelium Praelaturae, qui sicut ceteri clerici saeculares et laici, sibi aequales, in omnibus se gerunt, nascitur necessitas et veluti instinctus supernaturalis omnia purificandi, elevandi ad ordinem gratiae, sanctificandi et convertendi in occasionem personalis unionis cum Deo, cuius Voluntas adimpletur, et in instrumentum apostolatus.

81. § 1. Vitae spiritualis fidelium Praelaturae radix ac centrum Sacrosanctum Missae est Sacrificium, quo Passio et Mors Christi Iesu incruente renovatur et memoria recolitur infiniti eius amoris salvifici erga universos homines.

§ 2. Omnes proinde sacerdotes Sacrosanctum Missae Sacrificium quotidie celebrent eique cuncti laici devotissime assistant, Corporis Christi Dapem sacramentaliter vel spiritualiter saltem participantes. Praeterea Christum in SS. Sacramento alio diei tempore visitent.

82. Exemplum imitantes Apostolorum, qui erant perseverantes unanimiter in oratione, atque communitatum primaevorum christianorum Praelaturae fideles, dum ordinariis vitae ac laboris quotidiani vicissitudinibus se dedicant, continuam suae animae contemplativae unionem et conversationem cum Deo curare debent. Ad hunc finem necessario custodiendum ac fovendum:

1. singulis diebus, mane, post oblationem suorum operum Deo factam, orationi mentali spatio semihorae vacabunt; vespere autem aliam semihoram orationi dedicabunt. Praeterea lectioni Novi Testamenti et alterius libri spiritualis per aliquot temporis spatium vacent, et Preces communes Operis Dei recitent;

2. singulis mensibus spirituali recessui unam dedicent diem;

3. singulis annis longiori per aliquot dies recessui spirituali vacent;

4. semper et ubique recolant Dei praesentiam; meminerint filiationis divinae; communiones spirituales iterent; item gratiarum actiones, actus expiationis, orationes iaculatorias; foveant impensius mortificationem, studium, laborem, ordinem, gaudium.

83. § 1. Ut insidiac vincantur triplicis concupiscentiae, superbiae vitae speciatim, quae ex doctrina, ex condicione sociali et ex professionalibus laboribus ali posset, ascetismi christiani exigentiae a Praelaturae fidelibus firmiter et impense colendae sunt. Hic ascetismus nititur fideli ac perpetuo sensu humilitatis externae et intrinsecae, non tantum individualis sed etiam collectivae; candore connaturalis simplicitatis; familiari et nobili agendi ratione; expressione iugis serenae laetitiae, labore, sui abnegatione, sobrietate, actibus sacrificii atque statutis exercitus mortificationis etiam corporalis singulis diebus et hebdomadis peragendis, iuxta uniuscuiusque aetatem et condicionem. Haec omnia curantur ut media non solum purificationis personalis, sed praeterea veri ac solidi progressus spiritualis, iuxta illud bene probatum et comprobatum verbum: "tantum proficies quantum tibi ipsi vim intuleris." Curantur etiam ut necessaria praeparatio ad omnem apostolatum in societate peragendum eiusque perfectum exercitium: "adimpleo ea quae desunt passionum Christi in carne mea pro corpore eius, quod est Ecclesia" (Col. I, 24).

§ 2. Hic ascetismus et spiritus paenitentiae alias quoque exigentias in vita fidelium Praelaturae secum fert, praesertim quotidianam conscientiae discussionem, directionem spiritualem et praxim hebdomadariam confessionis sacramentalis.

84. § 1. Ament Praelaturae fideles et diligentissime custodiant castitatem, quae homines Christo eiusque castissimae Matri reddit gratissimos, pro certo habentes operam apostolatus castitate suffultam esse debere.

§ 2. Ad praesidium huius thesauri, qui vasis fertur fictilibus, summopere conferunt fuga occasionum, modestia, temperantia, corporis castigatio, SS. Eucharistiae frequens receptio, ad Virginem Matrem adsiduus ac filialis recursus.

85. Tenero amore et devotione Beatissimam Virginem Mariam, Domini Iesu Christi Matrem et nostram, Praelaturae fideles colant. Quotidie quindecim mysteria marialis Rosarii contemplentur, quinque saltem mysteria vocaliter recitantes, vel, iis in locis in quibus pia haec praxis usualis non sit, aliam aequipollentem marialem precationem pro hac recitatione substituentes. Ipsam Deiparam, uti mos est, salutatione Angelus Domini vel antiphona Regina coeli filiali devotione honorare ne omittant; et die sabbato mortificationem aliquam faciant, recitentque antiphonam Salve Regina vel Regina coeli.

86. § 1. Dominus hominem creavit "ut operaretur" (*Genes.* II, 15), ideoque haec laborandi lex pertinet ad generalem humanam condicionem. Attamen peculiaris character ac finis Praelaturae eius fideles ducit non solum ad colendum, verum etiam ad profunde amandum ordinarium laborem: in ipso enim vident tum insignissimum valorem humanum, necessarium quidem ad tuendam humanae personae dignitatem et societatis progressionem, tum praecipue miram occasionem atque medium unionis personalis cum Christo, imitantes eius operosam vitam absconditam generosi servitii aliorum hominum et ita cooperantes operi amore pleno Creationis et Redemptionis mundi.

§ 2. Peculiaris proinde character spiritus Operis Dei in eo consistit, quod unusquisque suum laborem professionalem sanctificare debet; in sui laboris professionalis perfecta adimpletione, sanctificari; et per suum laborem professionalem, alios sanctificare. Unde multae oriuntur concretae exigentiae in vita ascetica et apostolica eorum qui ad opera peculiaria Praelaturae dicantur.

87. § 1. Praelatura Operis Dei tota devota est servitio Ecclesiae, pro qua fideles Praelatur—plena, perpetua ac definitiva Christi Domini servitio deditione sese mancipando—relinquere parati semper erunt honorem, bona, adhuc autem et animam suam; numquam Ecclesiam sibi inservire praesumant. Sit ergo firmus ac exemplaris pius amor erga Sanctam Matrem Ecclesiam omniaque ad illam quoquo modo pertinentia; sint sincerae dilectio, veneratio, docilitas et adhaesio Romano Pontifici omnibusque Episcopis communionem cum Apostolica Sede habentibus, quos Spiritus Sanctus posuit Ecclesiam Dei regere.

§ 2. Praeter orationes quae in Sacrosancto Eucharistico Sacrificio et in Operis Dei Precibus quotidianis pro Summo Pontifice et pro Ordinario uniuscuiusque Ecclesiae localis effunduntur, omnes fideles quotidie intentiones eorundem Domino specialiter commendare ne omittant.

88. § 1. Praelatura fovet in suis fidelibus necessitatem speciali sollertia colendi oboedientiam illam illudque religiosum obsequium, quae christiani universi exhibere debent erga Romanum Pontificem et Episcopos communionem cum Sancta Sede habentes.

§ 2. Omnes fideles tenentur praeterea humiliter Praelato ceterisque Praelaturae auctoritatibus in omnibus oboedire, quae ad finem peculiarem Operis Dei pertinent. Haec oboedientia sit penitus voluntaria, ob motivum divini amoris et ut imitentur Christum Dominum, qui cum esset omnium Dominus, semetipsum exinanivit formam servi accipiens, quique factus est "oboediens usque ad mortem, mortem autem crucis" (*Philip.* II, 8).

§ 3. Ad professionalem autem actionem quod attinet, itenique ad doctrinas sociales, politicas, etc., unusquisque Praelaturae fidelis, intra limites utique catholicae doctrinae fidei et morum, eadem plena gaudet libertate qua ceteri gaudent cives catholici. Auctoritates vero Praelaturae a quibuslibet vel consiliis dandis his in materiis omnino abstinere debent. Proinde illa plena libertas tantum minui poterit a normis quas forsan dederint pro omnibus catholicis, in aliqua dioecesi aut ditione, Episcopus vel Episcoporum Conferentia; quapropter Praelatura labores professionales, sociales, politicos, oeconomicos, etc., nullius omnino sui fidelis suos facit.

89. § 1. Omnes Praelaturae fideles diligant atque foveant humilitatem non modo privatam, sed etiam collectivam; ideo numquam Operi Dei gloriam quaerant, quinimmo hoc unum animo alte defixum habeant: gloriam Operis Dei summam esse sine humana gloria vivere.

§ 2. Quo efficacius suum finem assequatur Opus Dei, uti tale, humiliter vivere vult: quare sese abstinet ab actibus collectivis, neque habet nomen vel denominationem communem quibus Praelaturae fideles appellentur; nec ipsi aliquibus publicis manifestationibus cultus, uti processionibus, intererunt collective, quin ex hoc occultent se ad Praelaturam pertinere, quia spiritus Operis Dei, dum fideles ducit ad humilitatem collectivam enixe quaerendam, quo impensiorem atque uberiorem efficaciam apostolicam attingant, omnino simul vitat secretum vel clandestinitatem. Quapropter universis in circumscriptionibus omnibus nota sunt nomina Vicariorum Praelati necnon eorum qui Consilia ipsorum efformant; et Episcopis petentibus nomina communicantur non solum sacerdotum Praelaturae, qui in respectivis dioecesibus suum ministerium exercent, sed Directorum etiam Centrorum quae in dioecesi erecta habentur.

§ 3. Huius humilitatis collectivae causa, Opus Dei nequit edere folia et cuiusque generis publicationes nomine Operis.

90. In sua vita professionali, familiari et sociali, fideles Praelaturae virtutes naturales, quae in humano consortio magni aestimantur et ad apostolatum peragendum iuvant, diligenter et fortiter colant: fraternitatem, optimismum, audaciam, in rebus bonis ac rectis sanctam intransigentiam, laetitiam, simplicitatem, nobilitatem ac sinceritatem, fidelitatem; sed eas semper et in omnibus supernaturales fideliter reddere curent.

91. Praelaturae fideles, memores normarum caritatis et prudentiae, exercere tenentur correctionem fraternam, ut, in casu, sese mutuo amoveant a moribus, qui spiritui Operis Dei repugnent.

92. Omnes maxima cura res etiam parvas cum spiritu supernaturali perficiant, eo quod vocationis ratio in diurno labore sanctificando consistit. Non semper res magnae occurrunt; parvae utique, in quibus Iesu Christi amor saepius demonstrari potest. Haec est una ex manifestationibus spiritus paenitentiae Operis Dei proprii, quae potius in parvis et ordinariis rebus est quaerenda et in labore quotidiano, constanti, ordinato.

93. In hoc suo ordinario labore adimplendo, maximo cum amore Dei et proximi, fidem vivam et operantem necnon filialem spem omnibus in adiunctis Praelaturae fideles colant; quac virtutes omnia superare faciunt obstacula in Ecclesiae animarumque servitio forte obvenientia: "omnia possum in eo qui me confortat" (*Philip.* IV, 13). Nihil ergo aut neminem formident: "Dominus illuminatio mea et salus mea, quem timebo?" (*Ps.* XXVI, 1).

94. § 1. Praelaturae fideles plena vivant personali cordis a bonis temporalibus libertate, unusquisque iuxta suum statum et condicionem, animis ab omnibus, quibus utuntur, alienatis; sobrie semper in vita sua personali et sociali iuxta spiritum et praxim Operis Dei se gerentes; omnem sollicitudinem de rebus huius saeculi in Deum proiicientes; atque in hoc mundo tamquam peregrini, qui civitatem futuram inquirunt, commorantes.

§ 2. Suo ordinario labore professionali, peracto cum mente et animo patris familiae numerosae ac pauperis, omnibus Praclaturae fidelibus officium est providendi propriis necessitatibus oeconomicis personalibus et familiaribus atque, in quantum ab ipsis fieri possit, iuvandi sustentationem apostolatus Praelaturae, remedium afferentes indigentiae spirituali ac materiali plurimorum hominum. Gaudeant simul quando effectus experiantur carentiae mediorum, scientes numquam in necessariis providentiam Domini defecturam, qui nos monuit ut primum Regnum Dei et iustitiam eius quaeramus, si volumus ut cetera omnia nobis adiiciantur.

§ 3. Praelatura tamen curat ne suis fidelibus necessarium adiutorium spirituale desit, atque Praelatus, per se vel per suos Vicarios, paterno affectu eos fovet, ab unoquoque ea ratione exigendo, prout varia cuiusque adiuncta suadeant. Propterea, quod attinet ad Praelaturae fideles atque personas, quae diu noctuque in Centris Operis Dei degunt, potest Praelaturae Ordinarius, iusta de causa, dispensationem concedere ab obligatione servandi diem festum vel diem paenitentiae, aut commutationem eiusdem in alia pia opera.

95. Praeter festa Domini, Beatae Mariae Virginis et Sancti Ioseph, a Praelaturae fidelibus speciali devotione celebrantur festa Exaltationis Sanctae Crucis; SS. Archangelorum Michaëlis, Gabrielis et Raphaëlis atque Apostolorum Petri, Pauli et Ioannis; aliorum Apostolorum et Evangelistarum; dies secunda octobris seu Angelorum Custodum festivitas, et decima quarta februarii. Hac postremae dies, pro Opere Dei , dies actionis gratiarum sunto.

CAPUT II

DE INSTITUTIONE DOCTRINALI RELIGIOSA

96. Sub aspectu doctrinali religioso, institutio quae fidelibus Praelaturae impertitur ipsis profundam cognitionem Fidei catholicae et Magisterii ecclesiastici, alimentum quidem necessarium suae vitae spiritualis et apostolicae, praestare contendit, ut in quocumque societatis ambitu personae adsint intellectualiter praeparatae quae, cum simplicitate, in ordinariis adiunctis quotidianae vitae atque laboris, exemplo ac verbis efficacem apostolatum evangelizationis et catecheseos exerceant.

97. In qualibet regionali circumscriptione a Vicario Regionali, de consensu sui Consilii et Praelato confirmante, erigantur, prout opus fuerit, Studiorum Centra pro omnibus cuiusque Regionis fidelibus, ut institutio doctrinalis religiosa impensa et assidua ad vitam spiritualem sustinendam et ad finem apostolicum Praelaturae proprium prosequendum cunctis congrue praebeatur.

98. Potest etiam Praelatus, audito suo Consilio, Interregionalia Centra Studiorum erigere, a seipso dependentia, ut in his instituantur Praelaturae fideles ab ipso Praelato selecti sive directe, sive respectivis circumscriptionum Vicariis id proponentibus. Haec Centra specialiter destinari possunt ad fideles, sacerdotes vel laicos, praeparandos, qui formationis officus in diversis Regionibus incumbant.

99. § 1. Institutio doctrinalis religiosa, praesertim quod attinet ad disciplinas philosophicas ac theologicas, impertietur a professoribus Centrorum Studiorum Regionalium vel Interregionalium quae hunc in finem eriguntur, quaeque diversa habentur pro viris et pro mulieribus.

§ 2. Programmata cyclica ita componentur, ut institutio continue impertiri ac perfici valeat, quin unusquisque fidelis, in adimpletione officiorum professionalium et familiarium, detrimentum patiatur.

100. § 1. Praelaturae fideles tempus institutionis perficere possunt extra Centra Studiorum iuridice erecta, si, attentis circumstantiis, audito proprio Consilio, Vicarius Regionalis hoc disposuerit.

§ 2. Tempore hoc perdurante, formationem accipiunt a professore vel professoribus a Vicario Regionali delectis.

§ 3. Iidem autem periculum debent postea subire in aliquo Centro iuridice erecto.

101. § 1. Omnes Numerarii, necnon illi Aggregati quorum personalia adiuncta id suadeant, integra studia biennii philosophici et quadriennii theologici peragant.

§ 2. Singuli anni biennii atque quadriennii dividuntur in duos cursus semestrales, quorum duratio, numerus nempe horarum quae lectionibus dedicantur, aequivalere debet illi cursuum semestralium apud Pontificias Romanas studiorum Universitates, quorumque programmata eadem amplitudine qua in iisdem studiorum Universitatibus explicentur.

§ 3. Duodecim curriculis semestralibus persolvendis, de quibus in praecedentibus, unusquisque alumnus tot annis incumbat, quot necessarii sint, iuxta adiuncta sua personalia atque sui laboris professionalis.

§ 4. Pro mulieribus Numerariis Auxiliaribus, Centra Studiorum cursus disponunt institutionis philosophicae ac theologicae ad earum personalia adiunctario amplecti debent integrum curriculum philosophicum-theologicum.

§ 5. Pro ceteris vero Praelaturae fidelibus institutio doctrinalis complectitur etiam congruam formationem doctrinalem religiosam, quae eos idoneos reddat ad suum apostolatum exercendum.

102. § 1. Pro Numerariis qui ad sacerdotium destinantur sunt specialia Centra Studiorum a Praelato erecta, ubi tamen semper alii Numerarii qui sacerdotes non erunt commorari debent, propriam ipsorum institutionem accipientes et vitam cum primis ducentes, quia una eademque pro omnibus spiritualis formatio requiritur.

§ 2. Attamen, post hoc satis longum tirocinium in Centris Studiorum peractum, durante uno tantum sacrae theologiae studiorum anno, candidati ad sacerdotium commorantur in Centro speciali ad ipsos solummodo destinato.

§ 3. Quoad Aggregatos qui pro sacerdotio recipiendo instituuntur, eaedem normae applicari possunt, congrua tamen congruis referendo.

103. Philosophiae rationalis ac theologiae studia, et alumnorum in his disciplinis institutionem, professores omnino pertractent ad Angelici Doctoris rationem, doctrinam et principia, eaque sancte teneant, iuxta normas a Magisterio Conciliorum et Sanctae Sedis traditas vel tradendas.

104. Quoad illos omnes, qui in posterum ad sacerdotium destinentur, studia de quibus in n. 101, ad normam iuris et Sanctae Sedis instructionum peracta, publica habenda sunt.

105. Omnes sacerdotes Praelaturae praediti sint oportet laurea doctorali in aliqua disciplina ecciesiastica.

106. § 1. Cuncti qui Praelaturae incorporari desiderant, ex quo admissionem expostulant, formationem doctrinalem religiosam, quae praevia vocatur, recipiant necesse est antequam eisdem incorporatio concedatur.

§ 2. Post incorporationem vero, perficere tenentur studia de quibus in n. 97. Hunc in finem frequentabunt cursus pro coetibus homogeneis dispositos, et assistent coadunationibus, conferentus aliisque id genus.

107. Expletis respectivis studiis institutionis doctrinalis religiosae,

quam recipiunt post incorporationem in Praelaturam, omnes suam institutionem modo permanenti et per totam vitam continuabunt iuxta rationem cyclicam repetitionis et adaequationis ad recens adquisitas cognitiones, quo profundius in dies suam formationem doctrinalem ipsi perficiant.

108. Pro Cooperatoribus catholicis, necnon pro aliis Cooperatoribus qui Ecclesiae Catholic doctrinam cognoscere desiderent, cursus, coadunationes aliaque similia promoveantur de re dogmatica ac morali deque ascetica christiana, ita ut ipsi formationem doctrinalem sibi adquirant vel perficiant.

109. Opus Dei nullam habet propriam sententiam vel scholam corporativam in quaestionibus theologicis vel philosophicis quas Ecclesia liberae fidelium opinioni relinquit: Praelaturae fideles, intra limites statutos ab ecclesiastica Hierarchia, quae Depositum fidei custodit, eadem libertate gaudent ac ceteri fideles catholici.

CAPUT III

DE APOSTOLATU

110. Praelatura sollicite suis fidelibus tradit congruam formationem apostolicam ac necessariam assistentiam pastoralem ad impensum laborem evangelizationis et catecheseos exsequendum, ita ut in vita omnium atque singulorum constanter ad effectum deducatur officium et ius christianorum exercendi apostolatum.

111. Haec semper Praelaturae christifideles in apostolatu meminerint:

1. zelus quo adurimur hoc unum quaerit, nempe ut omnes cum Petro ad Iesum per Mariam quasi manu ducamus;

2. pro multitudine constituti sumus. Nulla igitur est anima quam diligere et adiuvare non velimus, omnia omnibus nos facientes (cfr. I *Cor.* IX, 22). Vivere nequimus praetermittentes omnium hominum curas atque necessitates, quia nostra sollicitudo omnes animas amplectitur: vitam agentes absconditam cum Christo in Deo (cfr. *Col.* III, 3), esse debemus tamquam fermentum in massa humanae societatis latens et ipsi se immiscens donec fermentata sit tota (cfr. *Matth.* XIII, 33).

112. Praelaturae fideles sibi proponant, semper et super omnia, ad effectum deducere suum finem personalem sanctificationis et apostolatus, fideliter adimplentes normas asceticas, formativas ac disciplinares Operis Dei, quibus adiuvantur in nisu perfecte exsequendi propria officia professionalia, familiaria et socialia, constans ita testimonium christiani sensus vitae humanae praebentes, et nuntium Christi diffundentes apud omnes societatis ambitus, us non exclusis ad quos ordinarius labor apostolicus sacerdotum ac religiosorum difficile pervenit.

113. Praelaturae fideles, persuasum habentes suum peculiarem apostolatum procedere ex propria vita interiore atque ex amore erga humanum laborem, quae fundi ac compenetrari debent in unitate vitae, speciatim enitantur ut suum laborem sanctificent ipsumque quam maxima possint perfectione humana exsequantur, secundum divinam voluntatem ordinent atque ad animarum salutem dirigant, in primis vero suorum in professione collegarum. Ideo eorum actuositas apostolica non habet modum se manifestandi uniformem vel exclusivum, quia radicatur in ipsa circumstantiarum varietate, quam humanus labor secum fert.

114. Praeter apostolatum testimonii atque exempli, per congruentem vitam personalem unionis cum Domino exhibiti, fideles Praelaturae eniti debent ut aperto etiam sermone de Deo loquantur, veritatem cum caritate diffundentes constanti apostolatu doctrinali et catechetico, accommodato ad peculiaria adiuncta personarum cum quibus laborant et convivunt.

115. Apostolatus fidelium Praelaturae ad cunctos homines dirigitur, sine distinctione stirpis, nationis vel condicionis socialis, ut christiani invitentur, edoceantur atque adiuventur ad respondendum vocationi universali ad sanctitatem in exercitio suae professionis et in officiorum proprii status adimpletione, utque illi etiam qui Christum nondum agnoscunt testimonium de Ipso exemplo et verbis recipiant, et ita disponantur ad fidei gratiam recipiendam.

116. Sua divina vocatione, Praelaturae christifideles ad ordinem supernaturalem evehere satagunt sensum servitii erga homines atque societatem, quo labor quilibet professionalis exercendus est. Continenter prae oculis habebunt fecunditatem apostolatus apud personas condicionis intellectualis, quae, ob doctrinam qua pollent, vel ob munera quae exercent, vel ob dignitatem qua insigniuntur, magni sunt ponderis pro servitio societati civili praestando: ideo totis viribus Praelaturae fideles adlaborabunt ut etiam illae personae Christi Domini doctrinae et praeceptis adhaereant ipsaque in praxim deducant.

117. Praelaturae fideles qui ad apostolatum efficaciorem reddendum, exemplum christianum in exercitio proprii uniuscuiusque laboris professionalis, necnon in proprio ambitu familiari, culturali et sociali, dare conabuntur, suum personalem apostolatum exercent praesertim inter pares, ope praecipue amicitiae et mutuae fiduciae. Omnes nos amici sumus—"vos autem dixi amicos" (*Ioann.* XV, 15)—, immo eiusdem Patris filii ac proinde in Christo et

Christi una simul fratres: peculiare igitur Praelaturae fidelium apostolatus medium est amicitia et assidua cum collaboratoribus consuetudo, quin tamen ad hoc speciales associationes actionis externae religiosae constituantur.

118. Peculiaris etiam nota, qua labor apostolicus fidelium Praelaturae insignitur, est amor libertatis personalis cunctorum hominum, cum accuratissimo obsequio erga libertatem conscientiarum et desiderio cum omnibus convivendi. Quo spiritu fideles ducuntur ad sinceram caritatem semper colendam erga eos qui Christum sequuntur, quia pro Ipso laborant; necnon ad eos diligendos, recte quoque eorum mentes aestimantes, qui Christum nondum sectantur, exemplo ac doctrina eos ad Dominum trahere satagentes.

119. Praelatura a suis fidelibus quaerit impensam et constantem actuositatem apostolicam personalem, in ipso labore et ambitu sociali uniuscuiusque propriis exercendam, liberam ac responsabilem, spontaneitate plene imbutam, quae fructus sit actionis gratiae quaeque sese accurate accommodet fidei et moribus christianis atque Ecclesiae Magisterio.

120. In hac continua actuositate apostolatus personalis, Praelaturae fideles adhibent etiam, pro cuiusque peritia, media illa atque incepta quae in societate civili communia sunt, nempe circulos studiorum, coadunationes, frequentes conventus, sessiones, conferentias, cursus studiorum aliaque similia, modo quidem accommodato ad diversos ambitus civiles in quibus ipsi vitam agunt.

121. § 1. Praeter apostolatum personalem, quem Praelatura in suis fidelibus fovet cuique profecto locus praecipuus competit, Praelatura qua talis specificam assistentiam pastoralem praestat laboribus et inceptis indolis civilis ac professionalis, non confessionalis, persequentibus fines educativos, assistentiales, etc.

§ 2. Praelaturae Ordinarius, necessitate ductus adimplendi suam specificam missionem utque peculiaris Praelaturae finis quam melius in praxim deducatur, maxima cura eos seliget qui cappellanorum atque religionis magistrorum munere fungentur, tum in inceptis ab Opere Dei qua tali promotis, tum in iis quae a Praelaturae fidelibus una cum aliis suscitantur et pro quibus adiutorium spirituale ab Opere Dei postulant. In nominandis vero his cappellanis et religionis magistris, Praelaturae Ordinarius suum Consilium audire numquam omittat, atque nominationes ita factas loci Ordinario opportune communicet.

122. Praelatura numquam sibi assumit aspectus technicos et oeconomicos inceptorum de quibus in n. 121, neque de iisdem respondet; hi enim pertinent ad eorum proprietarios et gestores, utentes bonis et opibus ex propria industria vel aliis mediis similiter civilibus obtentis vel obtinendis. Ordinarie Praelatura non est proprietaria instrumentorum materialium eorum inceptorum, quorum spiritualem curam acceptat.

123. Pars Praelaturae in inceptis de quibus in numero praecedenti consistit in eorum christiana vivificatione, per opportuna media orientationis atque formationis doctrinalis ac spiritualis, necnon per congruam assistentiam pastoralem, accurate quidem servata alumnorum, convictorum ceterorumque omnium legitima conscientiarum libertate. Ad hanc curam de unoquoque incepto apostolico exercendam, Centrum Operis Dei erigetur, praevia opportuna venia Ordinarii loci, melius in scriptis data.

124. Cum aliquis Praelaturae christifidelis, ad Ordinarii loci petitionem et servata Praelaturae disciplina, adiutorium directe praestat in laboribus dioecesanis, idem incumbit illis laboribus explendis ad nutum et mentem eiusdem Ordinarii, ipsique tantum de peracto labore rationem reddit.

TITULUS IV
DE REGIMINE PRAELATURAE

CAPUT I
DE REGIMINE IN GENERE

125. § 1. Praelaturae regimen committitur Praelato, qui suis Vicariis et Consiliis adiuvatur iuxta normas iuris universalis et huius Codicis.

§ 2. Potestas regiminis qua gaudet Praelatus est plena in foro tum externo tum interno in sacerdotes Praelaturae incardinatos; in laicos vero Praelaturae incorporatos haec potestas ea est tantum quae spectat finem peculiarem eiusdem Praelaturae.

§ 3. Praelati potestas, sive in clericos sive in laicos, ad normam iuris universalis et huius Codicis exercetur.

§ 4. Nomine Ordinarii Praelaturae iure intelleguntur et sunt Praelatus necnon qui in eadem generali gaudent potestate exsecutiva ordinaria, nempe Vicarii pro regimine tum generali cum regionali Praelaturae constituti.

126. Praelatura distribuitur in circumscriptiones regionales, quarum unamquamque moderatur Vicarius, qui Consiliarius Regionalis appellatur, cuique respectiva Consilia assistunt.

127. Excepto Praelati officio, quod est ad vitam, alia omnia munera Praelaturae sunt temporaria; admittitur tamen iterata eorundem nominatio.

128. Universa Praelatura eiusque partes tantum a Praelato vel eius delegatis, etiam in omnibus negotus iuridicis, legitime repraesentantur; munere autem Praelati vacante vel impedito, ab eo qui regimen assumit ad normam n. 149, 1 et 4; unaquaeque vero Operis Dei circumscriptio regionalis, etiam a proprio Vicario.

129. § 1. Praelatura eiusque circumscriptiones personalitate iuridica praeditae adquirunt, possident, administrant et alienant bona temporalia ad normam iuris, iuxta praescripta a Praelato statuta.

§ 2. Ex omnibus bonis, undecumque ipsa proveniant, quae Praelaturae adscribi possunt, illa tantum ut vere ecciesiastica ad normam iuris habenda sunt, quae de facto ipsi Praelaturae a Praelato adscripta iam fuerint.

§ 3. Praelatura vel circumscriptiones de quibus in 1. respondent de obligationibus quas respective contraxerint, atque semper legitimas leges civiles regionis vel nationis de qua agatur fideliter observant, intra terminos ah ipsis constitutos operando.

CAPUT II
DE REGIMINE CENTRALI

130. § 1. Praelatus, qui interne dicitur Pater cuiusque officium est ad vitam, seligitur exciuso compromisso a Congressu Generali electivo hunc in finem convocato; electio vero Romani Pontificis confirmatione indiget.

§ 2. Congressus Generalis constituitur a Congressistis, qui etiam vocantur membra Congressus. Sunt Congressistae illi sacerdotes vel viri laici, triginta duos saltem annos nati et iam a novem saltem annis Praelaturae definitive incorporati, qui inter fideles ex diversis nationibus vel regionibus, in quibus Opus Dei suum laborem apostolicum exercet, nominantur ad vitam a Praelato, cum voto deliberativo sui Consilii, auditis etiam Commissione Regionali et Congressistis respectivae Regionis.

§ 3. Congressus, antequam ad Praelati electionem procedere iure valeat, requirere et recipere debet, ab omnibus atque singulis membris Consilii Centralis de quo in n. 146, propositiones circa nomen seu nomina illius illorumve quos ad supremum Praelaturae munus digniores et aptiores censeant.

§ 4. Acceptatione ab electo rite habita, ipse confirmationem electionis a Romano Pontifice per se vel per alium petere debet.

131. Ut quis possit Praelatus eligi requiritur:

1. ut sit sacerdos membrum Congressus Generalis, iam a decem saltem annis Praelaturae incorporatus, et a quinquennio

saltem in presbyteratus Ordine constitutus, filius legitimi matrimonii, bona existimatione gaudens et natus saltem annos quadraginta;

2. eluceat praeterea prudentia, pietate, erga Ecclesiam eiusque Magisterium exemplari amore et oboedientia, erga Opus Dei devotione, erga Praelaturae fideles caritate, erga proximos zelo;

3. praeditus sit speciali cultura etiam profana, immo laurea doctorali in aliqua ecclesiastica disciplina, aliisque qualitatibus ad agendum necessariis.

132. § 1. Praelatus, sicut christifidelibus suae curae commissis auctoritate praeest, unde etiam Praeses Generalis nuncupari potest, prae ceteris ipsum etiam excellere virtutibus et qualitatibus decet, iis praesertim quac propriae sunt Operis Dei, quaeque eiusdem spiritum consequuntur.

§ 2. In exercitio sui muneris pastoralis, Praelatus specialiter curare debet ut universum ius quo regitur Opus Dei ac omnes eiusdem legitimae consuetudines adamussim serventur, atque fideliter promovere exsecutionem dispositionum Sanctae Sedis Praelaturam respicientium.

§ 3. Sit ergo omnibus Praelaturae fidelibus magister atque Pater, qui omnes in visceribus Christi vere diligat, omnes effusa caritate erudiat atque foveat, pro omnibus impendatur et superimpendatur libenter.

§ 4. Curet praesertim ut sacerdotibus ac laicis sibi commissis assidue et abundanter praebeantur media et auxilia spiritualia atque intellectualia, quae necessaria sunt ad eorum vitam spiritualem alendam ac fovendam eorumque peculiarem finem apostolicum exsequendum.

§ 5. Pastoralem suam sollicitudinem manifestet consiliis, suasionibus, immo et legibus, praeceptis et instructionibus, atque si id requiratur, congruis sanctionibus; necnon visitationibus sive per se sive per alios a se delegatos peragendis, in circumscriptionibus ac Centris, in ecclesiis Praelaturae vel eidem commissis, et circa personas et res.

§ 6. Ut bono spirituali Praelati et eiusdem valetudini consulant, sint duo Custodes seu admonitores qui tamen, ratione huius muneris, Consilium Generale non ingrediuntur. Designantur ad periodum octo annorum ab eodem Praelato inter novem Praelaturae fideles de quibus in n. 13, a Consilio Generali praesentatos. Convivunt in eadem cum Praelato familia.

133. § 1. Praeter Congressum Generalem electivum, octavo quoque anno celebrari debent Congressus Generales ordinarii a Praelato convocati, ut de Praelaturae statu iudicium proferant et futurae actioni regiminis opportunas normas suadere valeant. Congressui praeest Praelatus vel, eius delegatione, dignior Consilii Generalis.

§ 2. Congressus Generalis extra ordinem convocandus est, cum rerum adiuncta de iudicio Praelati cum voto deliberativo sui Consilii id postulent; et ad Vicarium auxiliarem seu Vicepraesidem designandum vel revocandum, ad normam nn. 134, 2 et 137, 2.

§ 3. Pro Sectione mulierum adsunt etiam Congressus Generales tum ordinarii cum extra ordinem convocati, non autem Congressus electivi. His Congressibus praeest Praelatus, cui assistunt Vicarius auxiliaris, si adsit, atque Vicarii Secretarius Generalis et Sacerdos Secretarius Centralis. Congressistae nominantur pan ratione ac viri Congressistae.

§ 4. Audita Commissione permanenti sui Consilii, de qua in n. 138 2, Praelatus convocare potest Praelaturae fideles non Congressistas, diversis in materiis peritos, qui Congressui Generali intersint qua collaboratores, cum voce sed sine voto; quod etiam valet pro mulieribus, in propria Sectione.

134. § 1. Si Praelatus opportunam seu convenientem in Domino censeat Vicarii auxiliaris ad normam n. 135 designationem, libere, audito suo Consilio, ipsum nominare potest. Consilium Generale plenum potent etiam Praelato sincere suggerere opportunitatem Vicarii auxiliaris designationis, qui ipsum in regimine adiuvare ad octo annos valeat. Praelatus, nisi graves obsint rationes, Consilio facile morem gerat.

§ 2. Si vero Praelatus illo Vicario auxiliari egere videatur de quo in n. 136, tunc Consilium plenum, post rei maturam in Domino considerationem, Congressum convocare potent, cui huius Vicarii auxiliaris designatio ad normam n. 136 exclusive reservatur. Ut vero Consilium iure Congressum, hunc in finem, convocare possit, formalis requiritur deliberatio in qua duae tertiae partes Consilii pleni praedictam nominationem postulent et unus ex Custodibus. Tunc Vicarius Secretarius Generalis convocare tenetur Congressum extra ordinem Generalem, cui ipse Vicarius Secretarius Generalis praesit.

§ 3. In Vicario auxiliari, excepta aetate, eaedem requiruntur qualitates ac in Praelato.

135. Vicarius auxiliaris, si detur Praelato habili, hunc adiuvat, ipsum supplet absentem vel impeditum: alias autem facultates non habet nisi quas, vel habitualiter vel ad casum, Praelatus delegaverit. De omnibus peractis Praelato rationem fideliter reddat.

136. § 1. Si Praelatus senio, infirmitate aliave gravissima causa ad gubernandum, etiam ordinario Vicario auxiliari adiutus de quo in

n. 135, certo incapax ita evadere videatur ut ipsius regiminis continuatio in damnum Praelaturae practice converteretur, tunc Vicarius auxiliaris eligi a Congressu potest in quem omnia Praelati iura et officia, excepto tamen titulo, transferantur; electus confirmationem electionis a Sancta Sede per se vel per alium petere debet.

§ 2. Iudicium de exsistentia et gravitate causarum ad designationem huius Vicarii auxiliaris, ipsiusque si casus ferat electio, vel, ex adverso, iudicium de opportunitate Vicarii auxiliaris ordinarii designationis, vel mutationis, si hoc nempe sufficere videretur, Congressui reservatur, qui duabus ex tribus suffragiorum partibus quod magis, omnibus ponderatis, Praelaturae bono conveniat decidere debet.

137. § 1. Vicarius auxiliaris ordinarius ad nutum Praelati revocabilis est. Opportune Praelatus, sicut in nominatione, de qua in n. 134, 1, ita etiam in revocatione suum Consilium Generale audire potent.

§ 2. Vicarius auxiliaris vero qui in regimine Praelatum substituit usque ad novum ordinarium Congressum perdurat. Potent tamen Congressus extra ordinem convocatus ipsum revocare: et tam ordinarius quam extraordinarius Congressus, speciatim si rationes suspensionis regiminis Praelati non necessario perpetuae aestimari valeant, Consilio Generali pleno facultatem delegare ut ex morali unanimitate Praelati regimen, revocato Vicario auxiliari, instaurare possit; quae Sanctae Sedi communicentur.

138. § 1. Ad Praelatum adiuvandum in dirigenda atque gubernanda Praelatura est Consilium Generale, constans e Vicario auxiliari, si adsit, Vicario Secretario Generali, Vicario pro Sectione mulierum, qui Sacerdos Secretarius Centralis nuncupatur, tribus saltem Vicesecretarus, uno saltem Delegato cuiusque Regionis, Studiorum Praefecto et Administratore Generali, qui constituunt Consilium plenum et vocantur Consultores.

§ 2. Praelatus, Vicarius auxiliaris, si adsit, Secretarius Generalis, Sacerdos Secretarius Centralis et, prout casus ferant, vel unus e Vicesecretarus vel Studiorum Praefectus aut Administrator Generalis, constituunt Commissionem permanentem Consilii. Huius Commissionis aliqua membra laici esse valent, pro negotiis tractandis quae characterem Ordinis sacri non requirant; sed Vicarius auxiliaris, Secretarius Generalis et Secretarius Centralis, qui sunt etiam Vicarii Praelati, semper inter sacerdotes nominentur.

§ 3. Ad Consilium Generale admitti semper debent, ad normam tamen n. 139, Consultores illi, qui praesentes sunt.

Invitari possunt, iudicio Praelati, et invitati assistere debent etiam illi qui ex munere absunt.

139. § 1. Ad negotia illa resolvenda, pro quibus ad normam iuris requiritur votum deliberativum Consilii Generalis, invitari semper debent illi saltem Consultores qui non sunt absentes ex munere: et ad validam Consilii decisionem quinque saltem ipsius membra adesse necesse est. Si quinque Consultores invitari non possint, vel invitati adesse non valeant, Praelatus cum praesentibus aliquem vel aliquos designare ex Congressistis possunt, qui absentes pro illa vice substituant.

§ 2. Pro aliis vero quaestionibus Consilium competens est eiusdem Consilii Generalis Commissio permanens.

140. § 1. Munera Consilii Generalis hac ratione provideri debent: Praelatus statim ac sua electio a Romano Pontifice confirmata fuerit informationes, quibus in Domino egere censeat, accurate colligit indeque per ordinem singillatim nomina candidatorum ad diversa munera Congressui proponit. Proposito a Prelato unoquoque nomine, Congressus, ad normam iuris universalis, suffragium secretum fert. Si propositum nomen a Congressu non probetur, aliud usque ad optatum suffragationis exitum proponere Praelatus debet.

§ 2. Octavo quoque anno, Praelato excepto, munera regiminis generalis omnia et singula Congressus revisioni, eadem servata ratione, subiicienda sunt. Possunt iidem ad idem aliudve munus generale absque limitatione eligi. Magni tamen interest ut ex regula aliqua nova membra ad Consilium Generale designentur.

141. Vacante, qualibet canonica ratione, Consultoris alicuius munere, Praelatus ad Consultoris munus Consilio Generali candidatum proponit, quod suo secreto suffragio, ipsum, eadem ratione ac in Congressu Generali, acceptare vel relicere potent. Hac occasione Praelato liberum relinquitur, audito Consilio, munera aliqua Consultoribus adnexa, si opportunum videatur, inter Consultores mutare.

142. Secretarius Generalis, Sacerdos Secretarius Centralis et Administrator Generalis debent esse membra Congressus. Ad cetera munera Consilii Generalis tantummodo habiles sunt Praelaturae fideles de quibus in n. 13. Prae aliis debent prudentia, cultura et Operi Dei devotione fulgere.

143. Licet munus ad octo annos perduret, possunt nihilominus Consultores ob iustas causas et quoties bonum maius Praelaturae requirat, a Praelato, ceteris auditis, removeri. Liberum quoque sit omnibus muneri renuntiare, verum renuntiatio effectum nullum habeat donec a Praelato admittatur.

144. § 1. Inter Consultores primus est Secretarius Generalis. Est semper sacerdos, post Praelatum venit, si Vicarius auxiliaris non adsit, eumque absentem vel quocumque modo impeditum supplet. Praelatum praeterea specialiter adiuvat tum in iis quae ad regimen et incepta universae Praelaturae, tum in iis quae ad res oeconomicas attinent, sed illis tantum facultatibus gaudet, quas vel habitualiter vel ad casum Praelatus delegaverit.

§ 2. Secretarius Generalis ad criteria, mentem et praxim Praelati, in quantum fieri possit, negotia gerat atque expediat: nihil proinde eorum, quae a Praelato gesta vel praescripta sunt, innovare valeat, sed semper Praelato et Consilio erit quam maxime fidelis.

§ 3. Eius insuper est labores inter membra Consilii distribuere, ab eisque fidelem muneris adimpletionem exigere.

145. § 1. Ut Praelato adiumentum specialiter praestet in moderanda Sectione mulierum Operis Dei (cfr. n. 4, 3), est Vicarius, qui Sacerdos Secretarius Centralis nuncupatur.

§ 2. Post Secretarium Generalem venit et illis facultatibus gaudet, quas vel habitualiter vel ad casum Praelatus delegaverit. Debet esse quadraginta saltem annos natus.

146. § 1. Sectio mulierum regitur a Praelato cum Vicario auxiliari, si adsit, Vicario Secretario Generali, Vicario Secretario Centrali et Consilio Centrali, quod Assessoratus Centralis appellatur, et eundem locum habet in Sectione mulierum ac Consilium Generale in Sectione virorum.

§ 2. Assessoratus Centralis constat e Secretaria Centrali, Secretaria Assessoratus, tribus saltem Vicesecretariis, una saltem Delegata cuiusque Regionis, Studiorum Praefecta, Praefecta Auxiliarium et Procuratrice Centrali.

§ 3. Ad munera Assessoratus Centralis nominat Praelatus in Congressu mulierum, eadem ratione ac in Congressu virorum vocat ad munera Consilii Generalis. Secretaria Centralis et Procuratrix Centralis seligantur inter Congressistas; ad alia munera Assessoratus vocentur Numerariae de quibus in n. 13.

147. § 1. Pro quaestionibus oeconomicis, Praelato assistit Consilium ab ipso nominatum, quod vocatur Consultatio Technica cuique praeest Praelatus vel, eius delegatione, Administrator Generalis.

§ 2. Rei oeconomic rationes, saltem semel in anno, ab Administratore Generali subsignatae, Praelato eiusque Consilio sunt exhibendae.

§ 3. Consilium simile habetur pro quaestionibus oeconomicis Sectionis mulierum.

148. § 1. Quin ratione muneris Consilium Generale ingrediantur, adsunt etiam Procurator seu Agens precum, qui debet esse semper sacerdos, quique Praelaturam apud Sanctam Sedem ex delegatione habituali Praelati repraesentat; necnon Sacerdos Rerum Spiritualium Praefectus, qui directioni spirituali communi omnium Praelaturae fidelium, sub ductu Praelati et Consilii, praeponitur.

§ 2. In cura spirituali Aggregatis et Supernumerariis Societatis Sacerdotalis Sanctae Crucis praestanda eius Praesidem Generalem Praefectus adiuvat, iuxta facultates habitualiter vel ad casum ipsi a Praeside delegatas.

§ 3. Procurator et Praefectus a Praelato, audito Consilio, ad octo annos nominantur.

149. § 1. Vacante munere Praelati, regimen tenet Vicarius auxiliaris, si sit; aliter Secretarius Generalis vel, post eum, Vicarius Secretarius Centralis; usque omnibus deficientibus, sacerdos Congressista maiore suffragiorum numero ab iis designatus, quibus ius est constituendi Commissionem permanentem Consilii Generalis.

§ 2. Qui regimen assumit, tenetur obligationibus et gaudet potestate Praelati, iis exclusis quae ex rei natura vel iure Praelaturae excipiuntur. Congressum Generalem electivum convocare tenetur intra mensem a muneris vacatione, ita ut intra tres menses ab eadem vacatione celebretur, aut, si maiore de causa intra statutum tempus coadunari nequeat, statim ac causa impediens cessaverit.

§ 3. Vacante munere Praelati, qui muneribus funguntur regiminis, tum generalis Praelaturae tum circumscriptionum, in exercitio suorum munerum pergunt, donec, post novum electum Praelatum, in ipsis confirmentur vel substituantur.

§ 4. Praelato impedito, iuxta normas in 1. statutas procedendum est; si vero, in gravioribus rerum adiunctis, eaedem servari nequeant, coadunentur membra Consilii Generalis quae id facere valeant, sub moderatione dignioris, et sacerdotem quoad fieri possit membrum Congressus designent, qui regimen Praelaturae ad interim assumat.

CAPUT III
DE REGIMINE REGIONALI ET LOCALI

150. Praelati de consensu sui Consilii est circumscriptiones regionales, quae vocantur Regiones vel quasi-Regiones, erigere, mutare, aliter definire, et etiam supprimere.

151. § 1. Regimini uniuscuiusque Regionis praeponitur Vicarius, qui Consiliarius Regionalis nuncupatur, quemque nominat Praelatus cum voto deliberativo sui Consilii; Consiliario assistit Consilium, quod vocatur Commissio Regionalis, constans membris usque ad duodecim, designatis inter Praelaturae fideles de quibus in n. 13 pariterque nominatis a Praelato audito suo Consilio, cuius consensus requiritur in casibus de quibus in nn. 157, 1. et 159.

§ 2. Inter membra Commissionis peculiarem locum obtinet Defensor, cuius munus est adimpletionem normarum huius Codicis fovere.

152. § 1. Quando non sint omnia elementa necessaria ad novas Regiones constituendas, possunt etiam quasi-Regiones a Praelato, cum voto deliberativo sui Consilii, erigi. Eas moderantur Vicarii, qui Vicariis Regionalibus iure aequiparantur.

§ 2. Potest etiam Praelatus, audito suo Consilio, Delegationes erigere directe a se dependentes, Vicario delegato conferens facultates quas, iuxta casus, intra limites tamen facultatum Consiliariorum Regionalium, committendas censuerit.

153. Ad meliorem curam exercendam laboris apostolici in aliqua circumscriptione, Praelatus, audito suo Consilio eisque quorum intersit, erigere potest Delegationes a Commissione eiusdem circumscriptionis dependentes, quarum unicuique praeponatur Vicarius delegatus, cum proprio Consilio, opportunis facultatibus praeditus.

154. Ipso facto erectionis, Regiones, quasi-Regiones et Delegationes a Praelato dependentes iuridicam adquirunt personalitatem. Delegationes in circumscriptione regionali constitutae donari possunt personalitate iuridica in erectionis decreto.

155. Circumscriptiones personalitate iuridica gaudentes, de quibus in n. 154, quoad negotia iuridica et, in genere, quoad quaestiones omnes, repraesentantur, praeterquam a Praelato eiusque delegatis, tantummodo a respectivis Vicariis, qui agere possunt per se vel per alios opportuno mandato praeditos.

156. § 1. Munera regionalia conferuntur a Praelato, audito Consilio, exceptis tamen Consiliano, Sacerdote Secretario Regionis et Administratore Regionali, qui nominari debent ad normam nn. 151, 157, 1. et 159, et durant ad quinquennium, nisi pro omnibus vel pro aliquibus Commissionis membris tempus in munere ad octo annos prorogetur. Pro Delegatis autem Regionalibus valet praescriptum n. 140, 1. et 2.

§ 2. Ad munera Commissionis in quasi-Regionibus et Delegationibus vocat Praelatus, audito suo Consilio.

157. § 1. In singulis Regionibus, nomine et vice Praelati semperque ad ipsius mentem, respectivus Vicarius Consiliarius

Regionalis cum alio sacerdote, qui Sacerdos Secretarius Regionalis vocatur, nominato a Praelato cum voto deliberativo sui Consilii et audito Assessoratu Centrali, Sectionem mulierum moderantur, una cum Consilio regionali mulierum, quod Assessoratus Regionalis appellatur et eundem locum habet in Sectione mulierum ac Commissio Regionalis in virorum Sectione.

§ 2. Assessoratus Regionalis constare potest membris usque ad duodecim, selectis inter Numerarias de quibus in n. 13; nominatur a Praelato, audito Assessoratu Centrali, cuius consensus requiritur pro muneribus Secretari Regionalis et Procuratricis Regionalis.

§ 3. Ad munera Assessoratus in Quasi-Regionibus et Delegationibus vocat Praelatus, audito Assessoratu Centrali.

158. Si quando in aliqua Regione impedimentum obstiterit, quod impossibilem reddat cum Praelato eiusque Consilio communicationem et, perdurante hac impossibilitate, defuerit aliquod Commissionis membrum, ad eius munus ipsa Commissio alium Numerarium per maiorem suffragiorum partem eliget. Cum autem plus quam tria Commissionis membra defuerint vel cum ipsa Commissio, expleto tempore sui mandati, renovanda sit, Numerarii ad munera vocabuntur maioritate item suffragiorum a speciali coadunatione constituta ex omnibus Regionis Congressistis non impediris omnibusque membris Commissionis, cui coadunationi praeerit Congressista ordine praecedenti senior. Quodsi, quavis de causa, tres saltem Congressistae coadunationi adesse non potuerint, vocandi erunt etiam tres Numerarii ex iis de quibus in n. 13, ordine praecedenti seniores Regionis, non impediti: absentibus Congressistis, praeerit ordine item praecedentiae senior inter praesentes. Paritatem suffragionim dirimet praeses coadunationis.

159. § 1. In unaquaque Regione, pro rebus oeconomicis, Vicario Regionali assistit Consilium oeconomicum, seu Consultatio Technica, cuius membra ab eodem Vicario designantur, cuique praeest Administrator Regionalis, a Praelato nominatus cum voto deliberativo proprii Consilii.

§ 2. Consultatio similis habetur pro quaestionibus oeconomicis Sectionis mulierum.

160. In unaquaque circumscriptione, quin ratione muneris ad Commissionem pertineat, est Sacerdos Rerum Spiritualium Praefectus Regionalis, ad vitam spiritualem omnium Praelaturae fidelium sub ductu Consiliarii fovendam. Consiliario insuper adiumentum praestat in cura spirituali Aggregatis et Supernumerariis Societatis Sacerdotalis Sanctae Crucis danda, iuxta facultates habitualiter vel ad casum ipsi a Consiliario delegatas. A Praelato, auditis Consiliario et Defensore Regionis, ad quinquennium nominatur.

161. § 1. In singulis circumscriptionibus Centra erigantur, ad normam n. 177.

§ 2. Regimen locale constituitur a Directore cum proprio Consilio. Munera sunt ad triennium, et conferuntur a Consiliano, audito suo Consilio.

§ 3. Conceptus Centri, hoc in Codice, potius personalis est quam territorialis, et potius regionalis quam localis.

§ 4. Ut apta habeatur Praelaturae fidelium cura, ad idem Centrum adscribi possunt fideles, vel etiam fidelium Coetus, qui sive in eadem civitate sive in diversis civitatibus vel dioecesibus commorentur.

§ 5. Sunt proinde in Praelatura Centra autonoma et Centra ab aliis dependentia, quia adhuc canonice non sunt erecta.

CAPUT IV

DE ADUNATIONIBUS REGIONALIBUS

162. Ad impensiorem formationem fidelium Praelaturae et ad meliorem evolutionem actionis apostolicae, decimo quoque anno, in singulis Regionibus, Adunationes de more celebrentur, in quibus transactae periodi experientiae habitae perpendantur.

163. Praeter Adunationes ordinarias, possunt etiam extraordinari celebrari, in una vel in pluribus circumscriptionibus, quoties Praelatus, auditis Consilio Generali et Commissione Regionali, id expedire duxerit.

164. Adunationem, de mandato Praelati, convocat Vicarius circumscriptionis designans locum et tempus sessionis, tribus saltem mensibus ante eiusdem celebrationem.

165. Adunationibus praesunt Praelatus vel eius delegatus, cui assistunt Vicarius et Delegatus circumscriptionis. A secretis est junior laicus praesens.

166. § 1. Adunationi cuiusque circumscriptionis interesse debent:

1. omnes qui in Commissione aliquo munere funguntur, vel functi sunt;

2. omnes Congressistae circumscriptioni adscripti;

3. omnes eiusdem Regionis sacerdotes aliique fideles Praelaturae, qui cuncti inter eos de quibus in n. 13 adnumerentur;

4. Directores Centrorum Studiorum;

5. item, a Praelato designati, Directores locales.

§ 2. Vocari etiam possunt ad Adunationem alii Praelaturae

fideles diversis in materiis periti, ut eidem intersint qua collaboratores.

167. § 1. Fovenda est quam maxima omnium Praelaturae fidelium participatio in Adunationibus, requirendo eorum communicationes, notulas de experientiis habitis aliaque id genus.

§ 2. Eadem de causa, si adiuncta id suadeant, haberi queunt plures coetus diversis in sedibus, quo maior harum Adunationum efficacitas obtineatur.

§ 3. Notae vel schedae de experientiis habitis postulari quoque possunt ab Operis Dei Cooperatoribus, etiam non catholicis, qui suggestiones praebeant pro studio thematum laboris.

168. Omnes ad Adunationem convocati, mense saltem ante eiusdem celebrationem, mittant ad secretarium notas, schedas, animadversiones, etc., quas proponere conveniens eis videatur; ex ipsis autem atque ex omnibus propositionibus Adunationi transmissis (n. 167), commissio, a praeside nominata, elenchum quaestionum iis qui intersint submittendarum conficiat.

169. Conclusiones Adunationis vim praeceptivam non habent quousque adprobationem receperint Praelati, audito suo Consilio, nisi ex rei natura votum deliberativum ipsius Consilii requiratur. Ipse Praelatus opportunas etiam feret instructiones per organa directionis ordinaria.

170. Adunationes Sectionis mulierum celebrentur, congrua congruis referendo, iuxta normas in n. 162 et sequentibus traditas.

CAPUT V
DE RELATIONIBUS CUM EPISCOPIS DIOECESANIS

171. Praelatura Operis Dei immediate et directe subiicitur Sanctae Sedi, quae eius spiritum et finem probavit et eius quoque regimen ac disciplinam tuetur et promovet in bonum Ecclesiae universae.

172. § 1. Cuncti Praelaturae christifideles tenentur humiliter Romano Pontifici in omnibus oboedire: haec oboediendi obligatio fideles omnes forti ac dulci vinculo obstringit.

§ 2. Ordinariis quoque locorum subiiciuntur ad normam iuris universalis, eadem ratione ac ceteri catholici in propria dioecesi, iuxta praescripta huius Codicis.

173. § 1. Praelati est sollicite exsecutioni mandare omnia decreta, rescripta aliasque dispositiones Sanctae Sedis quae Praelaturam respiciant, itemque eidem Sanctae Sedi opportunas relationes praebere, ad normam iuris, de statu Praelaturae deque eiusdem apostolica activitate.

§ 2. Ipse Praelatus curabit, etiam quia spiritus Operis Dei maximo amore filialem unionem cum Romano Pontifice, Christi Vicario, colit, ut eiusdem Magisterii documenta et acta universam Ecclesiam respicientia ab omnibus Praelaturae fidelibus accurate cognoscantur, utque eorum doctrinam ipsi diffundant.

174. § 1. Universus labor apostolicus quem Praelatura, iuxta propriam naturam propriumque finem, exsequitur, ad bonum singularum Ecclesiarum localium confert, atque Praelatura debitas cum Auctoritate ecclesiastica territoriali relationes semper colit.

§ 2. Curet praeterea Praelatus ut, singulis in circumscriptionibus, Vicarius competens, per se vel per alios eiusdem Vicarii nomine, habituales relationes servet cum Episcopis in quorum dioecesibus Praelaturae christifideles resideant, et praesertim ut frequenter colloquatur cum illis Episcopis locorum in quibus Opus Dei Centra erecta habet, necnon cum iis qui muneribus directivis funguntur in respectiva Conferentia Episcopali, ad illas indicationes ab iisdem Episcopis suscipiendas, quas Praelaturae fideles filiorum animo in praxim deducant (cfr. n. 176).

175. Praeter orationes quas pro Romano Pontifice et Episcopo dioecesano eorumque intentionibus quotidie Praelaturae fideles recitare tenentur, maximam eis reverentiam et amorem demonstrabunt, quae etiam impense apud omnes fovere contendant.

176. Singulis in circumscriptionibus, auctoritates Praelaturae curent ut eiusdem fideles bene cognoscant normas directivas pastorales a competenti ecclesiastica Auctoritate territoriali, nempe a Conferentia Episcopali, ab Episcopo dioecesano, etc., statutas, ut unusquisque, iuxta propria adiuncta person alia, familiaria et professionalia, eas ad effectum deducere et in ipsis cooperari valeat.

177. § 1. Ut labor apostolicus Praelaturae in aliqua dioecesi incipiat, mediante canonica erectione primi Centri, ex quo exerceri possit apostolatus collectivus, debet prius informari loci Ordinarius, cuius venia requiritur, melius scripto data.

§ 2. Quoties laboris progressus aliorum Centrorum erectionem in dioecesi suadeat, procedendum semper est ad normam paragraphi praecedentis.

§ 3. Simplex mutatio domicilii alicuius Centri Praelaturae, intra terminos eiusdem civitatis, si Centrum non habeat adnexam ecclesiam, communicari debet in scriptis loci Ordinario, etsi novam veniam non requirat.

178. § 1. Erectio Centri secum fert potestatem erigendi aliud Centrum pro mulieribus fidelibus Praelaturae Administrationi prioris Centri addictis, ita ut de iure et de facto duo sint Centra in unoquoque Operis Dei domicilio (cfr. n. 8, 2).

§ 2. Secum fert pariter facultatem oratorium pro usu fidelium Praelaturae aliorumque in unoquoque Centro ad normam iuris habendi, ibique Sanctissimum Sacramentum asservandi atque functiones pro labore apostolico opportunas peragendi. In oratoriis sollemnis Sanctissimi Sacramenti expositio nocte primam feriam sextam uniuscuiusque mensis praecedenti fieri saltem debet.

§ 3. Concedere potest Ordinarius Praelaturae ut sacerdotes, iusta de causa, bis in die, immo, necessitate pastorali id postulante, etiam ter in diebus dominicis et festis de praecepto Sanctam Missam celebrent, ita ut non solum fidelium Praelaturae necessitatibus, sed etiam aliorum dioecesis fidelium, dum possibile sit, satis faciant.

179. Episcopus dioecesanus ius habet visitandi singula Centra Praelaturae canonice erecta (cfr. n. 177) in iis quae ad ecclesiam, sacrarium et sedem ad sacramentum Paenitenti pertinent.

180. Ad erigendas ecclesias Praelaturae vel, si res ferat, ad eidem committendas ecclesias in dioecesi iam exsistentes, fiat singulis in casibus opportuna conventio, ad normam iuris, inter Episcopum dioecesanum et Praelatum vel competentem Vicarium Regionalem. Iis in ecclesiis, una cum normis in unaquaque conventione statutis, servabuntur dispositiones generales dioecesis ecclesias saeculares respicientes.

TITULUS V
DE STABILITATE ET VI HUIUS CODICIS

181. § 1. Hic Codex fundamentum est Praelaturae Operis Dei. Ideo sanctae ems normae habeantur, inviolabiles, perpetuae, unique Sanctae Sedi reservatae tam quoad mutationem quam quoad novorum praeceptorum inductionem.

§ 2. Tantummodo mutationem alicuius Codicis praescripti, seu in eius corpus aliquam innovationem, aut denique temporariam vel perpetuam alicuius normae suspensionem vel expunctionem a Sancta Sede poscere valet Congressus Generalis Praelaturae, dummodo hic certitudinem habeat de necessitate huius mutationis, innovationis, suspensionis vel expunctionis.

§ 3. Ut haec certitudo iuridice exsistat, si agatur de textus expunctione, innovatione vel indefinita suspensione, requiritur diuturnum experimentum, duorum ordinariorum Congressuum Generalium auctoritate confirmatum, quod tertio ordinario Congressui Generali subuciatur et duabus saltem ex tribus suffragiorum partibus comprobetur.

§ 4. Si agatur vero de temporaria alicuins Codicis praescripti suspensione, Praelatus, cum voto deliberativo unius tantummodo Congressus Generalis, a Sancta Sede eam exposcere valet: requiritur tamen ut plane Sanctae Sedi manifestetur tempus ad quod postulata suspensio est protrahenda.

182. § 1. Auctoritates Praelaturae omnibus modis Codicis applicationem fovere, ipsamque prudenter et efficaciter exigere tenentur, scientes ilium medium esse certum sanctificationis fidelibus Praelaturae: quapropter adversus ipsum Codicem nec consuetudo aliqua, nec desuetudo, praevalere umquam poterunt.

§ 2. Facultas dispensandi ab adimpletione disciplinari Codicis, in his quae dispensari valent et non manent Sanctae Sedi reservata, competit tantummodo Praelato cum voto consultivo sui Consilii, si de rebus magni momenti agatur, vel dispensatio universae Praelaturae sit concedenda: secus, sufficit decretum Vicarii Regionalis, de consensu proprii Consilii.

183. § 1. Praescripta Codicis quae leges divinas vel ecclesiasticas referunt, propriam quam ex se habent obligationem retinent.

§ 2. Codicis praescripta, quae regimen spectant; item, quae definiunt regiminis necessarias functiones aut munera quibus exercentur, quoad nempe ipsorum cardinales normas; pariterque praescripta quae naturam et finem Praelaturae statuunt et consecrant, in Conscientia, pro gravitate materiae, obligant.

§ 3. Praescripta denique mere disciplinaria vel ascetica, quae sub praecedentibus paragraphis huius numeri non cadunt, per se sub reatu culpae directo non obligant. Insuper, quaelibet ex ipsis, vel minimis, ex formali contemptu violare, peccatum est; quod si transgressio ex ratione vel fine non recto fiat, vel ad scandalum moveat, peccatum contra respondentes virtutes secum fert.

184. Praelati cum voto deliberativo sui Consilii est illa omnia definire quae ad practicam huius Codicis interpretationem, applicationem et adimpletionem spectant.

185. Quae de viris hoc in Codice statuuntur, etsi masculino vocabulo expressa, valent etiam pan iure de mulieribus, nisi ex contextu sermonis vel ex rei natura aliud constet aut explicite specialia praescripta ferantur.

DISPOSITIONES FINALES

1. Quae ad haec usque tempora ab Apostolica Sede in favorem Operis Dei concessa, declarata vel approbata sunt, integra manent, quatenus cum eius regimine iuridico Praelaturae personalis componuntur. Pariter vim suam retinet venia ad haec usque tempora concessa a locorum Ordinariis, ut Operis Dei Centra canonice erigantur necnon successivus actus erectionis.

2. Hic Codex, quoad omnes fideles Operi Dei iam incorporatos, tum sacerdotes tum laicos, necnon quoad sacerdotes Aggregatos et Supernumerarios Societatis Sacerdotalis Sanctae Crucis, vim exserere incipiet a die 8 decembris an. 1982.

Hi omnes iisdem obligationibus tenentur et eadem servant iura, quae habebant in regimine iuridico praecedenti, nisi aliud expresse statuant huius Codicis praescriptiones vel de us agatur quae ex normis novo hoc iure abrogatis proveniebant.

INDEX

Index

Holy Spirit
  action of, 101
  and charisms, 39, 53, 54, 73
  and the Church , 20, 26, 39, 53–
    54
  God and, 35–36
homilies (Escrivá), 150
  "Christ Is Passing By," 158*n*20,
    172–73, 177, 178
  "Freedom, a Gift from God,"
    189*n*97
  "In Joseph's Workshop"/
    "Working for God," 156*n*16
  "Passionately Loving the World,"
    10, 162*n*29, 181*n*71
  "Richness of Ordinary Life, The,"
    157*n*17
  "Toward Holiness," 197
hypostatic union, 20, 38

Ignatius of Antioch, Saint, 79*n*171
incardination, 90–92, 143, 144
Incarnate Word, 38, 127
Incarnation of Christ, 105, 177,
    221
  grace in, 117
  mystery of, 53, 116
  salvation and, 22
"inklings," 54*n*92
International Theological
    Commission, 54, 64

Jesus Christ
  baptism and, 161, 167
  blood of, 101, 116
  command of, 20
  exousía of, 39, 73
  fidelity to, 187*n*94
  as Head, 45, 49
  human activities and, 116–17, 160
  identification with, 114
  imitation of, 24, 26
  as king, 38, 73
  as man, 20, 36, 177
  as Mediator between God and
    man, 38, 40, 44

mystery of, 26, 167
  Opus Dei members and, 26
  ordinary life of, 158
  preaching of, 79
  and redemption, 28*n*29, 176
  Resurrection of, 182
  sacramentum salutis and, 53
  sacred ministry and, 37
  salvation as work of, 26
  "soldiers" of, 125, 129
  in souls of the faithful, 10
John, Saint (apostle), 135*n*158
John Paul II, Pope
  on *communio*, 97
  on Escrivá, 221
  on man and Church, 22*n*17
  on ministry, 46, 50
  on mission of laity, 63
  on Opus Dei, 11, 13, 52
  prelature and, 11
  on priests, 107, 144*n*195

laity, 141–45
  clergy and, 66, 83–89
  Code of Canon Law on, 86
  Lumen gentium on, 164, 167–68
  mission of, 126
  priests and, 54–58, 62, 72,
    80*n*175, 132
  Statutes of Opus Dei on, 65
  and exercising of options, 70
  outlook of, 193–94
  in councils, 88
  in *munera*, 86, 87
  as ordinary Christians, 164–67,
    191–92
  in prelature, 84–85
  priests and, 209
  as sacristans, 60*n*106
  sanctification of world by, 117
"Life, Training, and Apostolate of
    the Prelature's Faithful," 66
"little flock," 30
love
  acts of, 196
  charity and, 114–15